Yellowstone & Grand Teton National Parks and Jackson Hole

Yellowstone & Grand Teton National Parks and Jackson Hole

A GREAT DESTINATION

Jeff Welsch and
Sherry L. Moore

The Countryman Press   Woodstock, Vermont

To Daisy and Cash,
future stewards of the
Greater Yellowstone ecosystem.

Interior photographs by the authors unless otherwise specified
Maps by Erin Greb Cartography, © The Countryman Press
Book design by Joanna Bodenweber
Composition by Eugenie S. Delaney

Published by The Countryman Press, P.O. Box 748, Woodstock, VT 05091
Distributed by W. W. Norton & Company, Inc., 500 Fifth Avenue, New York, NY 10110
Printed in the United States of America

Explorer's Guide Yellowstone & Grand Teton National Parks and Jackson Hole: A Great
Destination
Second Edition
978-1-58157-139-4

10 9 8 7 6 5 4 3 2 1

Acknowledgments

WE WOULD AGAIN LIKE TO THANK the many Greater Yellowstone residents and visitors who shared with us their special insights into the last great largely intact temperate ecosystem on the planet. We would also like to thank Countryman Press for the opportunity to share our affection for this region with the world.

Having lived in Yellowstone's backyard for eight years now and spending yet another year immersing ourselves in research for this book, the depth of our appreciation, admiration, and respect for this wild country has increased immeasurably. We are truly fortunate to be witnesses—and have access—to this magnificent place.

Jeff Welsch and Sherry L. Moore

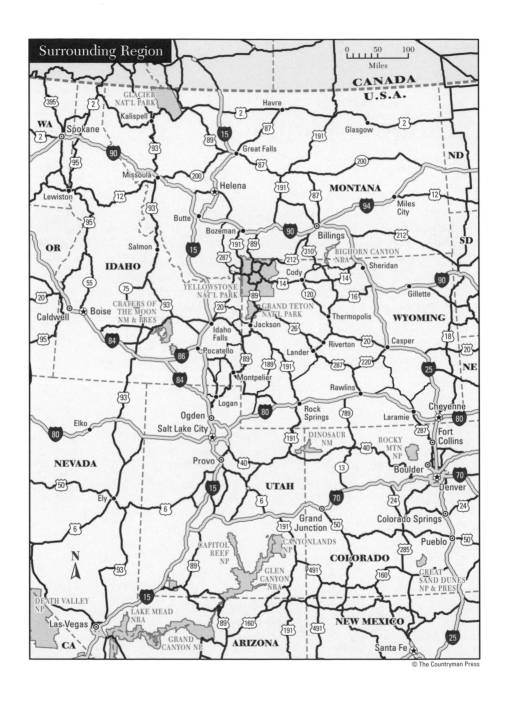

Contents

The Way This Book Works

SAME TITLE, DRAMATICALLY DIFFERENT FORMAT. In a nutshell, that describes the second edition of *Explorer's Guide Yellowstone & Grand Teton National Parks and Jackson Hole: A Great Destination.* Recognizing the realities of today's electronic age, we have narrowed the focus of our guidebook to provide more value.

Instead of giving a general overview of the parks and Jackson Hole, we take you along for the ride and share our insider knowledge of the well-known and obscure alike. Instead of listing all of the dining and lodging in the region, we give you our top choices under the headings of "Best Lodging" and "Best Dining." Instead of providing copious lists and information readily available on the Internet or your cell phone, we tell the stories behind the best places.

More than 3.5 million visitors come to Greater Yellowstone each year to appreciate the history, learn the geology, marvel at the scenery, and, above all, see iconic wildlife in its natural surroundings. Our book reflects these interests. In these pages you'll get history lessons you won't find in other guidebooks. You'll get easy-to-understand descriptions of the fiery world just beneath your feet and the wonders in front of your eyes. And you'll get the backstory on the challenges facing the region's charismatic megafauna: wolves, grizzly bears, bison, moose, elk, mountain lions, and more.

We have divided vast Yellowstone National Park into five chapters, one for each of the entrance stations. Within each chapter you'll follow the roads inside the parks that begin at those entrances. Each chapter also includes key information on the area's gateway communities while highlighting some of the can't-miss attractions and recreation outside of the parks. Grand Teton and Jackson Hole merit one chapter because they are largely one and the same. Keep in mind that Yellowstone alone encompasses parts of three states—Wyoming, Montana, and Idaho; Grand Teton is entirely within Wyoming. That's important to know in part because Wyoming and Idaho each have a sales tax, but Montana doesn't.

We have made every attempt to organize important information so that it is easily found and understood, but changes occur rapidly in tourist areas. What was true last week might not be so during your visit. Restaurants come and go, and change their hours, literally, with the weather. Motel and hotel rates fluctuate, sometimes dramatically, based on seasons and events; rates tend to be lower in the "shoulder seasons," spring and fall, and summers tend to be pricey.

Our dining choices are based on a number of factors, most importantly our own experiences. We also considered reputation, ambiance, quality and diversity of food, and local popularity. Among those we selected for the book, we have further included our best of the best—places we eagerly frequent—with an "Authors' favorite" icon 🎖. Dining codes ($) are based on the price of an average dinner entrée. In cases where we have two sets of dollar signs separated by slash, either most meals are in the lower range and a few are higher or there is a significant difference between breakfast and dinner.

Best Dining

$: Up to $10
$$: $11–20
$$$: $21–30
$$$$: Over $30
B/L/D: Breakfast/Lunch/Dinner

Our lodging codes are as follows: Where two or more $ symbols are listed separated by a slash, the lower number reflects off-season rates and the higher number denotes high-volume times. We have also included icons to denote 🐾 pet-friendly, ♿ handicapped-accessible, and 🍴 in-house restaurant lodging.

Best Lodging

$: Up to $75
$$: $76–125
$$$: $126–200
$$$$: Over $200

Because there are numerous dining choices in West Yellowstone and Jackson, we further arranged our best selections into different groups based on price. Again, because of the many options for lodging in those two towns, we have grouped them by style and rates. The exception to our "best of" dining and lodging criteria is in the parks, where we have included all that is available.

Finally, we have made every attempt to determine seasons for lodging, dining, and attractions and listed those along with the phone numbers and $ ranking in parentheses. No seasons are noted when facilities are open year-round.

Introduction

IF WONDROUS SCENERY, incomparable wildlife viewing, riveting geology, and the chance to witness a natural environment at work aren't enough incentive to put Yellowstone and Grand Teton national parks at the top of your vacation list, then how about this: It could all be gone tomorrow, obliterated in a cataclysmic instant.

We're not talking about climate disruption. Or the encroaching masses of humanity that threaten to love Yellowstone, Grand Teton, and Jackson Hole to death. Or a pen stroke from a Congress that appears determined to unravel decades and, in some cases, more than a century of conservation successes. We're not even talking about a recurrence of the dramatic 1988 fires that scorched ⅓ of Yellowstone's 2.2 million acres, from which the park has experienced an astonishing evolution.

> **Did You Know?** Yellowstone's more than ten thousand hot springs, geysers, fumaroles, mud pots, and travertine terraces represent half of the rest of the world's geothermal features *combined* and that the three hundred geysers are ⅓ of Earth's entire total.

It's far more ominous than that. It's megatons of pent-up geothermal fury, poised to unleash its ire on the planet much the way it did about 640,000 years ago . . . and about 700,000 years before that . . . and about 700,000 years before that.

Detect a trend here? Maybe. Or maybe not. Scientists can't say for sure when, or if, the molten rock just beneath Yellowstone's 1,500-square-mile caldera will erupt in such a violent manner as to make Mount St. Helens seem like a burp.

Of course, such natural shock and awe wouldn't bode well for those of us living downstream—downstream being everywhere from West Yellowstone to West Philadelphia. But truth be known, this uneasy alliance between man and nature is part of the allure of the world's first national park and its majestic younger sibling 8 miles to the south.

For as you marvel at the jagged, fault-blocked Tetons rising abruptly above Jackson Lake to a cloudless sky, you'll contemplate the silent rumblings underfoot and realize that Mother Nature sets the ground rules here. As you admire the

LEFT: The Grand Canyon of the Yellowstone from Artist's Point.   Michael McCubbin

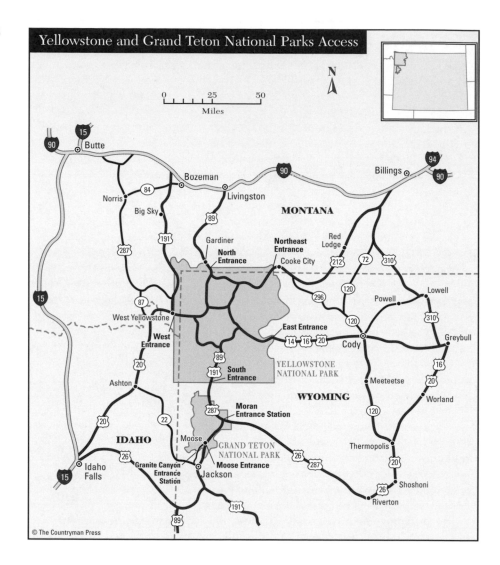

Yellowstone and Grand Teton National Parks Access

belching, hissing, and spewing of Yellowstone's ten thousand geothermal features, you'll respect just how alive and unpredictable this planet truly is.

As you perhaps glimpse a pack of wolves hunting down an ailing elk, or coyotes herding a frightened pronghorn, or a young bison and its mother suffocating in a bog, you'll begin to understand that the beauty of this extraordinary ecosystem lies partly in its cruelty. And that's just the point. Yellowstone and Grand Teton are not drive-thru zoos.

You'd never guess it by the summer "bear jams" and the occasional tales of camera-toting tourists gored by elk, charged by bison, or warned with an irritated snort by protective mother bears.

Many visitors forget this axiom and often pay a price, sometimes with their lives. Every year, people who treat this deceptively tranquil island of wilderness with cavalier hubris or carelessness tumble over cliffs, drown in swift rivers, fall into boiling geysers or, as occurred twice in Yellowstone's geographic center in 2011, meet a tragic fate at the paws or jaws of a startled grizzly bear.

It's understandable to a degree why some might disregard nature's laws. When the world's first national park was created in 1872, the idea was to preserve a place of natural beauty, yes, but purely for human benefit. Predators deemed contrary to this vision were eradicated, most notably wolves, mountains lions, and grizzlies. Hunting was allowed and poaching was common. Until the late 1960s, federal officials eradicated elk by the thousands because they grazed valleys and hillsides to the nubs. Bison were pushed perilously close to extinction by wanton slaughter. Two generations ago, bears routinely congregated at the parks' entrances for food handouts from tourists, a petting-zoo image perpetuated on Saturday morning television by Yogi and Boo Boo as they frolicked in Jellystone Park.

Ever since the Organic Act of 1968, efforts have been made to inch Yellowstone and the adjoining 310,000 acres of Grand Teton as close as humanly possible to their natural condition. Hunting is now prohibited, except for elk and bison in a small portion of Grand Teton. Fishing rules are strict on most streams. Animals within the park boundaries are protected. Wildlife-sensitive areas are off-limits to humans. Snowmobile use in the parks has been dramatically limited and regulated.

The crowning moment of this ecosystem-first philosophy came in 1995, when 14 gray wolves from Alberta, Canada, were introduced into Yellowstone's northern range, followed a year later by 17 from British Columbia. The controversial transplant brought the park's ecology full circle seven decades after a government-sponsored slaughter ended with the shooting of the last wolf.

Many scientists credit the thriving packs with restoring the health of the ailing Lamar Valley ecosystem. This so-called "trophic cascade" starts with the fear *Canis lupus* has reinstituted in elk, their favorite food. No longer able to casually browse, the elk have become more nomadic, allowing cottonwood, willow, and aspen to regenerate after 70 years of futility. The new plant growth in the Lamar has led to the return of songbirds and beavers, whose dams have created improved habitat for the struggling Yellowstone cutthroat trout. In turn, newly sprouted streamside berry bushes are providing forage for the endangered grizzly bear, whose existence may be jeopardized partly by beetle and fungus decimation of whitebark pines and their vital nuts.

Remarkably, much of this grand ecological experiment has taken place right in front of our eyes. Nowhere on the planet are wolves more readily visible to the public, and the result has been a year-round economic boon for the parks' gateway towns. An estimated 300,000 people have seen wolves in Yellowstone's wilds, and at least one wolf has been spotted literally every day since 2001—thanks largely to research collars worn by a select few.

It's true that visitors must tread lightly in Yellowstone and Grand Teton, but lest anyone find regulations in the parks too limiting, there is a rich assortment of outdoor and human-made indoor pleasures on the fringes of the parks and in the sage valley known as Jackson Hole.

River runners ply the Snake River's Class III rapids south of Jackson. West Yellowstone touts itself as the snowmobile capital of the world, with Cody and Cooke City not far behind; sledders miffed at tightening regulations inside Yellowstone have found rich playgrounds in the surrounding national forests. The Greater Yellowstone headwaters that contribute to America's three great river

History holds its place at the base of the Grand Tetons. Jon Sullivan/ Wikimedia Commons

systems—the Missouri, Columbia, and Colorado—offer the finest trout fishing on earth, with hundreds of guides eager to share their second-favorite holes. Five downhill ski resorts are within 50 miles of either park. Jackson Hole is a mountain biker's mecca worthy of mention in the same breath as Moab. And nearby federal wilderness areas provide adventure for hunters, anglers, hikers, campers, and packers wishing to see the land much the way Jim Bridger and John Colter saw it in the early 19th century.

The surrounding communities of Jackson and Cody in Wyoming; Ennis, Gardiner, Red Lodge, and West Yellowstone in Montana; and Driggs, Victor, Island Park, and Ashton in Idaho offer diverse restaurant fare and comfortable lodging ranging from the provincially rustic to cowboy-lux guest ranches.

Did You Know? About 98 percent of Yellowstone's visitors never go farther than 100 yards from a roadway, meaning that roughly 98 percent of the park is experienced by less than 2 percent of its visitors.

For those wanting the full park experience, semiprimitive lodging and basic dining are available inside both parks, from frontier luxury at historic Old Faithful Inn and Jenny Lake Lodge to no-frills rooms at Mammoth Hot Springs and bare-bones cabins at Tower Junction. Campgrounds are plentiful. And there's always the certainty of solitude in the backcountry.

Despite the millions of acres of wild country, these parks represent a mere island in a sea of humanity rapidly squeezing in from all sides. Their futures are by no means certain, even as current management practices nudge them toward more naturally functioning ecosystems where humans are expected to leave only footprints and dollars.

Today, those who put Yellowstone and Grand Teton at the top of their vacation lists can still discover that some of Earth's finest handiwork remains in northwest Wyoming and narrow slices of Montana and Idaho. That's true whether your tastes lean toward the towering backdrop of the snowcapped Tetons or the intricate web of life spun in front of your eyes in vast Yellowstone.

And part of this allure is in the understanding that what Mother Nature gives she can also take away—in a cataclysmic instant.

1

A Yellowstone, Grand Teton, and Jackson Hole Primer

GEOLOGY

Yellowstone National Park

Relax. You're not destined to be vaporized by a sudden rumbling from the Earth's most schizophrenic subsurface. When the time comes, scientists believe the fury beneath the Greater Yellowstone ecosystem will provide plenty of warning, in which case you'll want to book the first flight to Mars because the third rock from the sun quite likely will need some major restoration before humans can inhabit it again.

It's all because the earth under Yellowstone is tossing, turning, pushing, pulling, hissing, snorting, and heaving unlike anywhere else on the planet so accessible to humans. Yellowstone's ten-thousand-plus geysers, hot springs, fumaroles, travertine terraces, mud pots, and paint pots make for more geothermal activity than the rest of the globe's land mass combined. Some one to three thousand earthquakes are measured annually; there have been thirty rated 5.5 or higher on the Richter scale since 1900. And this activity offers a mere glimpse of the underground roiling from northwest Wyoming to northern Nevada since the first of three major eruptions 2.1 million years ago. The numbers from that initial blast are staggering. More than 600 cubic miles of ash rode air currents to what now is our Midwest, Gulf of Mexico, and Canada, covering thousands of square miles in minutes. Compare that to the minuscule 0.026 cubic miles of ash covering 11 states from the Mount St. Helens blast. And it surely wasn't the first major eruption. Specimen Ridge, which features 27 fossilized forests stacked on top of one another—including the preserved remnants of redwoods, oaks, mangrove, and breadfruit—has petrified trees as old as 50 million years.

LEFT: Old Faithful Geyser has entranced generations of visitors. NPS

17

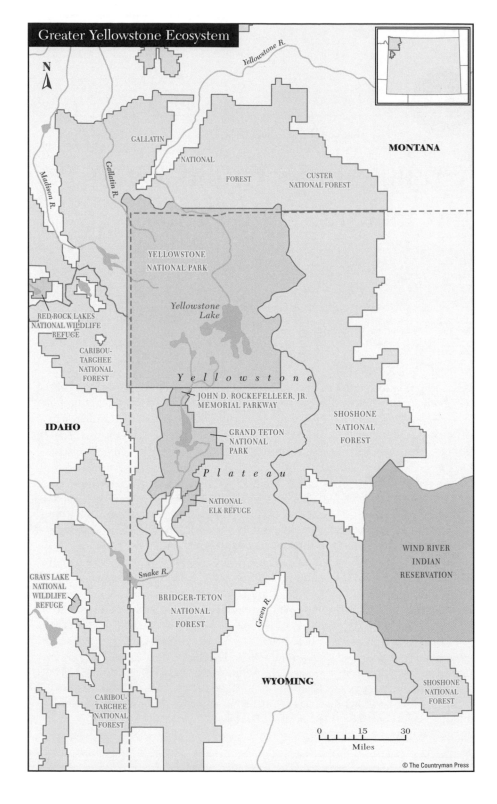

Greater Yellowstone Ecosystem

N

MONTANA

Yellowstone R.

Madison R.

Gallatin R.

GALLATIN

NATIONAL

FOREST

CUSTER
NATIONAL FOREST

YELLOWSTONE
NATIONAL PARK

Yellowstone
Lake

RED-ROCK LAKES
NATIONAL WILDLIFE
REFUGE

CARIBOU-
TARGHEE
NATIONAL
FOREST

Yellowstone

JOHN D. ROCKEFELLEER, JR.
MEMORIAL PARKWAY

SHOSHONE

NATIONAL

FOREST

IDAHO

GRAND TETON
NATIONAL
PARK

Plateau

NATIONAL
ELK REFUGE

WIND RIVER
INDIAN
RESERVATION

GRAYS LAKE
NATIONAL
WILDLIFE
REFUGE

Snake R.

BRIDGER-TETON
NATIONAL
FOREST

Green R.

WYOMING

SHOSHONE
NATIONAL
FOREST

CARIBOU-
TARGHEE
NATIONAL
FOREST

0   15   30
Miles

© The Countryman Press

Glacial erratics are scattered throughout the Lamar Valley.

The simple explanation for all this hyperterra activity is that Yellowstone is mostly a giant caldera sitting atop a combustible fire pit where molten rock, otherwise known as magma, is a mere 3 to 5 miles below the surface. In that initial blast, mountains were blown to smithereens and the land collapsed, creating a gaping 1,300-square-mile hole. By comparison, Oregon's Crater Lake, another volcanic mountain that collapsed when it erupted, is 37 times smaller. While Crater Lake filled with water after the collapse of Mount Mazama, Yellowstone's caldera was carpeted with lodgepole pine, rock, streams, plains, steamy vents, and large lakes.

What remains in Wyoming's far northwest corner is a circular thin and delicate crust stretching roughly from Lewis Lake on the south and Lake Butte on the east to Norris/Canyon Village on the north and the Montana-Idaho border on the west. The gaps and fissures in the Earth's surface, combined with the magma's shallow depth, ensure the meeting of fire and water. The result is hot spots ranging from Old Faithful geyser's dramatic eruptions every 90 minutes and the increasingly tempered hissing of steamy fumaroles at Roaring Mountain to gurgling mud pots scattered throughout Geyser Basin and the elegant travertine terraces of Mammoth Hot Springs—all different in appearance and definition.

Yellowstone's geothermal activity is also at least initially responsible for the park's most breathtaking feature: the Grand Canyon of the Yellowstone. At 20 miles long, up to 1,200 feet deep, and ranging from 1,000 to 4,000 feet across, the Grand Canyon's story begins with the arrival of glaciers whose impact would be felt as far south as the Tetons. The glaciers dammed the Yellowstone River, forming lakes. When they retreated, water poured forth and eroded lava rocks made vulnerable by the hot gasses just beneath the surface. The rocks, called rhyolite, weren't so submissive to the onrushing water in two notable spots—one at the edge of the caldera, the other at the meeting point of two different types of rhyolite. These spots are now recognized as the Lower Falls (308 feet) and Upper Falls (109 feet) of the Yellowstone. Both are favorites of the tourist's camera because of the dramatic drops, colorful hues of the canyon walls, and mists that can create surreal light. It's no wonder that the most popular viewpoints are named Inspiration Point, Artist's Point, and Grandview.

Also inspiring is the Northern Range, generally the one part of the park where visitors will find the type of towering mountain ranges they might expect from a Western vacation. This region is no less extraordinary for the dramatic gap in age between the Gallatin and Absaroka mountains on the west, north, and east, and the Washburn Range and Red mountains to the south. Both tower above the Yellowstone, Gardner, and Lamar river valleys. Yet the Gallatins and Absarokas are about 50 million years old, while the area between the Washburns and Reds, best seen from 8,859-foot Dunraven Pass, is a product of Yellowstone's most recent major eruption 640,000 years ago. The hike to the top of 10,243-foot Mount Washburn provides a dramatic look at this explosive past. Rivulets of water cascade from these high peaks into the Lamar River, which cuts across a sagebrush and grass plain renowned for its wildlife.

Grand Teton National Park

Some of America's most dramatic, rugged, and wild mountain ranges surround Yellowstone National Park. Though each is unique in its splendor, none has captured imaginations and photographers' lenses like the Tetons, which tower abruptly from the floor of Jackson Hole in a jaw-dropping display of glacier-carved rock and ice. It's fitting that Grand Teton National Park is 57 years younger than Yellowstone just to the north because in geological time it's a mere baby.

The youngest of the Rocky Mountains were born in a geological nanosecond some 9 to 13 million years ago, when the east and west sides of a 40-mile north-south fault decided, mostly via earthquakes and other released tensions, to go their separate ways—up on the west, down even more dramatically on the east. Imagine an aboriginal photographer's nirvana then. By the time the fault-blocking and glacial carving had concluded, Grand Teton had risen from 6 miles underground to more than 5 miles above what would eventually be named Jackson Hole.

In the millions of years since, the limestone peaks of Grand Teton, Middle Teton, Owen, and Moran have eroded considerably. Much of the sediment has filled in Jackson Hole, signaling a likely reunion. Grand Teton has slipped to a mere 13,770 feet above sea level, less than 1.5 miles above the rising town of Jackson. Along the way, glaciers carved the jagged ridges and outcroppings that left the Tetons with unique contours once the last ice fields disappeared about 13,000 years ago. Today, the Tetons are one of the world's most spectacular visual wonders, especially from the east—where the fault-blocked rise and fall left few foothills to mar the views for the likes of such photographers as Ansel Adams and William Henry Jackson.

Every few thousand years or so, the gap between the valley floor and the top of the Tetons increases by a few feet due to a gentle temblor. But eventually Jackson Hole will rise and meet the tips of the Tetons—until the next great earthquake separates them again. Of course, when Yellowstone finally blows its top, any movement to the south may be the geological equivalent of rearranging the *Titanic*'s deck chairs.

Those of us living in the vicinity can at least hope that Yellowstone's caldera will keep its relative cool just a little longer. After all, the "hot spot" underfoot is moving southwest at the expeditious rate of about 1 inch per year. In no time at all, it'll be Nevada's problem.

CULTURE

Yellowstone National Park

Imagine that you've migrated across the frozen Bering Strait, crossed the wilds of what is now Alaska and British Columbia, and ventured south into what would be called—in about 11,000 years—Montana. Along the way, you've traversed retreating glaciers from an ice age, evaded saber-toothed cats, and feasted on woolly mammoths. Suddenly you come across a trembling landscape unlike any you've ever known. Hissing, steaming, snorting—all just reemerging after thousands of years trapped restlessly in icy seclusion.

Thus was the genesis of the physical and spiritual reverence humans have held for Yellowstone. The awe continued with latter-day Indians and the first Anglos who arrived in the 18th century. Food riches beckoned those first humans, known as the Folsom and Clovis cultures. If archeologists are correct, the earliest residents used obsidian to hunt mammoth, camels, mastodons, beaver, and bighorn bison that, compared to today's descendants, would've looked as if they were on steroids. Those first humans might also have used the same tools to fend off attacks from lions, bears, and wolves that also scarcely resembled the carnivores now roaming Greater Yellowstone.

After the ice departed, it probably ushered in a two-thousand-year period where the land was delicate tundra. Only after gradual warming did Yellowstone begin to take on its current profile, about nine thousand years ago. Lodgepole pine appeared, along with Engelmann spruce and whitebark pine, whose nuts became a favorite of the grizzly bear. Blood found on arrowheads, knives, rocks, and other tools scattered throughout the region suggests that deer, elk, rabbit, sheep, and bear were plentiful. In an ominous precursor of our current overconsumption habits, evidence also suggests that these cultures pillaged their bounty. The decline of game populations caused dramatic social restructuring and forced a focus on smaller game and plants for food.

Today's visitors would be surprised to learn they might not be the first to complain about summer crowds, though climates were so harsh that only the Sheepeaters—bighorn-eating ancestors of Idaho's Shoshone and Bannock tribes—made permanent homes in Yellowstone and the Grand Teton region. Hundreds of fire rings, wickiups, campsites, petroglyphs, tipi rings, obsidian points, burial grounds, and buffalo kill sites have been discovered, and archeological mapping has barely begun. Researchers also believe that most evidence of those long-ago residents has been lost to harsh climes and time. The whereabouts of other

Did You Know? The Folsom culture is named for fossilized points found in bison bones near what is now the town of Folsom, New Mexico. Similar remnants have been found in Greater Yellowstone, including the Little Bighorn Battlefield.

A Shoshone teepee near Mammoth has braved Yellowstone's winters for 140 years.

existing remote religious sites remain a mystery in part because today's native inhabitants, mostly the Crow and Shoshone, still use them, and in part because the Park Service guards the secrecy of their locations lest vandals or geo-cachers exploit them.

To the south, lack of hot springs, geysers, and other warming features apparently limited human winter habitation of the Grand Teton/Jackson Hole area even more than Yellowstone, mostly because large game migrated to lower elevations and less-harsh climes. The ancestors of what would become the Crow, Bannock, Shoshone, and Blackfeet would feast on summer roots on the plateaus and then cross the Continental Divide to wait out the deep snows of the Little Ice Age that ended in the decades just before Yellowstone was established in 1872. Other Indians would winter in the broad valley north of what is now Gardiner, where buffeting winds scoured the Yellowstone River Valley of its snow and left a paradise of native grasses and small animals. As the climate continued to warm in the past two thousand years, large game returned and human populations followed.

The Anglos who first arrived in the late 1770s were French-Canadian fur trappers in search of beaver pelts. They came up the Missouri River and dispersed up its tributaries—including the Yellowstone, Madison, and Gallatin rivers, which are birthed on the Yellowstone Plateau. Their legacy remains in some of the names still gracing towns, rivers, and mountains. The Yellowstone, known by the Indians as Elk River, was named *Rive des Roche Jaunes* (literally "river of yellow rock") by the French. It is assumed that it's because of the amber rimrock near present-day Billings, Montana, but possibly because of similarly hued outcroppings near the Yellowstone's confluence with the Missouri in North Dakota. The French influence is most notable in the Tetons themselves, christened *Les Trois Tetons*—the three breasts—by trappers perhaps yearning for female companionship (the Shoshone called these mountains *Teewinot*, or "Many Peaks").

The trappers and Indians had the woods and rivers to themselves in a tenuous détente until the Lewis and Clark Corps of Discovery passed through the region in 1803, after President Thomas Jefferson ordered exploration of the Louisiana Purchase country. Lewis and Clark never saw the Yellowstone or Teton area, but they heard Shoshone and Nez Perce tales of rolling thunder emanating from the mystical land to the south; indeed, by this time many Indians were reluctant to sleep near the geyser basins because they believed spirits inhabited them. Lewis and Clark's reports of bountiful resources in the area began to pique a nation's interest, and one of the trip's members, John Colter, returned to Yellowstone five years after the expedition to trap beaver. But it wasn't until 1827 that Americans on the East Coast received their first detailed description of Yellowstone-Teton, thanks to trapper Daniel Potts's vivid accounts in a Philadelphia newspaper. Colter and Potts were just two of many fur-trapping mountain men whose tales of the Northern Rockies grew to mythical proportions back East. Though their era lasted only until about 1840, such names as Jim Bridger, Jedediah Smith, and the Sublette boys live on, their legacies perpetuated in Western art, folklore, and such movies as *Jeremiah Johnson*. For about 15 years, Anglo and Indian trappers would gather for annual rendezvous that were whiskey-drinking, arm-wrestling, skirt-chasing, gun-dueling, poker-playing precursors to some of the tamer frontier-day festivals many small Western towns stage today.

The next wave of explorers came after the Civil War. Easily the most significant was a group formed at the behest of the Northern Pacific Railroad, which sought a route across Montana and needed publicity to entice investors. In 1870, the railroad bankrolled the 19-member Washburn-Langford-Doane Expedition. The group planned to follow a route detailed a year earlier by the Folsom-Cook-Peterson expedition, whose account of the region in a popular magazine had rekindled flagging interest. East and West Coast media tales of the Washburn expedition ensured that Yellowstone would forever be in the national consciousness. Annual tourist visits began to skyrocket past the average of five hundred who soaked at Mammoth Hot Springs during the Civil War era.

In 1872, thanks to further attention drawn to the area by the compelling images of landscape painter Thomas Moran and photographs of the aforementioned William Henry Jackson, the U.S. Congress was moved to designate Yellowstone as the world's first national park. President Ulysses S. Grant signed the Yellowstone Act into law that year. The region was ultimately and ironically saved from development by its own ruggedness. Amid the nation's headlong rush to exploit the West's resource wealth, Yellowstone was deemed so remote and inhospitable that protecting it couldn't possibly hinder progress.

"Protection" was a misnomer, however. For nearly a decade after its formation, the park was under such siege from poaching, squatters, and vandalism that the U.S. Army was called in to quell the lawlessness and land grabbing. For three more decades, the cavalry patrolled the park on horseback, first from Camp Sheridan and then from Fort Yellowstone, now the park's current headquarters at Mammoth. Their role was a far cry from Yellowstone's current mission. The cavalry built roads and fought fires. It also protected elk and bison from poaching, and

Until 1916, the cavalry oversaw the park from Fort Yellowstone (now Mammoth). NPS

eliminated such natural predators as coyotes, wolves, and mountain lions by using poisons. The cavalry's presence ended in 1916 with the formation of the National Park Service.

The next major players in the Yellowstone region were the railroads. By the early 1880s, Jay Cooke's Northern Pacific had reached Livingston, Montana, and Averill Harriman's Union Pacific had driven its golden spike in northern Utah. Despite opposition from hunters, railroad spurs were built from Livingston to Gardiner and from Pocatello, Idaho, to present-day West Yellowstone, Montana. At the turn of the century, more than 80 percent of tourists arrived by train and entered the park in carriages or on horseback. Railroad barons had grand visions of development within Yellowstone's borders, including building a dam at the falls in the Grand Canyon of the Yellowstone River. But others vehement about keeping the park in its natural state stonewalled their attempts.

The railroads' era lasted about as long as that of the mountain man. Construction of the Grand Loop Road was finished in 1905 and the first car entered Yellowstone legally in 1915. Within a quarter-century, more visitors had entered the park via car than by train, and rail service ended in 1960. Today, all that remains of the railroad's influence are visible remnants of the old grades, renovated historic stations at West Yellowstone and Gallatin Gateway, and the Railroad Ranch along the Henry's Fork of the Snake River, a world-renowned dry-fly fishing shrine. Meanwhile, Yellowstone now has 370 miles of roads and five entrances, with one, the north station at Gardiner, open year-round to automobile traffic.

The park's mission continues to evolve and the age-old debate over recreational values versus intrinsic values has been shifting. No longer is the prevailing sentiment "how can the park serve the people?"; now it has evolved to, "how can people serve the park?" Perhaps nowhere is this attitude reflected more than with

Until the 1960s, bears were routinely fed garbage by tourists and park employees. NPS

the controversial restoration of wolves to Yellowstone in 1995 and 1996. When the 14 gray wolves were released from a pen above the Buffalo Ranch in the Lamar Valley, it marked the first time in seven decades that wolves howled in the park. The last wolf had been shot in the 1920s after an all-out war against the predator. Researchers had no idea what to expect with what was termed a "nonessential experimental" population of wolves. To their surprise, the wolves have been highly visible, seen by thousands of visitors through scopes, binoculars, and often out of car windows as they romp along the road through the Lamar Valley.

Another example of a shift in attitudes: Where once park officials attempted to extinguish fires, now fire is viewed as essential to the park's

Camp Sheridan (now Mammoth, circa 1900) was where the cavalry resided before Fort Yellowstone was completed. NPS

health. The controversial "let-burn" policy made national headlines in the summer of 1988, when the media descended on the unprecedented inferno that Yellowstone had become. Images of towering smoke, vast wastelands with the ghostly spire remnants of lodgepole pine, and flames nipping at the fringes of Grant Village and Cooke City dominated TV screens. Once the anxiety died with the last smoldering ember, and after an astonishing 800,000 acres was scorched, cooler heads eventually prevailed. Turns out the devastation was partly a function of the failed old Smokey the Bear doctrine that the only good fire is an extinguished fire. Ever since the first humans arrived, nature had cleansed the ecosystem of bugs, disease, and deadfall with fire; suppression had created the perfect recipe for devastation. Well before 1988, scientists recognized that prescribed burns were necessary for the health of the forest, and that what happened that summer was inevitable.

The drama began subsiding as early as the next spring, when the park's "recovery" was already evident in the tender shoots of wildflowers and grasses. More than two decades later, the spires of two-hundred-year-old lodgepoles stand over verdant understories that provide browse for wildlife. Teenaged pines rise in the shadows. Wildflowers are abundant. Animals are thriving and the park is closer to a natural balance than at any time since the post–Civil War era. Scientists say conflagrations akin to 1988 had happened before, and they surely will happen again—probably with more frequency, given the realities of global warming—regardless of

A gray wolf from Alberta eyes a visitor outside its acclimation pen shortly after its arrival for reintroduction into the park in 1995. NPS

One of the five major Yellowstone blazes in 1988 rages near Grant Village. NPS

man's intentions. The good news is that nature heals quickly and provides an education along the way.

Other challenges remain as well. Limited funding has created infrastructure concerns. Ancient whitebark pines dying from beetles and fungus cast an ominous shadow over the threatened grizzly bear; many biologists think the high-elevation tree will be functionally extinct in Greater Yellowstone by 2020. The endangered Yellowstone cutthroat trout's future is further at risk because of the illegal introduction of voracious lake trout into the frigid waters of Yellowstone Lake.

Though only 1 percent is intensely developed and 90 percent of visitors limit themselves to these areas, the park is increasingly challenged by the number of summer visitors—a record 3.6 million in 2010. Perhaps even greater threats are coming from outside the park's borders. Logging and mining have subsided, but oil and gas operations cover northern and western Wyoming in unprecedented numbers, threatening wildlife corridors and pristine waters. Housing developments are sprouting on the fringes of both parks, compromising the wildness and isolation that lured people here in the first place.

Perhaps most ominous is the specter of a warming climate. In the past seven decades, the average temperature at Gardiner, Montana, has risen 3.7 degrees. Models from the first comprehensive study of Greater Yellowstone's climate, released in late 2011, show that if emissions of heat-trapping gasses aren't reduced globally, temperatures could rise as much as another 9.7 degrees by 2100—giving Yellowstone a climate akin to the Los Angeles suburb of Culver City.

Above all, even at 2.2 million acres, Yellowstone is an island, cut off from the connected ribbons of wild country to the north, its ecosystem fragile and its wildlife vulnerable. And yet, though many challenges remain, Americans can take

More than two decades after the 1988 fires, a lodgepole forest is reborn. NPS

great pride that the world's first national park and the lands surrounding it form the last great largely intact temperate ecosystem on the planet—where the natural world works as it was intended.

Grand Teton National Park

One look at the jagged peaks of Grand Teton, Middle Teton, and Mount Moran would seem sufficient evidence to instantly declare the awe-inspiring area south of Yellowstone a national park. And in fact, early Yellowstone superintendents and Wyoming politicians periodically proposed expanding Yellowstone's boundaries southward; the U.S. House of Representatives even approved setting aside the rock and ice of the Teton Range plus eight glacial lakes as a national park in 1929.

If only it were that easy.

More than 75 years of controversy, political wrangling, and compromise would pass after the rubber-stamp creation of Yellowstone before an increasing tide of tourists empowered Washington in 1950 to create the Grand Teton National Park we know today. As much as wilderness purists blanch at the growth of the town of Jackson and its trendy faux-Western boutiques, they would've cringed at what Jackson Hole had become at the beginning of the 20th century.

The utilitarian vision for the region south of Yellowstone began in 1910 with the construction of 70-foot-high Jackson Lake Dam on the Snake River. The dam flooded 7,200 acres of lodgepole pines and backed up enough water to supply potato and beet farmers on the other side of the mountains in Idaho. In an ironic twist, the dam might've planted the seed for the park's creation a half-century later. An ugly shanty town for construction workers sprang up overnight. Dead and dying trees poked through the surface of Jackson Lake. The scene quickly sparked an emotional preservation versus development debate.

Like those who appreciated Yellowstone's wonders, some entrepreneurs gazed at the grandeur of the Tetons and envisioned multitudes coming west to escape life's workaday pressures. The vacation dude ranches so prevalent in the region today actually had their genesis at the time the dam was built. Their owners saw the value of preserving the scenic value of the area and began the long, winding, and bumpy road to protection.

The first phase wasn't so challenging: In 1929, the rock-and-ice parts of the region—the Teton Range—were made into a national park. But proponents weren't done. In 1926, a visit by millionaire John D. Rockefeller, at the behest of Yellowstone superintendent Horace Albright and a coalition of dude ranchers, cattlemen, and others who feared exploitation of the valley, spurred further action. Rockefeller purchased 35,000 acres of delinquent ranches with the intent of donating the land to the newly created Park Service to add to the existing park. Knowing a giveaway to the federal government wouldn't sit well with cattlemen who used the rocky valley as a cattle thoroughfare between summer and winter grazing lands, he bought the land covertly, under the name of a company that implied his group might operate it as a ranch.

The deal was complete in 1930 before locals knew what hit them, and many of the state's politicians and ranchers were furious. After Rockefeller's end run, opposition to protection of surrounding lands intensified. The ire was so fierce that the feds wouldn't even accept his donated land. Park opponents opined that expanding the boundaries would lock up the land from development and put ranches out of business. For 13 years, they had their way with Congress.

In 1943, with the country distracted by World War II, President Franklin D. Roosevelt used his popularity to override Congress and accept Rockefeller's 35,000-acre gift. Roosevelt took another 130,000 acres of U.S. Forest Service land and created the Jackson Hole National Monument, again with a predictable reaction. Wyoming politicians repeatedly introduced legislation to overturn the monument, only to be rebuked in Washington, D.C.

Ultimately, tourists saved a valley now challenged by their very passion for it. The money they brought during a celebratory post–World War II travel boom eased local economic fears. In a move that would aid in the creation of future national parks and wilderness areas, the federal government compromised by "grandfathering" in the right of ranching families to run cattle and hunters to pursue elk within certain parts of the expanded park's borders. On September 14, 1950, Rockefeller's donated land and the national monument both were incorporated, bringing Grand Teton National Park to its present size.

Today nobody is more grateful that the land was preserved than the residents of Jackson Hole. Until the recent gas-and-oil boom, no region of Wyoming had a more bustling economy. Tourism flourishes at unprecedented levels. Jackson consistently ranks among the top communities in America for wealth, partly due to its scenic beauty and partly because only 3 percent of the county is privately owned. Though sprawl is evident, the park boundary, mountains to the west, and the National Elk Refuge to the north have limited Jackson's growth and kept it more intimate than other destination resorts. And even that old eyesore, Jackson Lake Dam, was rebuilt in the late 1980s so that it better meshes into the landscape. Above the dam, visitors to sprawling Jackson Lake Lodge now gaze over Willow Flats and shimmering lake waters to towering mountains that form one of the most breathtaking backdrops in America.

Grizzly bears have made an extraordinary recovery in Greater Yellowstone. NPS

WILDLIFE

For all the beauty, recreation, and awe-inspiring natural features of Yellowstone and Grand Teton national parks, wildlife viewing surely ranks at the top of any list of reasons to come. For millions of people, Yellowstone is where they'll see their first wild bison, probably their first elk, almost surely their first bear, and definitely their first wolf. Every day offers a new gee-whiz moment.

As noted earlier, wildlife management has undergone dramatic changes in both parks, but especially Yellowstone. Elk were hunted relentlessly and bison nearly went extinct from wholesale slaughter until the 1894 Lacey Act prohibited hunting of wildlife in the park. The law didn't prevent the concerted extirpation in the 1920s of the wolf, which as a predator was deemed a "bad" animal for its perceived threat to "good" animals, namely elk and deer. Bear-feeding shows were conducted until 1941 and feeding from cars at entrance stations was allowed until the early 1970s. Though Yellowstone can still feel like a theme park at times in the summer, the evolution to a more natural management—beginning with the Organic Act in 1968—has both enhanced the wildlife experience for visitors and improved habitat.

Because wildlife appear so docile, it's easy to be lulled into complacency. Don't be. As park literature constantly reminds visitors, these are wild animals. Don't leave your car and traverse a meadow to get closer to bear cubs; their mama won't like it. Don't put your young daughter on the back of a bison for a photo op; chances are you'll be gored and/or your daughter will be tossed like a rag doll. Don't try to get personal with a rutting bull elk; you might lose body parts and the elk will lose its rack. Sound ridiculous? All of these scenarios have actually happened in Yellowstone. The park says to give all animals at least 25 yards distance (we think it should be 50), and make it 100 yards for bears and wolves. Don't feed any wildlife, even chipmunks or ravens, because it'll habituate them to human handouts—with deadly consequences come winter. And don't even think about trying to call animals closer by bugling an elk or howling at a wolf.

Most visitors come to Yellowstone in the summer, which happens to be the least likely time for a wildlife bonanza because most are in the high country. The best time is spring, with autumn a close second. For our entrance-fee money, there is nothing quite like a visit to the park in May, before the high-country snows melt. Most of the wildlife—elk being an exception—have their young tailing them, and it isn't unusual to see bears, wolves, bison, elk, coyotes, and pronghorn all in one 360-degree panorama in the Lamar Valley. Truly, the American Serengeti.

Early morning and dusk are the best time to view animals, when they often feed in the open. By midafternoon, most have curled up for a nap. If you do decide to stop, you're required to have all four tires off the roadway to keep traffic flowing smoothly.

Bears (Black): The black bear appears to be on solid ground in Yellowstone, with roughly five hundred roaming the park and surrounding areas. The black bear doesn't inspire the same fear or awe in people as grizzlies, but it's imperative to give them space. You're more likely to see a black bear near one of the roads than a grizzly. And black bears generally try to avoid any place they associate with grizzly bears. They can be viewed just about anywhere, but one place where they seem

Black bears are relatively common in the Tower Junction area, also called "The Bearmuda Triangle."

particularly common is in the Tower Junction area—or, as some park naturalists call it, "The Bearmuda Triangle."

Bears (Grizzly): Though wolves certainly are garnering their share of interest these days, grizzly bears remain the embodiment of wild Yellowstone. Hiking in grizzly country heightens the senses like few other adventures. Remarkably, three decades ago biologists feared that such experiences were destined to become a tragic memory. Grizzlies were on the verge of extinction in Greater Yellowstone after garbage dumps were abruptly closed and a familiar food source dried up. Many grizzlies starved, others had to be euthanized because they were approaching campgrounds and community dumps looking for food. Populations dropped perilously close to the point of no return. However, thanks to Endangered Species Act protections, the grizzly bear has evolved to become one of the region's most astonishing conservation success stories. Roughly six hundred roam Greater Yellowstone and their territory is expanding into places they haven't been seen in decades or, in some cases, more than a century. Carrying bear spray should be as much a part of a hiker's arsenal these days as trail mix, good boots, and water.

The grizzly's future is still debated. The precipitous decline of two of the bear's most important food sources—the whitebark pine nut and Yellowstone cutthroat trout—have pushed grizzlies out of Yellowstone's interior in search of food. One unfortunate result, for both bears and people, is an increase in human-bear conflicts. Bear attacks remain exceedingly rare and both grizzly and black bear would just as soon avoid you, but it's imperative to follow all food-storage regulations, travel in groups of three or more, and know how to use bear spray—some people have actually sprayed it on themselves thinking it's a repellent. According to the Park Service, if you do happen to startle a grizzly and it charges, stretch out and play dead on your stomach, cover your neck, and keep your backpack on. Don't run; they'll be on you in a New York second. And always remember that a fed bear is a dead bear. Leaving food out will acclimatize a bear to humans, ultimately resulting in the animal's demise. If you plan to camp in the backcountry, hang your food at least 15 feet off the ground and at least 200 feet from your camp. Most backcountry sites provide food poles, but if not, use a long rope and gunnysack to hang your food from a tree.

A grizzly bear gnaws away at bison remains under the Yellowstone River Bridge.

The best time to see grizzlies is in the spring, when they're stirring from hibernation, and in the fall, as they're preparing for their winter sleep. Look for them moving in and out of tree lines and meadows.

Bighorn Sheep: Like many of Yellowstone's creatures, these muscular animals nearly lost their toehold in the park four decades ago. Though hunting played a role, the bighorn was most

Bighorn sheep rams laze on a hillside above the Lamar Valley.

challenged by a lack of nutrition, due largely to exorbitant populations of elk. Bighorn sheep like the high country and other rugged areas inaccessible to most humans, but it's not uncommon to see some of the 250 or so residing in Yellowstone, especially just south of the North Entrance in the Gardner River Canyon. They are recognizable by the curled horns used to do battle in mating season in November and December. Consider yourself extremely fortunate if you happen to come across two males ramming each other at high speeds as if auditioning for a Discovery Channel documentary.

Bison: This is one iconic Yellowstone creature you're virtually guaranteed to see, even though many leave for higher ground in summer. At one time they were reduced by wanton slaughter in the region to a total of 24—yes, 24—at the Buffalo Ranch in the Lamar Valley. Today, the last genetically pure remnants of the herds that thundered across the Great Plains by the millions generally fluctuate between 2,800 and 5,000 in the park. And it can be argued that the bison is the most persecuted wildlife in the nation despite being a revered symbol of the American frontier. The issue is that during harsh winters, many bison wander out of the park to the north and west, where they are "hazed" back into Yellowstone to protect cattle from a disease called brucellosis, which is found only in Greater Yellowstone and causes cows to abort calves. Though there has never been a documented case of a wild bison transmitting brucellosis to cattle (elk are the known purveyors), and

A bison herd forages on fresh grasses at the Blacktail Ponds.

though brucellosis was brought to the region by cattle in the first place, until the winter of 2010–11 bison were nevertheless hazed and even rounded up for slaughter. The goal of many conservation groups and state agencies is to restore free-roaming, disease-free bison to wildlife refuges and tribal lands where there are no cattle. By the spring of 2011, some progress was being made: Bison were allowed to roam the entire Gardiner Basin north of the park—the first time in four decades they were allowed to leave Yellowstone alive—and in December 2011 Montana Fish, Wildlife & Parks approved moving "surplus" Yellowstone bison to two Indian reservations in northeast Montana. If you drive US 89 south of Livingston, just before you reach Gardiner you'll notice four fenced-off areas on the east side of the highway. These are quarantine pens where bison are kept with an eye on turning them free on the prairie one day.

Bison are deceptively docile. For that reason, and because they are so readily visible, bison are the park's most dangerous animals. When provoked, they can charge at speeds of up to 35 mph. Give them room. If you're driving US 191 north of West Yellowstone, be on the lookout for bison crossing the road in the winter and spring—especially at night, when they are barely visible in the blackness. Unlike deer and elk, their eyes don't reflect headlights.

In Grand Teton National Park, nearly 1,000 mingle with elk for easy meals at the National Elk Refuge, creating the largest bison herd in any refuge. These bison are different from Yellowstone's in that they carry cattle genes and are not considered genetically pure.

Coyotes: Though not as commonly seen as the bison or elk, the wily coyote is still a Yellowstone fixture even as wolves have dramatically reduced their numbers. This resilient rascal has survived eradication programs to flourish throughout the park. It isn't uncommon to see them ambling along roadways looking for rodents or an unwitting pronghorn to herd. Some visitors confuse them with wolves, though once you've seen a wolf you won't make that mistake again. Both look like large dogs, but coyotes are smaller, less sturdy, and have more pointed ears. Instead of howling like wolves, they yip and yap.

Eagles: America's symbol, and perhaps best-known Endangered Species Act success story, is commonly seen in and around Yellowstone. Bald eagles are more numerous because golden eagles spend more time riding thermals in rugged mountains. Yellowstone has more than two dozen nesting pairs, compared to ten in 1986. Many of the younger birds tend to migrate out of the park in winter to Oregon and California, then return. One excellent

The bald eagle is an iconic symbol of America commonly seen in Yellowstone. NPS

place to see nesting eagles is between West Yellowstone and Madison Junction, in a dead tree, or "snag," on the south side of the road. In the Tetons, thermals created by the mountains plus an abundance of prey make an excellent home for eagles. Look for golden eagles at elevations above 10,000 feet.

Elk: No animal has had more impact on Yellowstone than the elk. And in a sense, no creature sparks more contentious debate. The stately ungulate, once essentially extinct in the region, is again prevalent thanks mostly to the efforts of hunting groups. In fact, for many years elk were so prolific that the Park Service was forced to either slaughter or relocate them to other areas of the country. Hunting free-for-alls were regular occurrences just outside the park's north boundary, in Montana. With the restoration of wolves and other factors, the population of Yellowstone's Northern Range herd has dropped by ⅔—to levels that most biologists say is just about right but hunters argue is too few. Either way, a ravaged landscape is healing, enabling the return of many other species, such as deer, bighorn sheep, pronghorn, and beaver, which became rare without lush grasses and trees.

If you come to Yellowstone during the mating season (rut) in late autumn, you'll be treated to the primal sounds of males bugling and fighting each other with their massive racks. Such warfare often takes place on the grasses between the buildings in Mammoth. In winter, the big bulls hang together, often near the road between Mammoth and the Northeast Entrance.

Elk are equally controversial in Grand Teton, where *wapiti* are a routine site in winter thanks in large part to them congregating by the thousands for an artificial buffet of hay and pellets in the neighboring National Elk Refuge. In summers, they tend to disperse into the high country, though they are commonly seen

A bull elk checks for danger near Canyon Village.

amid the sage and aspen in the park. It's not uncommon to see a herd crossing Willow Flats.

Moose: The stately moose is an unpredictable animal to be watched from a safe distance. A moose will come after you for no apparent reason, especially a cow with a calf or a bull courting a female. Look for moose around water, especially marshy areas where willows and aquatic plant life abound. These animals were perhaps hurt most by the prolific 1988 fires, which burned about ⅓ of Yellowstone's forests. Moose migrate to higher elevations in winter, where tree branches collecting snow make for easier movement. Without those trees, there is less prime moose habitat. They are also suffering from a type of parasite that is affecting population sustainability. Their dwindling numbers in the region are a major concern for biologists.

Mountain Lion: Once hunted nearly to extinction in the park, these elusive and secretive cats, also called cougars, are rarely seen, even though one might be watching if you venture into rocky areas. Like the wolf, the mountain lion was part of a predator-eradication program in the park at the turn of the previous century. Perhaps 25 of the animals live in Yellowstone, primarily in the Northern Range. They can be found wherever mule deer roam. Consider yourself lucky if you see one from a distance because cougars avoid humans if at all possible. No cougar attack on a human has ever been reported in Yellowstone.

Mule Deer: Midwesterners and easterners are often surprised to discover that elk are more commonly seen than deer in Yellowstone. Mule deer, also called black-tailed deer because of the black tips on their tails, are fairly abundant; about 2,500

The crafty coyote continues to thrive in Yellowstone.

reside in the park. But because they tend to spend summers in the forest and high meadows, they're not as readily spotted.

Others: The fortunate visitor might see the extremely rare wolverine, lynx, pine marten, or pika. More prevalent are the badger, fox, beaver, and sandhill crane. More commonly seen are white-tailed deer (especially outside the parks, in river valleys), marmots, hawks, ravens, red squirrels, osprey, river otters, white pelicans, and chipmunks. The mountain goat, a snow-white favorite of visitors in Glacier National Park, is an introduced species now routinely seen in the Absaroka Range in Yellowstone's northeast corner.

Pronghorn: Commonly—and mistakenly—known as the antelope, this graceful, speedy, and colorful creature is a denizen of sage prairies and is the region's lone true native—a survivor of the last ice age. Reaching speeds of up to 60 mph, they are the second-fastest land animal on the planet, behind the

A badger peers warily at an intruder from his home near Specimen Ridge.

cheetah—and the pronghorn would smoke a cheetah after 40 yards. The Grand Teton herd also performs the second-longest overland mammal migration in North America every year, up to 180 miles from its summer grounds through the Gros Ventre River Valley to the Red Desert south of Pinedale; only the caribou of Alaska and Canada roam farther. You'll see pronghorn by the hundreds if you arrive from Wyoming, which has a herd of about 400,000. About 5,000 live in and around Yellowstone, though only a few hundred typically are within the park's borders. Once there were seven major pronghorn migrations, and now there is but one because of habitat loss. The pronghorn is a creature of habit and won't jump even though it is extremely athletic, so when it meets a fence or other obstruction on its traditional path, it stops—and often dies.

Trumpeter Swans: Yellowstone is critical habitat for the largest water birds in North America. Anywhere from 30 to 60 live there in summer; nearly twice that many convene in winter. These elegant white birds were nearly hunted to extinction in the 1800s for plumage used to decorate women's hats. The park and wildlife refuges in surrounding areas have facilitated a tenuous rally. Prime viewing is available at Madison and Firehole rivers and the Yellowstone River near Canyon Village. In winter, look for them on the Henry's Fork of the Snake River in Island Park.

Wolves: Nowhere in the world is the wolf so readily visible in the wild than Yellowstone. The gray wolf was restored to the park (and the wilds of central Idaho) in 1995 after a seven-decade absence. Park naturalist James Halfpenny, a noted author on wolves, called it "the greatest ecological experiment of our time." There were 14 brought to Yellowstone from Alberta in 1995, and another 17 from British Columbia in 1996; still another 35 were released in Idaho over those two years. From those first 66, there are now about 1,700 in the Northern Rockies, and a profound impact has been evident ever since. Start with tourism. Thousands of visitors come to Yellowstone each year, especially in the slower winter months,

A gray wolf saunters near the confluence of Soda Butte Creek and the Lamar River.

simply to see wolves. Such communities as Gardiner, West Yellowstone, and Cooke City have savored a winter economic boon tallying $35.5 million annually. Scientists also believe the wolves are having a positive impact on the health of the ecosystem, thanks to what they call "trophic cascade." The wolf's place at the top of the food chain has rippled down to songbirds, beaver, pronghorn, trout, and other species. The explanation—the presence of *Canis lupus* has instilled a long-lost fear in their favorite cuisine, the elk, which no longer can safely browse in the same places for hours. This "ecology of fear" has enabled the rebirth of aspen in the Northern Range and cottonwood and willow in ailing valleys.

Still, the wolf is fighting for tolerance, acceptance, and appreciation. In 2011, the animal became the first ever to be removed from Endangered Species Act protections by politicians. Some ranchers have struggled with livestock predation from packs that have spread well beyond the parks' borders. Hunters and outfitters blame declines in populations of elk on the wolf. And some people just loathe wolves. The states surrounding Yellowstone have always been allowed to remove problem wolves because of their "nonessential experimental" status; now Montana and Idaho have hunting seasons, and Wyoming was expected to take over wolf management in 2012. In Yellowstone, wolf numbers have fluctuated based on prey, from a high of more than 170 a few years ago to fewer than 100 by

Rick McIntyre, aka The Wolf Man, shares the latest news on wolves in the Lamar Valley with attentive tourists.

2010 and back to about 125 in 2011. Contrary to fairy-tale lore, there has never been a documented attack by wolves on humans in the lower 48 states, and only twice since 1995 have individual animals been removed from Yellowstone for being too acclimated to people.

As for Grand Teton, it took three years for reintroduced wolf packs in Yellowstone to proliferate and migrate south. In 1999, the Teton pack took hold and gave birth to pups, the first in the park in more than 50 years. Wolves are still infrequently seen in Grand Teton, though they continue to increase as the number of packs moving in and out of the park has expanded to six.

If you want to see a wolf in Yellowstone, your best strategy is to look for "The Wolf Man," Rick McIntyre, either very early in the morning or late in the day, typically in or near the Lamar Valley. McIntyre, who studies the wolves literally every day and loves sharing information with visitors, uses radio telemetry to locate collared wolves and record their habits for the Yellowstone Wolf Project. And he is easy to spot as well: He drives a conspicuous yellow Nissan Xterra and inevitably has a devoted following of "wolfers."

2

Yellowstone: West Entrance

West Entrance to Madison Junction/Madison Junction to Norris/
Norris to Canyon Village/Madison Junction to Old Faithful/
The Bechler Region

GETTING HERE

There isn't much big about West Yellowstone—except its airport runway. The 8,400-foot strip of asphalt is one of the longest in Montana, a necessity when you play host to such dignitaries as the president of the United States. Yes, Air Force One has landed here, and so can you if you take SkyWest from Salt Lake City between late June and late September. You can also rent a car from Avis or Budget. The more common arrival point via the air is Bozeman Yellowstone International Airport at Gallatin Field (BZN) in Belgrade, Montana, about 8 miles northwest of Bozeman. The state's second busiest airport, served by United, Delta, Horizon, and several regional airlines, underwent a major expansion in 2011. Those who arrive via Bozeman get the added treat of the serpentine 90-mile drive south through the Gallatin Canyon to West Yellowstone. Dramatically different from the sweeping Yellowstone and Madison river valleys on either flank, the Gallatin is narrow, winding, and beautiful, and you'll have 20 fee-free miles of driving in Yellowstone. If the picturesque Gallatin River seems familiar, you might recognize it from the movie *A River Runs Through It*, much of which was filmed in the lower canyon near Storm Castle. Wolves, grizzly bears, and moose live along the upper stretches, where US 191 slices off the northwest corner of the park. The Gallatin might be the premier road-accessible whitewater-rafting stream in Montana when the water's high in the spring and early summer. At House Rock, just below a bridge over the river, you can pull into a parking area and watch rafters and kayakers navigate the Mad Mile. US 191 is also one of Montana's most dangerous stretches, as evidenced by the more than 100 white crosses denoting deaths along the road. Many locals prefer the longer but safer 70-mph drive on US 287 through Ennis to West Yellowstone.

LEFT: A field of arrowleaf balsamroot brightens the Bechler Region.

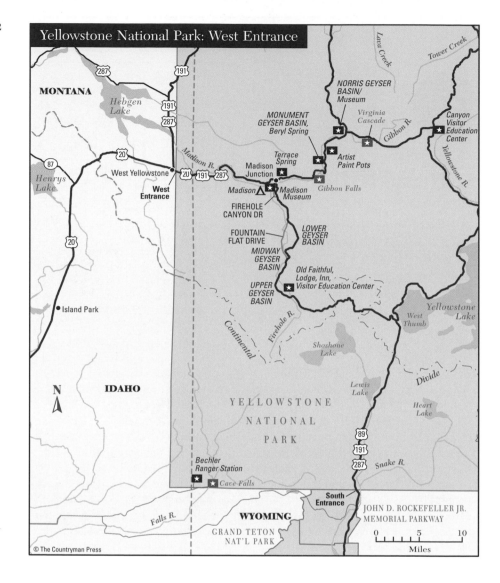

Yellowstone National Park: West Entrance

MONTANA

Hebgen Lake

Henrys Lake

West Yellowstone

West Entrance

Madison R.

Madison Junction

Terrace Spring

Madison

Madison Museum

FIREHOLE CANYON DR

FOUNTAIN FLAT DRIVE

MIDWAY GEYSER BASIN

UPPER GEYSER BASIN

LOWER GEYSER BASIN

Old Faithful, Lodge, Inn, Visitor Education Center

MONUMENT GEYSER BASIN, Beryl Spring

NORRIS GEYSER BASIN/ Museum

Virginia Cascade

Artist Paint Pots

Gibbon Falls

Gibbon R.

Canyon Visitor Education Center

Yellowstone R.

Lava Creek

Tower Creek

Firehole R.

Continental

Shoshone Lake

West Thumb

Yellowstone Lake

Lewis Lake

Divide

Heart Lake

IDAHO

Island Park

YELLOWSTONE NATIONAL PARK

N

Bechler Ranger Station

Cave Falls

Falls R.

WYOMING

GRAND TETON NAT'L PARK

South Entrance

JOHN D. ROCKEFELLER JR. MEMORIAL PARKWAY

Snake R.

0   5   10
Miles

© The Countryman Press

Another option is to fly into the regional airport serving Idaho Falls, Idaho. SkyWest, United Express, Allegiant, and SeaPort airlines serve Idaho Falls Regional Airport. If you're driving, at Idaho Falls take the West Yellowstone exit off I-15 onto US 20 and drive northeast through the potato fields of the Upper Snake River Plain to Rigby, Rexburg, St. Anthony, and Ashton. US 20 continues north through a few more miles of farmland before crossing the Henry's Fork of the Snake River and rising into the mountains toward Island Park and West Yellowstone. If time permits, we highly recommend turning east through Ashton on ID 47 and driving the especially picturesque Mesa Falls Scenic Byway. Most visitors zoom past this area without giving much thought to what they're missing in the lush forests to the east. Stop and smell the pines, and experience the grandeur of Upper and Lower Mesa Falls on the Henry's Fork of the Snake River on this

Take a detour to Upper Mesa Falls on the Henry's Fork of the Snake River in Idaho.

29-mile paved detour. The river drops dramatically out of Yellowstone's caldera onto the Snake River Plain at Upper Mesa Falls. It's believed to be the last falls undisturbed by humankind in the Columbia River system. ID 47 returns to US 20 just north of the Osborne Bridge across the Henry's Fork, on the south end of Island Park.

OVERVIEW

If there's any doubt which Yellowstone entry point gets the most intense traffic in the summer, one look at the wide entrance station settles the question. Rebuilt in 2008, the West Entrance looks like a toll booth on an urban interstate, and sometimes traffic is backed up just as far—all the way back to the town. West Yellowstone sits hard on the park's lodgepole-blanketed western boundary, and the contrast is striking coming or going. What's the attraction here? Two words: Old Faithful. Yellowstone's signature landscape feature is a mere 30 miles from the West Entrance, a stretch that often has a bumper-to-bumper rush-hour feel thanks to frequent plodding herds of bison. And this image is further accentuated at Old Faithful itself, where the Park Service built a cloverleaf interchange to accommodate the masses of automobile traffic.

This region is the heart of Yellowstone's geyser country, featuring not only Old Faithful but the world's largest geyser—Steamboat—and the spectacularly colorful Grand Prismatic Spring. The Madison, Firehole, and Gibbon rivers are the park's

Cave Falls plunges toward a meeting with the Snake River in Yellowstone's Cascade Corner.

most popular fly-fishing streams, the settings for many a photo of an angler with a bison and geothermal feature as a backdrop. In addition, this country provides the most discernible example of the Yellowstone caldera, especially at Madison Junction and Gibbon Falls. Wildlife are frequently seen in the geyser basins and in the meadows across the Madison River, most notably bison and elk but also the occasional wolf or grizzly bear. One more reason to like this part of Yellowstone: The 14-mile newly paved road between Madison Junction and Norris, upgraded because of necessary repair work around Gibbon Falls, is easily the smoothest and safest stretch for bicycling. It's a welcome addition for riders weary of worrying about getting whacked by Winnebago mirrors on shoulderless roads in the rest of the park.

The west side of Yellowstone has two roads entering the park that provide free access. As noted in "Getting Here," US 191 slices for 20 miles through the northwest corner along the Gallatin River and Grayling Creek. Several trails lead away from the busy highway into the park, all of them into exceedingly wild country with wolves and grizzly bears.

The other entrance is into the little-explored, underappreciated Bechler Region in the southwest corner of the park. It is 26 miles from Ashton, Idaho, to the Bechler Ranger Station, and another mile or so to the picnic area at Cave Falls. Those who have been to this area, also known as Cascade Corner, never forget the array of waterfalls, feeling of isolation, and prolific clouds of seasonals mosquitoes.

GATEWAY COMMUNITIES

West Yellowstone, Montana

No gateway community has more of a theme-park atmosphere than West Yellowstone, which seems to have sprung from a lodgepole pine forest simply to serve park tourists. Which is precisely what happened. In the late 1800s, visitors to the West Entrance came to this broad, forested bowl via wagon from Virginia City,

Montana, about 70 miles to the northwest. After the turn of the century, Union Pacific president E. H. Harriman saw a business opportunity and punched a rail line through from Pocatello, Idaho, to the town's current site. The line was finished in 1907 and West Yellowstone was carved out of Forest Service land in 1908. The town originally was named Riverside after a soldier's station inside the park, even though the Madison River is 2 miles away from town. However, having two Riversides was confusing, so in 1910 the town was renamed Yellowstone. But that only created more confusion between the town and park. So in 1920, "West" was added to the name. In the early years, heavy snows and temperatures that frequently were the lowest in the nation sent residents scurrying for warmer climes in winter.

The isolation also made it a place for some of the characters from Las Vegas, savory and otherwise, to hide out; this bygone era today is kept alive only in the name of a single motel: Best Western Desert Inn. Once the state began plowing US 191 north to Bozeman in winter, the town grew into a year-round playground. Rail passenger service ended in 1960, but the introduction of snowmobiles a few years later created new prosperity. That lasted for four decades, until tourist complaints about noise, pollution, and stress to animals moved the Park Service to ban the machines in the park. Today, a limited number of quieter, clean machines are allowed in Yellowstone, albeit only with guides. Thus, West Yellowstone has had to diversify. In the summer, West Yellowstone is a fly-fishing hub, renowned for such angling legends as Bud Lilly and Bob Jacklin, and the shops named for them. Lodging is functional, with many small operations that contribute to the town's western persona. West Yellowstone does have a central reservations system for lodging (1-888-646-7077 or 406-646-7077), providing easy access to more than five hundred rooms.

Island Park, Idaho

Island Park boasts of having "The Longest Main Street in America," a 33-mile north-south ribbon of US 20 that cuts a narrow swath through lodgepole pine roughly paralleling the Henry's Fork of the Snake River, once a fly-fishing shrine.

West Yellowstone was originally named Riverside in 1908. NPS

The town, no more than 500 feet wide in places, was incorporated in the 1940s for ease of licensing businesses scattered throughout the area. From the name, you'd expect to see a series of islands in the Henry's Fork, but the moniker is actually for the meadows, or "islands" of open land, amid the thick lodgepoles of the Yellowstone caldera. Travelers through the country would "park" in these meadows for overnighters before moving on to the next "island."

Much of the area's focus was resource extraction—mining, timber, ranching—until a gradual realignment of values beginning in the 1970s. The area south of town was heavily logged right up to Yellowstone's western boundary, an image still visible from space in satellite photos. The practice was discontinued to protect grizzly bear habitat. Today, Island Park has an interesting mix of tourists. Harriman State Park and the Box Canyon section of the Henry's Fork lure fly anglers and their Orvis togs from the world over. Toward the north at Macks Inn, the woods are a labyrinth of snowmobile and ATV trails. The "town" is still a place with land "islands" in which to "park," only now those parks feature motels, gas stations, and sporting goods stores. The area is chock-full of private cabins for rent.

HITTING THE ROAD

West Entrance to Madison Junction (14 miles): Much of this section of road is in lodgepole forest. About 2 miles after the entrance the hallowed Madison River appears like a shimmering jewel to the left of your vehicle. You'll also see remnants of the famous 1988 fires, mostly in the bleached ghostly spires of old lodgepoles poking above thick stands of 20-year-old trees (see sidebar on the 1988 fires). Bison frequently travel the roadway during their annual migrations to and from lower-elevation grasslands outside the park, often stopping traffic.

Elk frequent grasslands and the areas near the Madison River. NPS

This is also the most heavily used entrance by snowmobilers, and the most hotly debated. For about three decades beginning in the 1960s, sledders had free reign in the park during the long winter. It was not uncommon to see sleds careening across the snow at 80 mph, disturbing wildlife. Today, regulations are much stricter and winter traffic is gradually evolving to snowcoaches. Nobody is more grateful than the rangers at the entrance station who remember having to wear gas masks to combat air thick with carbon monoxide. Don't feel bad for the sledders: They have thousands of miles of trails just outside of West Yellowstone and Island Park, and with ever-improving technology they can reach places far more exciting than the relatively mundane 30 road miles to Old Faithful.

About 6 miles in, an active eagle

Montana Department of Livestock wranglers haze bison back to the park, an annual spring rite on Yellowstone's west side.

nest sits high in a dead Douglas fir, a perfect perch from which mom can scour the Madison River for trout and bring home dinner; when eaglets are in the nest, you're not allowed to stop here. For a closer and slower-paced look at the broad and shallow Madison's sparking riffles, take the clearly marked 1-mile Riverside Drive that parallels the main road. At the 7-mile mark is the aptly named **Seven Mile Bridge** over the Madison. Before you get to the bridge, look at the sage embankment on the other side of the river. You'll notice a heavily trafficked game trail, used by bison, wolves, elk, and other wildlife after fording the river. Bison are especially fond of this spot because they can safely coax their calves across, positioning them upstream so they can brace against the current by leaning against their mothers' flanks. Upstream from the bridge on the south side of the road is a broad meadow where bison and elk are almost always browsing in the shadow of 8,235-foot Mount Haynes, and moose are occasionally seen as well. And wherever elk are, wolves won't be far behind. Bears like this country, too. By the way, Mount Haynes and 7,500-foot National Park Mountain provide the first glimpse of the rim of the Yellowstone caldera, the boundary of which is on their south flanks. Before reaching Madison Junction, you'll arrive at **Madison Campground**, a buzz of activity in the summer. The junction is at the confluence of the famed Gibbon and Firehole rivers, which join to form the Madison.

Madison Junction to Norris (14 miles): Once one of the more rugged sections of highway in the park, this stretch was tamed considerably in 2010 when it was repaved, rebridged, and rerouted. A larger parking area was fashioned out of the rock above 84-foot Gibbon Falls at the edge of the caldera. Once renowned for its traffic jams, now Gibbon Falls offers plenty of room for viewing without slowing those in a hurry to get to Norris and beyond. Only the road between Madison Junction and Old Faithful has more thermal features. In fact, many people prefer Norris Geyser Basin because it tends not to get the crowds found at Lower and Midway geyser basins. Norris also is the hottest, oldest, and most rapidly changing thermal area in the park, and home to the mighty Steamboat Geyser.

The first few miles of this drive follow the meandering **Gibbon River**, a magnet for trout fishers—humans, sandhill cranes, and herons. In barely a mile is **Terrace Spring**, a thermal area that features the hot Terrace Spring and cooler Bath Spring. There are two picnic areas along the route, one at **Tuff Cliff** and the other at **Gibbon Falls**. The falls will look familiar to longtime visitors, but the road won't; since reconstruction it is difficult to even picture where the old route went. Once you arrive at the spacious new parking area above the falls, you're again on the rim of the caldera.

The next noteworthy stop is blue-green **Beryl Spring**, at the edge of the road, which vents (literally) at passing vehicles. At almost 200 degrees Fahrenheit, the spring is one of Yellowstone's hottest, and it likes to spew its boiling waters to heights of 4 feet. Nearby hissing fumaroles add to the feistiness of this thermal area. Up next is the trailhead for **Monument Geyser Basin**, where several petering-out geysers reside after a mile-long climb. Beyond that trailhead and past sloshy Gibbon Meadow—a great place to scan for elk, bison, and more exotic critters—is the turnoff for the colorful **Artist's Paint Pots**, one of our favorite places to take

Gibbon Falls tumbles 84 feet off the Yellowstone caldera between Madison Junction and Norris.

Winter visitors are shrouded in steam at a geyser near Norris.

visitors. Even the most serious guests, newcomers and Yellowstone veterans alike, find themselves giggling at the gurgling, cream-colored pots reached via a short trail up a hill.

Finally, save plenty of time for **Norris Geyser Basin**, with more than 50 thermal features viewed from a labyrinth of trails adding up to more than 2 miles. Grab a brochure at the free **Norris Geyser Basin Museum** (307-344-2812, June to September) and take one or both of the loop trails—Porcelain Basin or Back Basin—through an otherworldly landscape that offers a sensory feast with its aromas, colors, soundscapes, and constant activity. The Black Growler Steam Vent is a classic fumarole, Ledge Geyser shoots its waters more than 200 feet sideways, Whirligig Geyser swirls its waters, Emerald Spring has riveting colors, and then there's Steamboat. It doesn't show its fiery wares often, but when it does it's the most spectacular geyser in the world in terms of sheer height (more than 350 feet). In modern times, Steamboat went from 1911 to 1961 without a single eruption—but blew seven times after 2000 before going quiet again from 2005 to 2011. When it does go, water shoots more than 300 feet for up to 40 minutes, with a cooling-off period in which the geyser lets off steam for a couple days. Steamboat has two vents, about 15 feet apart. For the record, until 1985 the Excelsior Geyser in Midway Geyser Basin claimed the mantle as world's tallest, but it went dormant that year and is now listed as a hot spring.

It's difficult to believe today, but the Grand Loop Road once cut right through the heart of Norris Geyser Basin. Thankfully, the Park Service rerouted the road in 1966, to the benefit of visitors and the geysers themselves. This is an extraordinary place to come in winter via snowcoach, when the heated water mixes with frigid air to create a surreal atmosphere. At the

Gurgling mud pots elicit giggles from even the most sophisticated visitors. NPS

museum, you can purchase literature from the small Yellowstone Association bookstore.

Norris to Canyon Village (12 miles): This largely forested stretch is the middle section of the figure-eight Grand Loop highway in central Yellowstone, most of it on the north edge of the caldera. A route sometimes called the Norris Cutoff is relatively nondescript by park standards, but it offers a handful of modest hikes, is a good place to examine the scorched remnants of the famous 1988 fire, and has an exhibit describing a 1984 windstorm that has been reported as a tornado.

The drive from west to east is also a steady climb. It isn't unusual to start amid bare ground and wind up 12 miles later in a field of snow at Canyon Village, the gateway to some of the park's most spectacular overlooks.

Less than 2 miles into the drive from Norris is the turnoff for **Virginia**

Steamboat Geyser towers nearly 300 feet in this rare 1963 eruption. NPS

Cascade, a 60-foot drop on the Gibbon River that, like Gibbon Falls, drops spectacularly from the caldera rim. The difference: a twisting, descending 1.7-mile loop drive on pavement to view the falls, with precious little parking for those who want to gape at the waters plunging into the canyon. A picnic area at the end of the loop

Many touring companies offer snowcoach expeditions into Old Faithful, Norris Geyser Basin, and Canyon Village in the winter. NPS

Did You Know? The most violent high-elevation tornado in recorded U.S. history occurred on July 21, 1987, uprooting more than a million trees between 8,500 and 10,000 feet in elevation. The twister cut a 24-mile-long, 1.5-mile-wide swath across Yellowstone's southern region. Nobody was hurt and there is no evidence of the carnage today because the downed timber burned the next year during the great fires.

is one way to stretch your legs and see the cascade. Back on the main road, look for the parking area for the exhibit about fire and the freakish July 7, 1984, tornado in which hundreds of lodge-pole pines blew down. Nobody was hurt, but a few folks on the Virginia Cascade Road were stranded for several hours.

On the final 8.5 miles of the drive, you'll rise onto the Solfatara Plateau past five trailheads (see "Hiking") that lead to such places as Ice Lake, Little Gibbon Falls, and Grebe Lake before reaching Canyon Village. This is a busy hub where the sprawl is masked by the thick pine forest. The sparkling **Canyon Visitors Education Center** (307-344-2550, May to September), opened in 2007, offers the usual assortment of information along with exhibits about the area's stunning topography and geology. The rest of Canyon Village looks like an L-shaped misplaced strip mall, with tacky gift shops, a deli, grill, lounge, and the check-in desk for the lodging dispersed throughout the area.

Madison Junction to Old Faithful (16 miles): Geysers, geysers, geysers. That's the synopsis of this mystical section of busy road that follows the aptly named Fire-hole River to Lower Geyser Basin and Fountain Flat Drive. The route begins at the confluence of the Firehole and Gibbon rivers, which join to form the Madison. Both are coveted by fly anglers.

Within a few miles, you'll have access to Lower, Midway, and Upper geyser basins—the latter being home to Old Faithful itself—and a fourth thermal area called Fountain Paint Pots. Though Old Faithful is known worldwide, equally impressive and infinitely more colorful are Grand Prismatic Spring and Excelsior Geyser, both at Midway Geyser Basin. It's easy to be mesmerized for hours gazing at nature's hissing handiwork.

Before embarking on this route, wander through the free **Madison Museum** (307-344-2821, June to September). This National Register of Historic Places building (1929) contains a handful of touchable items and also serves as an information station and Yellowstone Association bookstore. If you're not in a hurry—and you shouldn't be; it's Yellowstone, after all—we recommend taking the 2.2-mile **Firehole Canyon Drive**, which begins less than 0.5-mile south of Madison Junction. The route winds through lodgepole forest past several cascades, including some excellent places to fish and one of the park's three sanctioned swimming holes. A mile into the detour is 40-foot Firehole Falls; it's another mile to the swimming hole, a delightful 75 degrees and often crowded on warm days.

Back on the main drag 3 miles later, an old freight route now called **Fountain Flat Drive** heads west across a picturesque plain toward **Lower Geyser Basin**. At 11 square miles, it is Yellowstone's largest geyser area. It's a 1.5-mile drive to a parking area where hikers and bicyclists may continue on to **Midway Geyser**

The 1988 Fires: Rebirth of the World's First National Park

The morning of June 21, 1988, arrived with characteristic sun-kissed bliss in Yellowstone National Park. One flick of a woodcutter's cigarette on the Targhee National Forest west of the park boundary permanently changed the landscape.

Before the day was out, howling winds, high temperatures, and the worst drought in Yellowstone's history conspired to set 460 acres ablaze. Before the week ended, lightning started two more fires in different corners of the park, creating an eerie glow that would last for months. Before the summer breathed its last, more than 800,000 acres—about ⅓ of the park—were consumed by 51 conflagrations, the devastation sensationally transmitted into America's living rooms each night by network television.

For nearly three months, from the moment that first blaze was ignited until September's snows blanketed the park, the "tragedy" in Yellowstone was the buzz of an upset and anxious nation. Government officials argued over policies that had ranged from the old Smokey The Bear suppress-every-fire philosophy to the inaccurately nicknamed "Let Burn" doctrine of 1972, which guided decisions made 16 years later. Residents of such gateway communities as Cooke City and West Yellowstone expressed anger as they watched the flames draw near, their livelihoods and homes threatened. Tourists in the park and folks back home watched in shock and sadness as America's first and most cherished national park went up in smoke, never to look the same again.

They saw the tens of millions of scorched trees. They saw the charred remains of fleeing elk. They saw the smoldering remnants of cabins. And they saw more than 25,000 firefighters living in grimy tent cities battle the flames in utter futility, at an astronomical $125 million cost to the taxpayer. By August, some 25 fires were burning a mosaic across the park. Ash fell 100 miles to the east and smoke plumes 27,000 feet high could be seen 500 miles away. On August 20, called Black Saturday, hurricane-force winds forced officials to close the park completely for the first and only time in its history. On September 7, almost 100,000 acres burned, taking 20 cabins near Old Faithful in the process.

How could this happen, Americans wondered, and more to the point, how could the Park Service let this happen? When the winter snows mercifully halted the carnage, reporters packed their notebooks, TV trucks lowered their satellite dishes, and government officials turned to other matters, leaving the rest of the Yellowstone

Basin. The prettiest of the 17 springs in Lower Geyser Basin might be the blue-green **Ojo Caliente** (Spanish for "hot spring"). Believe it or not, a stately park-style hotel—the Fountain—stood here from 1891 until 1917, when the automobile made it possible to zip through the area to Old Faithful, rendering it obsolete.

Next up on the Grand Loop Road is the **Fountain Paint Pot Trail**, where you can see all four of the park's geothermal-feature types. This is probably the best place in the park to observe mud pots, but there are six geysers, a handful of hissing fumaroles, and some pretty pools—including 200-degree Celestine Pool.

The most famous geyser in this area is across the main road from Fountain story untold. What Americans wouldn't see on TV or in the headlines for the next 20 years—except on nature programs and in reports buried in newspaper travel sections—was the miracle of regeneration, a turnaround so rapid and remarkable that even many biologists were awestruck. Missed all along, though, was the irony: The fires were exacerbated not only by record winds, stifling heat, and 20 percent of normal rainfall, but by years of fire suppression that allowed for dense undergrowth, acres of timber dying in aging forests, and beetle infestations that killed lodgepole and whitebark pine.

Regardless of human efforts, the siege wasn't about to end until nature counter-punched with cooler temperatures and precipitation. Finally, three months and 1.4 million charred Greater Yellowstone acres later, the embers began to flicker and die after a snowfall on September 11, leaving those who cared about the park fearful for its future. Yet they didn't have to wait long for their first hopeful news. Fewer than four hundred large mammals perished, about ⅔ of them elk. Less than one out of every one thousand elk in the park were lost. Only a handful of bison, bear, moose, and deer were killed, most from smoke inhalation.

Two decades later, Yellowstone's rebirth is astonishing. Wildflowers like fireweed and Indian paintbrush, along with grasses and forbs, were the first flora to come back, providing forage for deer, elk, and bison in places where they once wouldn't roam because of the tangled understory. Millions of lodgepole cones opened and rooted, creating stands now 20 feet tall. Weaker wildlife ultimately perished at the paws of predators in the harsh winter of 1988–89, leaving the fit to survive, leading to today's flourishing populations.

Though at first area residents feared Yellowstone would cease to be one of America's favorite destinations, visitors come in greater droves than ever. The still-visible burned areas are more a source of fascination than disappointment. Wildlife gravitate to the burns, making them more visible to happy gawkers. Gateway communities thrive as never before. The upshot—the ecosystem works and self-regulates. Even cataclysmic fires are part of the process—always have been, always will be. A typical plot of Yellowstone land has burned at least 30 times since the last ice age some ten thousand years ago. An average year will see 22 lightning-caused fires.

A year later, at least one prominent media outlet offered a mea culpa for the industry's sensationalist coverage. "Reports of the park's death," the Washington Post wrote, "were greatly exaggerated."

Paint Pot Trail on **Firehole Lake Drive:** the entertaining and relatively predictable **Great Fountain Geyser.** Its half-hour eruptions, which spit steamy water anywhere from 100 to 220 feet, occur roughly every 12 hours—and you can watch from your car. Check the board at the site or Old Faithful Visitor Center for the next estimated eruption time.

Dubbed "Hell's Half-Acre" by the famed writer Rudyard Kipling is **Midway Geyser Basin,** with its two showcase thermal features. One is the extinct **Excelsior Geyser,** which once sent water and rock an astonishing 300 feet into the air and now dispatches 4,050 gallons of scalding water per minute into the Firehole River.

Excelsior was the largest geyser in the world before likely muting itself through the sheer force of it own violent eruptions. The other is the wonderfully colorful **Grand Prismatic Spring**, where the blue and turquoise in the center is dramatically offset by the reds, browns, and oranges on the perimeter. At 370 feet in diameter,

Did You Know? At least 19 people have died from falling, slipping, or jumping into geothermal features, a tragic reminder to adhere to Park Service signs cautioning visitors to stay on trails.

Grand Prismatic is the largest hot spring in the park. Though a boardwalk hugs an edge of the spring, it is more fully appreciated by hiking a short trail to the flanks of the burned slope to the south. Also camera-worthy here is the picturesque **Turquoise Pool.**

About 2 miles south of Midway Geyser Basin is **Upper Geyser Basin**, where the prime attraction needs no introduction. Before venturing into the madness at **Old Faithful**, you might check out two quick walking tours: **Biscuit Basin** and **Black Sand Basin**. Biscuit Basin, named for the small biscuit-shaped formations that once surrounded Sapphire Pool, is a 0.75-mile walk on a boardwalk amid numerous pools and geysers. In the same neighborhood, Black Sand Basin has an equally impressive collection of thermal features.

Your arrival at **Old Faithful Village** is announced by the sight of the decidedly out-of-place cloverleaf interchange leading to the historic **Old Faithful Inn** and other services in the area, including two gas stations, lodging, restaurants, cafeterias, gift shops, employee dormitories, and bleachers in a crescent shape around the **Old Faithful Geyser.** The cathedral-esque, gold-level LEED-certified, $27 million **Old Faithful Visitor Education Center**, completed in August 2010, is a treat not to be missed. The sparkling center covers a tremendous amount of ground, but its primary purpose is to provide a thorough and compelling education

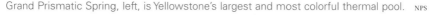

Grand Prismatic Spring, left, is Yellowstone's largest and most colorful thermal pool. NPS

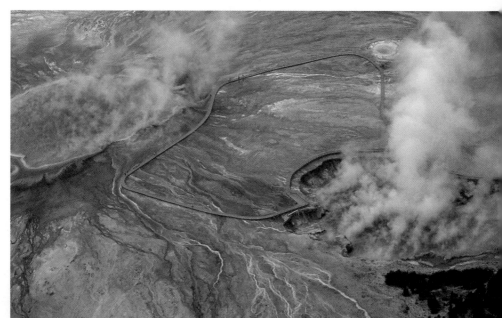

Great Fountain Geyser erupts about every 12 hours, and when it does it's a sight to behold. NPS

about the world-famous geothermal features. Once you've seen the eruption millions come to witness, take some time to walk on the trail from **Geyser Hill** behind Old Faithful back to the northwest toward Midway Geyser Basin. There are dozens of pools and geysers, and you'll escape some, though not all, of the crowds.

The Bechler Region

Far from the hordes, the Bechler Region, also known as Cascade Corner, is a well-kept secret that provides a memorable experience if you're a hiker, horseback rider, fisherman, waterfalls aficionado, or simply enjoy a refreshing swim on a warm summer day. Yellowstone's wettest region has more waterfalls than the rest of the park combined, a handful of hot springs suitable for soaking, and spectacular fishing.

The Bechler is Yellowstone's "other" entrance, hard against the southwest corner. The park boundary is 18 miles east of Ashton, Idaho, much of it on gravel, with the gentle side of the fault-blocked Tetons initially serving as a riveting backdrop. To get here, head due east out of Ashton on ID 47. About 4 miles out of town, the road bends to the northeast in wide-open country, and you'll see a sign at the intersection of Marysville Road for the park. Veer east and continue as the road becomes Cave Falls Road and turns to gravel. Just south of the park, the road forks, with the option of a left turn destined for **Bechler Ranger Station** or continuing straight to **Cave Falls** on the aptly named Falls River. If you only have a short time, choose the falls. They are nearly as spectacular as nearby Mesa Falls on the Henry's Fork of the Snake River. The upper falls are the showstopper, though the lower drop is worthy of a photo op too.

It takes some intestinal fortitude to fully immerse yourself in the region, which is why the folks at the small ranger station office are wont to waive the $25 entrance fee if you simply want to poke around on the trails leading toward the

Pitchstone Plateau and Old Faithful. After all, you can't get anywhere else in the park from here unless you're up for some serious hiking or packing. And for much of the short summer and autumn seasons, the prolific amounts of water and massive numbers of mosquitoes make this inhospitable for many.

The ranger station, which turned one hundred years old in 2011, is the place to get information on the backcountry and serves as the trailhead for a handful of hikes. The list of waterfalls accessible from here is impressive: Bechler, Ouzel, Dunanda, Iris, Union, and Colonnade, just to name a few of the dozens. This is a haven for wildlife that likes marshy areas, especially sandhill cranes, moose, and both types of bears. The area has many black bears and a few grizzlies; sometimes problem

Entry fees are sometimes accepted at the Bechler Ranger Station. NPS

bears are relocated here because of the region's remoteness. Because many trails require fording streams and because the mosquitoes are brutal, it's highly recommended you wait until late summer or early fall to explore this region.

Cave Falls is the most prominent of the waterfalls in Yellowstone's Cascade Corner. NPS

Bechler Meadows are rarely visited—but are a treat for those who do. NPS

Pick Your Spot

LODGING INSIDE THE PARK

Old Faithful Area: ♿ Old Faithful Inn ($$$/$$$$, 307-344-7901, May to September)—the Grand Dame of Yellowstone and now a National Historic Landmark—turned 100 in 2003 and remains the most visited human-made attraction in Yellowstone, thanks partly to a somewhat-popular geyser with the same name just out the back door. As such, it's also the most difficult lodging to secure in the park. Inside the lobby, it's Swiss Family Robinson meets *Jeremiah Johnson.* The inn's original log structure, fondly called "The Old House," towers seven stories with a mosaic of lodgepole staircases and walkways designed by architect Robert C. Reamer to reflect nature's perfect imperfections. The centerpiece is a massive floor-to-ceiling stone fireplace. At the top, some 92 feet from the floor, is a crow's nest where musicians once played. Despite the heavy foot traffic

between Memorial Day and Labor Day, it's still possible to find a cozy corner in which to sit in a log rocker and read a book by the fire. Wings were added in the two decades after the original construction. The lodge now has 327 rooms, many with original plumbing, including clawfoot tubs. The old building has survived the area's frequent earthquakes, including the famed 1959 temblor that collapsed the dining-room chimney. Old Faithful Inn came perilously close to being reduced to cinders in the 1988 fires—remnants can still be seen from the inn—but she has endured. The inn offers a restaurant and deli, and interpretive tours can be arranged.

For the budget-conscious who want the amenities of the Old Faithful Inn and access to the geysers and fishing on the Firehole River, check into ♿ Old Faithful Lodge Cabins ($$, 307-344-7901, May to September) next door. The lodge might be the stepchild of the Old Faithful Inn, but it certainly isn't ugly. It has the best views of the geyser from its cafeteria. There are no rooms in the lodge itself, it simply serves as the hub for 130 cozy cabins. The primitive Budget cabins are standard motel-style units with a sink, toilet, and communal showers in the main lodge; the Pioneer cabins are also rustic, but have showers. A store, gift shop, and recreation hall are in the main lodge.

&. ♨. **Old Faithful Snow Lodge and Cabins** ($$/$$$, 307-344-7901, May to October/December to March) is Yellowstone's newest lodge, constructed in 1999 to blend in seamlessly with its lodgepole and geyser surroundings. What sets the Snow Lodge and Cabins apart is that it's open for the winter season. From the warm and cozy confines, winter adventurers are destined for a treat: solitude amid steamy geysers and congregating wildlife, especially bison. Getting here in winter is the challenge. Snowcoaches and snowmobiles bring in most tourists from West Yellowstone about 30 miles away, though some intrepid visitors will arrive via cross-country skis. The lodge holds 100 attractive rooms with full baths. The Western cabins are akin to staying in a comfortable motel room. The Frontier cabins are duplexes and more vanilla, but still comfortable. A relatively upscale dining room and store also are on-site.

BEST LODGING OUTSIDE THE PARK

West Yellowstone: Because West Yellowstone has so many lodging options, we have divided our selections into three categories based on rates: Budget, Middle of the Road, and Higher End.

In the *Budget* category, a favorite is **Al's Westward Ho** ($, 1-888-646-7331 or 406-646-7331, May to October), which looks directly across the street into the lodgepole forest of Yellowstone National Park. Al's has been a part of the community fabric for more than six decades. A few kitchen suites are available—and in keeping with the philosophy of the area, there are no phones. The **Lazy G Motel** ($/$$, 406-646-7586), open all year except for April and early November, has 15 rooms containing fridges and phones, but no air-conditioning. A bonus: It is on the quieter west end of town. The **Madison Hotel** ($/$$, 1-800-838-7745 or 406-646-7745, May to October) is a one-of-a-kind experience in West Yellowstone. Built in 1912, the Madison offers a variety of options for the budget-minded traveler: 14 hostel and economy rooms with a shared bathroom down the hall, plus 17 standard and deluxe motel rooms, all with private baths and Internet access. Former president Warren G. Harding and actors Wallace Beery and Gloria Swanson have stayed at this hotel. The gift shop is reputed to offer Montana's largest selection of regional knick-knacks. The Timberline Café is adjacent to the hotel.

For *Middle of the Road* lodging, the Best Western chain has three options in West Yellowstone, each with a slightly different flavor. The &. 🐾 **Cross Winds Motor Inn** ($$$, 1-877-446-9557 or 406-646-9557, May to October) is a recently remodeled two-story on the north edge of town with 70 rooms, indoor pool, spa, and continental breakfast. &. 🐾 **Desert Inn** ($$, 1-800-574-7054 or 406-646-7376)—so named because of the town's Las Vegas influence six decades ago—is a comfortable three-story with 74 rooms and an indoor pool two blocks from the park entrance. The &. 🐾 **Weston Inn** ($/$$$, 1-800-599-9982 or 406-646-7373, May to October) is also a three-story structure, with 66 nonsmoking rooms, heated outdoor pool, and hot tub four blocks from the park entrance. & ☀ Pop's Brandin' Iron Inn ($$, 1-800-217-4613 or 406-646-9411) is another local favorite for the economy-minded. Each of the 80 rooms has a fridge, and there are two indoor hot tubs. & ☀ Clubhouse Inn ($$, 1-800-565-6803 or 406-646-4892, May to October), with 77 recently renovated rooms near the Grizzly and Wolf Discovery Center, is one of the more plush for the price and they have a heated indoor pool, whirlpool, and exercise room.

& ☀ Holiday Inn SunSpree Resort ($$/$$$, 1-877-834-3613 or 406-646-7365) is one of the town's most popular motels, especially in winter, thanks partly to an indoor pool, exercise room, and sauna. There are two-room luxury suites with jetted tubs and wet bars, and snowmobile rentals and snowcoach tours are available in winter. One of the more unique properties is the & ☀ Hibernation Station ($$/$$$, 1-800-580-3557 or 406-646-4200), which thinks of itself as more of a village. There are 50 newer cabins with homey log interiors—some with kitchenettes and fireplaces, all with satellite TV. A family condo unit sleeps eight and features a fireplace, kitchen, and jetted tub; enjoy the outdoor spa. Snowmobile rentals are available for winter fun. Sleepy Hollow Lodge ($$, 406-646-7077, May to October) has 14 snuggly cabins, including 7 with hand-hewn logs and homemade log furnishings; 9 cabins have kitchens. & ☀ ¶ Stagecoach Inn ($/$$$, 1-800-842-2882 or 406-646-7381) is a large, modernized facility with 88 Western-style rooms and heated underground parking. The lobby's old stone fireplace, sweeping staircase, and stuffed mounted heads let you know you're in the Northern Rockies. Amenities on-site include two hot tubs, dry sauna,

Mexican restaurant, and lounge that underwent renovations in late September 2011.

To escape the intensity of West Yellowstone's summer, try the & ☀ Super 8 Lionshead ($$$, 1-800-800-8000 or 406-646-9584, May to October), a 44-room facility 8 miles west of town. You might suffer from sticker shock assuming lower prices at a Super 8; welcome to summer in West Yellowstone. You do get a continental breakfast, sauna, and guest laundry. & ☀ Yellowstone Lodge ($$/$$$, 1-877-239-9298 or 406-646-0020) is an attractive three-story with 80 spacious rooms, a continental breakfast with waffle maker, indoor pool, and hot tub. North of West Yellowstone about 35 miles is ☀ ¶ Cinnamon Lodge & Adventures ($/$$$$, 406-995-4253), which has cabins in a wide variety of shapes, sizes, and rates in the Gallatin River Valley. They also offer fabulous meals, mountain biking adventures, and an excellent location—the closest lodging to Yellowstone's northwest corner.

If you desire more *Higher End* options, The Clubhouse Inn's sister property, the & ☀ Kelly Inn West Yellowstone ($$/$$$$, 1-800-635-3559 or 406-646-4544), has 78 spacious rooms, a handful of Jacuzzi suites, a large indoor pool, sauna, hot tub, and an above-average continental breakfast; summer rates are roughly double winter rates. & ☀ Gray Wolf Inn and Suites ($$/$$$, 1-866-539-8117 or 406-646-0000) has a heated underground parking garage, unheated indoor pool, hot tub, sauna, and breakfast buffet. Though it doesn't look like much from the outside, the & ☀ ☀ ¶ Three Bear Lodge ($$$/$$$$, 1-800-646-7353 or 406-646-7353) has some stunning features. There are 73 diverse rooms, some of them fairly luxurious and all of them updated. A February 2008 fire destroyed the historic hotel portion, but much of the salvaged wood from the blaze has been handcrafted into furnishings and other distinctive decor. The Three Bear is another popular hangout for snowmobilers. For personal and intimate touches, the 🐾 Yellowstone Inn ($$/$$$, 406-646-7633, May to October) ranks among the best in West Yellowstone. There are 10 units, including three separate cabins with full kitchens and fireplaces.

Hebgen Lake Area: The 🐾 ☁ ¶ Hebgen Lake Mountain Inn ($$$, 1-866-400-4564 or 406-646-7281) is a two-story motel with a non-Western motif across US 287 from Hebgen Lake. Each of the 15 rooms has a fully equipped kitchen and semiprivate deck; an indoor pool and spa complete the scene. The infamous rowdy and slightly raunchy Happy Hour Bar and Restaurant is directly across the highway, overlooking the lake, and open for lunch and dinner. 🐾 ☁ Yellowstone Village Condominiums ($$/$$$, 1-800-276-7335 or 406-646-7335) is a collection of 1980s furnished one-, two-, and three-bedroom condos with kitchens and fireplaces on a forested peninsula pushing into Hebgen Lake about 10 miles northwest of West Yellowstone. There is a summer outdoor pool and year-round hot tub. During winter and spring, your neighbors quite likely will include bison.

Island Park, Idaho: 🐾 ¶ Anglers Lodge at Henry's Fork ($$/$$$, 208-558-9555) is an attractive 15-room motel with log accents that sits hard on the east bank of the Henry's Fork, with all rooms and the restaurant overlooking the meandering stream—which stays ice-free in winter. Three cabin rentals and a vacation home also are

available through Angler's Lodge, which is a short distance and visible from US 20. Snowmobiles are available for rent in winter. 🐾 Last Chance Lodge ($/$$, 1-800-428-8338 or 208-558-9675) has 10 lodge rooms and 12 stand-alone cabins across the street from the Henry's Fork, with an on-site fly shop. Guided fishing trips on the Henry's Fork, Madison, and Teton rivers can be arranged.

🐾 ¶ The Pines at Island Park/ Phillips Lodge ($$/$$$$, 1-888-455-9384 or 208-558-0192) is a selection of one-, two-, and three-bedroom handcrafted log cabins tucked into forested grounds near Island Park Reservoir and Henry's Lake, each touting satellite TV and private hot tubs. ¶ Trout Hunter Lodge ($$/$$$, 208-558-9900) is another clean, attractive log structure with 11 rooms on the banks of the Henry's Fork. It also offers special rates for the budget-minded angler. Each room has a fly-tying desk, guided fishing trips are offered, and a vast array of fly-fishing equipment is available in the full-service store. The Last Chance Bar & Grill is open seasonally and serves lunch and dinner. ¶ Pond's Lodge ($/$$/$$$$, 208-558-7221) is a work in progress and looks weary from US 20, but it appears to have great potential. There are motel rooms, duplexes, and two large, spacious cabins that sleep up to 12. The cabins have fireplaces, hand-peeled log furniture, great views, and hot tubs. A restaurant on-site boasts a San Francisco–trained chef with aspirations to make this a destination stop.

BEST ALTERNATIVE LODGING OUTSIDE THE PARK

West Yellowstone: The 🐾 ☁ ¶ Bar N Ranch ($$$$, 406-646-0300, May to October) 6 miles west of town is cowboy lux lodging at its finest, right down to the fluffy bathrobes. The seven lodge rooms, four one-bedroom cabins, and three two-bedroom cabins all have private outdoor hot tubs. A country-style breakfast is served each morning and the ranch has a gourmet restaurant with a wine list that's open daily in the summer and from Wednesday to Sunday the rest of the year. The South Fork of the Madison River flows through the 200 acres for blue-ribbon trout fishing. Located on a historic Bannock Indian migration route, **Parade Rest Guest Ranch** ($$/$$$, 406-646-7217, May to September) is 10 miles north of West Yellowstone, a mile from the junction of US 287 and US 191. There are 14 cabins, a dining hall, recreation room, outdoor hot tub, and equestrian facilities; the cabins range from the original 1912 Homestead Cabin to more modern buildings. Some of the cabins are in the main ranch area and others are on a ridge overlooking a horse pasture and a creek. Many guest ranches like to mix an Old West feeling with creature comforts, but not so the **Elkhorn Ranch** ($$$$, 406-995-4291, June to September), also in the upper Gallatin River Valley. At the request of many of its repeat guests— some of them regulars since the 1950s—the Elkhorn has remained largely unchanged for six decades, retaining its genuine rustic feel. The cabins and main lodge are plenty comfortable, and the meals are outstanding, but they serve mostly as a backdrop for visits to Yellowstone, riding horses into some of the region's prettiest country, fishing for trout in the Gallatin and Taylor Fork, or simply sipping a cold beverage on the porch of your 1930s cabin—one of 15 on a property that's just a long cast from the park's northern boundary.

Camping

West Yellowstone: There are plenty of camping opportunities in West Yellowstone, starting with **Yellowstone Holiday RV Campground and Marina** ($/$$, 1-877-646-4242 or 406-646-4242, May to September), which caters to families and reunions, and includes a central cooking facility for large groups. There are 24 camp cabins, some with private baths, and an apartment sleeps up to 10 and has a kitchen. There are 36 large RV sites with full hook-ups accommodating rigs up to 75 feet, some on the lake with beachfront access. **Yellowstone Cabins and RV Park** ($/$$, 866-646-9350 or 406-646-9350) has eight RV sites (limited to 40 feet and shorter) and seven duplex camp cabins with private bathrooms and cable TV. Gas grills and picnic tables are available for guest use. Perhaps the best manicured of the group is the **Rustic Wagon RV & Campground** ($/$$, 406-646-7387), with 50-amp service for RVs up to 70 feet—plowed in winter. Also available are one-, two-, and three-bedroom cabins set amid lodgepole pines. About 7 miles west of town, the **Lionshead RV and Resort** ($/$$, 406-646-7662) is tucked into the Gallatin National Forest. The pretty site has 175 RV pads, tent sites, standard camping cabins, and a deluxe cabin ($225) furnished with the works.

Hebgen Lake Area: 🐾 **Kirkwood Resort and Marina Cabins** ($/$$, 1-877-302-7200 or 406-646-7200) has 11 cabins, some with kitchens and some with multiple rooms. At the marina on the property Pete Owens runs **Paddle On Adventures** (406-209-7452), offering recreational kayak rentals with hard-top carriers and guided trips on the lake. **Madison**

Arm Resort ($/$$, 406-646-9328, May to October) is 9 miles north of the West Entrance, just off US 20/191 at Hebgen Lake. The busy property features 20- and 30-amp full hook-ups with a couple of pull-throughs, tent sites on the lake, and relatively modern cabins and cottages. A variety of boat rentals are available at the resort's marina. **Yellowstone Grizzly RV Park and Cabins** ($/$$, 406-646-4466, May to October) offers three types of RV sites, tent camping, and three styles of cabins. RV sites range from 30- to 100-amp in premium 70-foot pull-throughs with full hook-ups. Expanded in 2006, much of the RV park backs up to the Gallatin National Forest.

Local Flavors

DINING INSIDE THE PARK

Old Faithful: No doubt you've seen photos of the tall interior log infrastructure at **Old Faithful Inn Dining Room** ($$/$$$, 307-545-4999 or 307-344-7311, B/L/D, May to October), with its classic Western parks theme, log furnishings, huge stone fireplace, and original oil paintings. Meals will be more memorable for the grand ambiance than for the food. Breakfast and lunch are first-come, first-served and dinner is by reservation; all three meals have a buffet option. An ample spread can be found at the breakfast buffet along with an à la carte menu. A lunch buffet may include pan-fried trout, a chicken sandwich, bison chili, salad, soup, beans, coleslaw, etc.; hot and cold sandwiches may be ordered off the menu. Dinner specialties can include a game Bolognese, Alaskan salmon, elk medallions, beef rib-eye, pork, fish, and chicken along with starters and salads. If you just want a light bite, choose drinks and appetizers at the **Bear Pit Lounge.** The **Old Faithful Lodge Cafeteria** ($/$$, L/D) will suffice for less formal lunches and dinners, and seating near the windows may offer a peek of the geyser when it's gushing. The **Bear Paw Deli** ($, L/D) has room for 70 and is fine for sandwiches, salads, and scoops of ice cream through the evening. In the Old Faithful Snow Lodge, the **Obsidian Dining Room** ($$/$$$, 1-866-439-7375 or 307-344-7901, B/Br/D, May to October /December to March) is a place to get away from crowds at the inn, and truth be told, may have slightly better food. Breakfast and lunch are the usual, with a few variances: the vegan breakfast burrito and grilled Reuben with apple sauerkraut. Bison ribs braised in Moose Drool beer, and nonmeat choices of spicy peanut linguine, ratatouille risotto, or wild mushroom ravioli are a few of the atypical dinner selections. The décor is definitely Western with wildlife accents; reservations are not taken. Service can be spotty, but that's true of many park dining rooms; there just isn't a lot of personal investment toward captive diners. The **Firehole Lounge** makes for a good warming hut with its large fireplace and the **Geyser Grill** ($, B/L/D) is a quick fix for the hungry with sandwiches, soup, salads, burgers, and the ubiquitous huckleberry ice cream.

BEST DINING OUTSIDE THE PARK

West Yellowstone: If you're looking for fine dining with ambiance, this isn't the place. The whole idea of being *in here* is to experience *out there,* and restaurants in West Yellowstone are in lockstep with that theme. Functional food along with mostly nondescript and noncreative menus won't encourage anyone to linger. That said, we've enjoyed plenty of meals in West Yellowstone. You just have to look a little harder. We'll start with our favorites.

To get the day started or for a lunch to take to the park, ❧ Ernie's Bakery and Deli ($/$$, 406-646-9467, B/L) is one of a handful of eateries you can count on for good eats, being open year-round, and homemade breads—not to mention a Web site with updated earthquake activity for the area. For an afternoon pick-me-up, stop in the Freeheel & Wheel Nordic ski and bicycle shop for Mocha Mamma's ($, 406-646-7744, B/L) espresso bar, where you can "belly up and they'll fill yer cup" with coffee, chai, tea, or hot chocolate seven days a week. You can also fill your belly with bagels, burritos, cookies, or gourmet chocolate. It claims to be a cool store in a historic building, and we agree. Plus, they're genuinely nice folks. Check for their hours online but pretty much count on 9 AM to 6 PM. After a day of wildlife touring, ❧ Wild West Pizza ($$$, 406-646-4400, L/D) calms the hunger pangs and gets our WOW award—for consistently Wonderful Out of this World pizzas made from scratch, starting with Wheat Montana flour and their own recipe sauce. Also on the wonderful list are the salads, Montana beer selections, and spot-on service. We remember them as the tiny, dingy, alternative joint—now they're all decked out in spacious new digs, including a centrally located bar with lots of TVs. ❧ Sydney's Mountain Bistro ($$/$$$, 406-646-7600, D) is a true delight that doesn't fit the mold of West Yellowstone eateries. A limited menu allows

the chef to focus on fresh and flavorful ingredients; Sherry loves the squash ravioli and Jeff the burger. It has a shoe-box-sized kitchen that doesn't handle large output, so slow down and savor the moment and anticipation.

New on the scene is the ❧ Café Madriz ($$/$$$, 406-646-9245, D, May to September), one of the few truly ethnic choices in town. It's small, slightly crowded, reminiscent of tapas bars in Spain, and, true to form, you may order small plates or meals. Seating is on picnic-style tables, more in line with the town, but the food is the real deal—we love the paella and papas bravas. Probably the most upscale dining in town is at the Madison Crossing Lounge ($/$$, 1-866-500-5050 or 406-646-7621, D)—the only place to get sushi (Wednesdays, and once a month in the winter). It is decidedly fine dining at non–fine dining prices. Try the bison meatloaf, bison short-ribs (Friday nights), or cedar-plank-cooked trout. If we just want a burger and fries, we go to Bullwinkle's Saloon and Eatery ($/$$, 406-646-7974, L/D). The crowded dining room serves wild game, steaks, burgers, and seafood, and is suitable for families, though not always known for the friendliest service.

Other mainstays that usually get favorable reviews include the breakfast served all day—yes, get the pancakes—at the Running Bear Pancake House ($/$$, 406-646-7703, B/L). Prominent on the food scene in West Yellowstone is the Geyser Grill ($$, 406-646-4745, B/D), with summers-only family-style meals and good pizza any time of year. Speaking of pizza, it's not surprising you'll find many selections in a family vacation town like this, and you can't go too wrong with Pete's Rocky Mountain Pizza Company ($$, 406-646-7820,

L/D), which has take-out and delivery. **Gusher Pizza and Sandwich Shoppe** ($/$$, 406-646-9050, L/D, May to October/December to March) has, well, pizza and sandwiches, along with salads, electronic entertainment (poker and keno), take-out, free delivery, and decent pies. The unpretentious **Beartooth BBQ** ($$, 406-646-0227, L/D, May to October) specializes in BBQ and brats, pulled pork, country-style baked beans, and serves beer and wine. **Canyon Street Grill** ($/$$, 406-646-7548, B/L/D) is a popular 1950s-style café complete with black-and-white checkered floor, red-and-chrome booths and table sets, and a reputation for local Wilcoxson ice-cream malts and shakes.

A couple of coffee or breakfast stops we frequent include ⊛ **Morning Glory Coffee & Tea** ($, 406-646-7061, B/L), in part because of the fair-trade coffee beans from around the world roasted there, to be supped in-house or shipped to your home. **Three Bear Restaurant** ($/$$$, 1-800-646-7353 or 406-646-7353, B/D, May to October /December to March) is part of the ecoconscious Three Bear Lodge, and the dining room is favored for good reason. Breakfasts are above average and under $10—with the exception of the New York steak and eggs—and are served promptly. Steak and seafood dinners are equally popular in the summer, but in winter meat 'n taters are favored, especially the 10-ounce bison rib-eye and 16-ounce bone-in cowboy cut. Delaware North Company, one of Yellowstone's concessionaires, took over the Holiday Inn and **Branch Restaurant & Bar** ($$/$$$$, 406-646-7365, B/L/D), formerly Oregon Short Line and Iron Horse Saloon. Rebranded and remodeled, the restaurant-bar combo touts "open range cuisine," meaning creative and

unfenced American. Signature burgers include the Big Sky, a thick beef patty with smoked bacon and bleu cheese draped in Moose Drool–caramelized onions, or the Branch burger—a mix of bison, elk, and pork under a huckleberry glaze. Popular with the out-of-towners is the bison pot roast and smoked prime rib. Outside of town 6 miles west on US 20, check out **Bar N Ranch's** ($$/$$$$, 406-646-0300, B/D, May to October) new and intentionally rustic dining room loaded with animal mounts, much like the inside of a Cabella's. Chef Ryan Smith is slinging plenty of Bar N Burgers (8-ounce patties stuffed with cheese and topped with smoked bacon and onion curl), their signature baby clam and spicy elk sausage fettuccini, and pork chops stuffed with local goat cheese and green onions. Vegetarians may not be the primary crowd, but aren't forgotten with handmade pesto ravioli. Omelets are good day starters meant to fill you up for a day's worth of outdoor activity. North of West Yellowstone, after passing through the northwest corner of the park on US 191, is ⊛ **Cinnamon Lodge & Adventures** ($$/$$$, 406-995-4253, D), which has the typical steak fare but also the best Mexican food between West Yellowstone and Bozeman. Whatever you choose to eat, be sure to have a prickly pear margarita and save room for the decadent sopapilla cheesecake for dessert.

Hebgen Lake Area: The legendary **Happy Hour Bar** ($$$, 406-646-5100 or 406-646-7281, L/D, May to October /December to March) serves hand-cut steaks, bison and beef burgers, and shrimp scampi under pinned-up brassieres, panties, and boxers, creating a one-of-a-kind ambiance; a rickety deck overlooking the lake and dock adds more character. The top-selling

Happy Hour steak special, a hand-cut top sirloin, baked potato, and corn on the cob, comes out sizzling on a hot skillet and topped with grilled onions for under $20. Another favorite, the hand-pattied garlic burger made from a house recipe, tastes exceptionally good with a secret family recipe bloody Mary or margarita. Also famed is their summer refresher, a Moscow Mule (vodka, ginger ale, and lime juice in a copper cup). Just down the road is the more family-friendly **Longhorn Saloon** ($$/$$$, 406-646-0196, D, May to October), where apps, burgers, sandwiches, pasta, steaks, ahi tuna, and walleye can be ordered starting at 4 PM. They host live local music periodically.

Island Park: At Angler's Lodge Restaurant ($$/$$$, 208-558-9555, B/L/D) you may be able to watch fly anglers or trumpeter swans on the Henry's Fork of the Snake River while dining in a great atmosphere that includes log walls and a front-and-center stone fireplace. During warmer times, sit on the deck paralleling the river. Some of the house favorites are the Angus steaks, chicken Marsala, and chicken Chablis. We've always enjoyed

meals and lodging at the Angler, where the Eby family works hard to make it a rod above. At the Pines Resort's **Lodgepole Grill** ($$/$$$, 1-888-455-9384 or 208-558-0192, L/D) burgers come in variations, most notably the Black and Bleu or Phillips, which is topped with ham. In the Phillips Lodge at the Pines Resort, where history creaks from the planked floors of the rebuilt lodge, dinner choices range from steak and St. Louis–style ribs to pasta and fish. There is a full bar and decent wine list. If you're a fan of surf and turf, Friday and Saturday nights are renowned for smoked prime rib, Alaskan king crab legs, and homemade clam chowder for around $30. The very busy cluster of cabins, boats, and anglers right next to US 20 and in the center of Island Park is Mack's Inn. High on the "if you're in the area" list is an evening of local talent at **Mack's Inn Dinner Theater** ($$$, 1-888-558-7272 or 208-558-7272, May to September), in the form of spoofs or Western plays. For dinner you may choose between slow-smoked prime rib, roasted chicken, or veggie pasta they promise to be delicious. Reservations are required.

To Do

ATTRACTIONS

West Yellowstone: The town's two most popular attractions are the neighboring **Grizzly & Wolf Discovery Center** (1-800-257-2570 or 406-646-7001) and **Yellowstone IMAX** (406-646-4100), almost adjacent to the West Entrance. The center is the easy—and safe—way to get up close and personal with two of Yellowstone's more famous denizens. The center features nine grizzlies, including "101," who lived in the wild for 20 years before human carelessness allowed her and her cubs access to pet food. Eleven wolves form three packs, all born in captivity and thus unable to survive in the wild. The center feels somewhat like a zoo exhibit, but it does provide educational information on the two key predators' struggles to coexist with humans. The IMAX is a six-story theater that offers a bird's-eye view of the park on its giant screen. Among the features regularly playing is *Yellowstone.* Look for films on wolves and bears as well. Movies about places

The Day the Earth Shook

Quake Lake (406-682-7620, May to September), about 25 miles northwest of West Yellowstone, is worth the drive for an eerie perspective on recent geological history. On August 17, 1959, two faults just outside of Yellowstone moved simultaneously and caused an earthquake that registered 7.5 on the Richter scale. A massive landslide into the Madison River west of Hebgen Lake roared down Sheep Mountain at 174 mph, killing 23 unsuspecting campers in eight seconds. Five more campers were washed away in a flood as waters raged over the dam at Hebgen. Some 370 aftershocks were counted, and 298 geysers in the area erupted, some for the first time in recorded history.

The landslide became a natural dam on the Madison and created a 38,000-acre lake 190 feet deep and 6 miles long. The spires of drowned trees still stand like sentinels above the water and the site of the landslide is still obvious. Just how powerful was the quake? Water-softener magnate Emmitt Culligan had a home on Hebgen Lake built to withstand a nuclear attack. Unbeknown to Culligan and his architect, the home was built on a fault line. When the earth quit trembling, one side of the house was 15 feet higher than the other. A Forest Service visitors center has been built at the site of the slide, with a boardwalk, exhibits, and video room helping visitors marvel at Mother Nature's awesome power.

farther away, such as Grand Canyon National Park and the Louisiana Bayou post-Katrina, also play. The **Museum of the Yellowstone** (406-646-1100, May to September), in the stately old Union Pacific Building, provides a closer look at the cultural history of the park and the events that have shaped it.

Island Park: About 3 miles south of the town with America's longest Main Street is **Harriman Railroad Ranch** (208-558-7368), where a serene ranch was founded amid sage and lodgepole in 1902 by the Guggenheim family and Averill Harriman, owner of the Union Pacific Railroad. Harriman, who also founded Idaho's Sun Valley Resort, built a spur line from Pocatello, Idaho, to West Yellowstone. The ranch has 27 buildings and is renowned for its world-class dry-fly fishing on the Henry's Fork of the Snake River, which serpentines through the property. Today the land is owned by the State of Idaho. A bunkhouse can be rented for weekend retreats for groups of 15 to 40.

RECREATION INSIDE THE PARK

Fishing

Never heard of the **Bechler River?** Not many people who visit Yellowstone have, largely because few ever visit the remote southwest corner of the park. And for fishermen, it isn't what you catch, but where you are and the effort required in getting there. The Bechler is accessible only from Ashton—or a 30-mile hike south from Old Faithful. For as few people as the cutthroats and rainbows here see, they're surprisingly wary. You'll have much more company on the **Firehole River,** which epitomizes the pure dry-fly Yellowstone fishing experience, especially in June and July. On cloudy days, pale morning duns and caddis flutter above the river and entice trout to the surface. The fish aren't big, but they're feisty. The hatches tend to occur late morning, but get there early because others will stake out prime holes and wait for the water to boil with activity. No doubt you've seen photos of fly anglers casting with geysers, bison, and elk in the background. That's the Firehole.

Farther downstream, the **Madison River** and "trout fishing" are inextricably linked, like Bogey and Bacall. Famed local angler Charles Brooks once described the Madison as the world's largest chalk stream, a reference to its nutrient-laden calcium bicarbonate. Birthed at the junction of the Firehole and Gibbon, the Madison meanders westerly and leaves the park north of West Yellowstone before turning north after leaving Hebgen Lake. Though fishing in the park is solid, the river is best known for a 40-mile stretch between Quake Lake and Ennis that produces large rainbows and browns. The **Gibbon River** is another angler favorite all the way from its source at Grebe Lake to its confluence with the Firehole; fish the meadows for rainbows, browns, and even some grayling.

Hiking

Madison Junction Area: The brisk, easy 1-mile **Harlequin Lake** about 1.5 miles west of Madison Campground meanders through charred lodgepoles to a small lake, and definitely requires mosquito repellent. **Purple Mountain**, which begins 0.25-mile north of Madison Junction, is a moderate trail through burned pines,

Fly anglers are drawn to the Firehole River for its trout and surreal backdrop. NPS

with better views at the end than Harlequin—and fewer mosquitoes. The route climbs 1,500 feet and offers a good look at where the Firehole and Gibbon rivers join to become the Madison. **Two Ribbons** is a short, pretty, wheelchair-accessible boardwalk through regenerated forest along the Madison River 5 miles east of the entrance; watch for bison and elk.

Old Faithful Area: The easy **Fairy Falls/Twin Buttes** hike ends at 197-foot Fairy Falls on Fairy Creek, one of the highest in the park. The creek meanders and drops through a lush forest where elk, bison, coyotes, and eagles are known to roam or soar. With several options for access, it's suitable for those wanting a leisurely 5-mile stroll or more exertion from a 7-mile jaunt. The trailhead is reached via the Steel Bridge parking area 1 mile south of Midway Geyser Basin or at the Fountain Flats parking area. **Fountain Paint Pot**, 8 miles north of Old Faithful, offers close-up views of geysers, hot springs, fumaroles, and mud pots on an easy, short loop trail. Few trails offer a better perspective of geothermal activity than **Geyser Hill Loop**, which winds by Beehive, Castle, Daisy, and Firehole geysers. Some geysers in the area, such as Anemone, erupt every few minutes. Beehive shoots higher than Old Faithful and has a cone shaped like a beehive. Castle is shaped like its name and erupts about every 12 hours, shooting spray up to 75 feet. The Morning Glory Pool was once one of the park's most brilliant, though years of tourists tossing coins and other junk from the road have tempered its hues and helped spur algae growth. Be wary of bison and elk in the area.

Popular with bicyclists, the **Lone Star Geyser** trail is a flat 5-miler through lodgepole pine on an old paved road to one of the park's more powerful geysers. Lone Star erupts about every three hours and never disappoints. The trailhead is 3.5 miles southeast of Old Faithful at Kepler Cascades parking area. Slip away for some solitude amid pines, meadows, rock, and burnt timber on a moderate 6.8-mile jewel called the **Mallard Lake** trail, reached from the cabin at Old Faithful. For a terrific perspective on Old Faithful, take the 2.4-mile **Mystic Falls** hike. Many visitors turn back after reaching the 70-foot falls, but it's worth veering to the right where the trail forks for a climb up a series of quad-testing switchbacks to an overlook. The Upper Geyser Basin fans out below you, with Old Faithful in the background. Finally, another excellent way to get an overview of the Old Faithful area without too much exertion is the **Observation Point Loop**, a 1.1-mile trail that rises 200 feet above Upper Geyser Basin to an overlook. Keep an eye out for bison and check out the forest regeneration from the 1988 fire.

Swimming

Of the three designated swimming areas in the park, two are near the West Entrance. The **Firehole River Swimming Area**, off Firehole Drive south of Madison Junction, is another popular spot where hot runoff warms the river to just the right temperature downstream. The swimming hole is between modest rapids and it is an adrenaline rush to get to the calm water by riding the waves. The area closes when high, swift water makes it too dangerous. **Madison Campground Warm Springs** is just that—warm. A 100-degree spring trickles into the Madison River, where the 50-plus temperatures are better suited for trout. The convergence near the bank makes for temperatures between 80 and 90. It is dandy for a refreshing dip on a warm summer day, but you won't find anybody here in winter.

The Firehole River has one of the park's three sanctioned swimming holes. NPS

RECREATION OUTSIDE THE PARK

Fishing

Twisting through a canyon between the more renowned Madison and Yellowstone, sometimes the **Gallatin River** is overlooked, even by residents. The fishing isn't as publicized, but it merits attention on several counts. One, it's the first river in Montana to be declared navigable (meaning it belongs to the public below the high-water mark, even where it goes through private property). Two, this is *the* river that ran through it, at least for much of the film *A River Runs Through It*. Best of all, the fishing for rainbows and browns is outstanding, especially during the harshest of summer months. While the sun bakes the broad Madison and Yellowstone, the Gallatin's emerald-green waters stay cool in the shade of the canyon and commonly render 20-inch trout.

To the south, Idaho's nutrient-rich **Henry's Fork of the Snake River** was birthed from an Idaho spring southwest of Yellowstone. Once upon a time, the Henry's Fork moved even the greatest of fly anglers to genuflect. To get a taste for the mammoth trout that lurk in the Henry's Fork, drive east of Island Park to Big Springs and peer over the bridge railing at the fat rainbows gorging themselves near the river's crystal-clear birthplace. Downstream from Island Park Reservoir, the Henry's Fork has two prime angling areas: Box Canyon and the Railroad Ranch. The 3-mile Box Canyon stretch between Island Park and Last Chance is briskly moving water where nymph anglers go deep in pocket water for big rainbows. Farther downriver, at Railroad Ranch, is the world-renowned dry-fly portion, where rising fish tease the best anglers and shrug off any less-than-perfect presentation. Fishing remains excellent until the river warms when it arrives at the Snake River Plain below Ashton. For a less-crowded but nevertheless rewarding experience, try fishing for cutthroats, rainbows, and brookies in the **Falls River**, which pours out of the southwest corner of the park and tumbles brightly toward

Rafters ease past House Rock on the Gallatin River north of Yellowstone.

the Snake. You can fish the section in the potato fields east of Ashton, or follow Marysville Road until you nearly arrive in Wyoming, and head down the rugged Forest Service road to exceptional fishing uninterrupted by anything but an occasional moose or grizzly.

Skiing (Alpine)

Big Sky: **Big Sky Resort** (1-800-548-4487 or 406-995-5000), the vision of former NBC newsman Chet Huntley, has become Montana's poshest ski destination. Towering Lone Mountain receives 400 inches of snow each year. The 85 named runs, including a whopping 6-miler, ensure short lines at the lifts. Vertical drop is 4,350 feet and skiable terrain is 3,600 acres. The resort also has a family-oriented snowtubing park. Neighboring **Moonlight Basin** (1-888-362-1666 or 406-993-6000) provides Big Sky visitors a more affordable option with plenty of elbow room. The resort on Lone Mountain features 4,150 vertical feet and 1,900 acres, most notably a 2.8-mile run.

Bozeman: **Bridger Bowl** (1-800-223-9609 or 406-587-2111) is a nonprofit area cherished by locals who kept one eye on work and kept one eye on the blue flashing light atop Bozeman's Baxter Hotel, which until 2007 told skiers that Mother Nature had been kind again. Lift tickets are remarkably reasonable for such an outstanding ski area. Bridger is sandwiched between two bowls with 2,600 acres and a 1,500 vertical. Average snowfall is 350 inches annually, and most of the runs

Snowmobiles: A Quarter-Century of Furor in Yellowstone

Snowmobiles arrived on the Yellowstone scene relatively late, in 1963. Once the Park Service made the decision to allow Yellowstone to be the country's only national park to allow snowmobiles inside its boundaries, it didn't take long for the sleds to become a part of the gateway communities' economic fabric. Certainly this was true in Gardiner, Cody, and Jackson, but especially in West Yellowstone and Island Park. By the 1990s, as many as 2,000 were entering the park on peak weekends, queuing up more than 30 or 40 deep at the West Entrance. For many years the whine of snowmobiles cruising the streets of West Yellowstone was more prevalent than auto traffic. But by the late 1990s, an increasing number of visitors were coming for winter solitude and quiet. Snowshoers, Nordic skiers, wolf watchers, and snowcoach riders were growing increasingly disenchanted with the noise and air pollution. On some days the air over West Yellowstone and park corridors was so dirty it rivaled major metropolitan areas; Park Service employees collecting fees at the West Entrance wore gas masks. Biologists also feared snowmobiles were causing stress to the park's animals. The winters were harsh enough, and riding inside the park was a free-for-all. In 2000, mindful that some 75,000 snowmobilers were entering Yellowstone over hundred-day periods, the Park Service under the Clinton administration created a furor by announcing it intended to phase out snowmobiling inside the park. Panicked, the city of West Yellowstone, which contributed about 60 percent of the park's snowmobile traffic, filed suit. For about a decade since, the battle has raged, with the pendulum swinging between pro and con, depending on court decisions and park environmental impact statements. The Park Service is seeking a permanent solution. As of 2011, all people entering the park on snowmobiles must be with certified guides aboard four-stroke sleds equipped with so-called Best Available Technology (BAT). Interestingly, studies show that when people come on a weeklong snowmobiling vacation to West Yellowstone they spend one day in the park and the other five or six riding the labyrinth of trails outside the park.

are geared toward intermediate and advanced skiers, though there's plenty for beginners. Those literally wanting a walk on the wild side trudge another 400 feet to "The Ridge" for extreme skiing, and folks schuss here long after the resort closes because snow often lingers well into July.

Skiing (Nordic)

West Yellowstone: There has been so much emphasis on snowmobiles here that it's easy to forget that the area has some of the best cross-country snow around, especially at **Rendezvous Ski Trails** (406-646-7097). There are 35 miles of groomed trails on gently rolling terrain through lodgepole pine forest on wildlife-filled national forest land. Passes are required from November 1 to March 1. Thanks to a cooperative effort between the Forest Service, the West Yellowstone Chamber of Commerce, and the Ski Education Foundation, a season-long pass is $25 and a one-day pass is $5.

Upper Mesa Falls on the Henry's Fork of the Snake River.

Big Sky: About ⅔ up the hill toward the downhill resorts is **Lone Mountain Ranch** (406-995-4644), featuring about 46 miles of groomed trails on a variety of terrain that's easily navigated by novices.

Sled Dogs

Big Sky: **Spirit of the North Adventures** (406-682-7994) runs half-day trips daily out of Moonlight Basin at Lone Mountain. Spirit of the North even lets you operate your own dog-sled team of Alaskan huskies. Trips are also run out of West Yellowstone.

Snowcoaches

West Yellowstone: No fewer than eight companies offer these treks into the park's interior, most notably to Old Faithful but also to Norris Geyser Basin and the Grand Canyon of the Yellowstone. Increasingly conservationists and others in the community have been pushing for snowcoaches as a cleaner, quieter, warmer, and more efficient way for groups of people to see Yellowstone's majesty in winter.

West Yellowstone: Outside the park there are hundreds of miles of trails, with rugged mountain terrain ever more accessible as technology improves. West Yellowstone, which still fancies itself as the "Snowmobile Capital of the World," has no fewer than 13 rental facilities and plenty of information at the Chamber of Commerce (406-646-7701).

Island Park: Trails dip and bob through the lodgepole forests between the "islands" and push up against Yellowstone's western boundary on the Caribou-Targhee National Forest. Another popular playground is in the Centennial Mountains to the west. The Idaho side is easily accessible; be sure to obey the signs prohibiting entry onto the wilderness study area on the Montana side.

3

Yellowstone: North Entrance

North Entrance to Mammoth/Mammoth to Norris/Mammoth to Tower Junction

GETTING HERE

The drive to the North Entrance on US 89 south of Livingston, Montana, might be the most riveting of the park's five entrances. Even though the northern end of the gorgeous Yellowstone River Valley has been carved into ubiquitous 20-acre ranchettes with trophy homes, and the river has been unnaturally channeled in places to fend off flooding, these distractions pale against a backdrop of the magnificent Absaroka and Gallatin mountains rising to the east and west. Livingston is reached via I-90; it is about 30 miles east of Bozeman Yellowstone International Airport at Gallatin Field (BZN) in Belgrade and 100 miles from Billings's Logan International Airport (BIL). Turn south on US 89 at exit 333, squeeze through a narrow slot where the Gallatin and Absaroka mountains pinch together, and enter some of the most eye-pleasing developed landscapes in Greater Yellowstone.

It's easy to see why this 50-mile stretch is called Paradise Valley. People have long been drawn to the valley, for evolving reasons. Indigenous peoples came in the winter to hunt game, which was plentiful because the notorious winds blowing ferociously off the Yellowstone Plateau to the south scoured the valley of snow. Today it is the scenery and lifestyle that lure people from all over the world. Livingston doesn't look like much from the freeway, but it has a pretty backdrop and unparalleled redbrick character, thanks to its reinvention as an artists' colony after the Burlington Northern Railroad pulled out in the mid-1980s. More professional writers per capita ply their trade here than anywhere in the United States, including Thomas McGuane, Tim Cahill, David Quammen, and Jim Harrison. Livingston's denizens spend much of their summers in the valley, floating the serpentine river as it winds gently amid the cottonwoods. Living here does require

LEFT: Minerva Terrace at Mammoth Hot Springs is a classic example of a travertine terrace. NPS

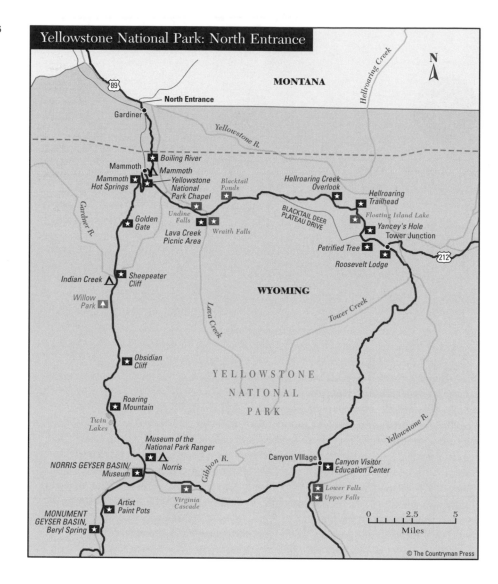

Yellowstone National Park: North Entrance

MONTANA

89

North Entrance

Gardiner

Yellowstone R.

Boiling River

Mammoth

Mammoth

Mammoth Hot Springs

Yellowstone National Park Chapel

Blacktail Ponds

Hellroaring Creek Overlook

Hellroaring Trailhead

Gardner R.

Golden Gate

Undine Falls

Lava Creek Picnic Area

Wraith Falls

BLACKTAIL DEER PLATEAU DRIVE

Floating Island Lake

Yancey's Hole

Tower Junction

Petrified Tree

Roosevelt Lodge

212

Indian Creek

Sheepeater Cliff

Willow Park

WYOMING

Lava Creek

Tower Creek

Obsidian Cliff

YELLOWSTONE

NATIONAL

PARK

Roaring Mountain

Twin Lakes

Museum of the National Park Ranger

NORRIS GEYSER BASIN/ Museum

Norris

Gibbon R.

Canyon Village

Canyon Visitor Education Center

Yellowstone R.

Artist Paint Pots

Virginia Cascade

Lower Falls

Upper Falls

MONUMENT GEYSER BASIN, Beryl Spring

N

Hellroaring Creek

0   2.5   5

Miles

© The Countryman Press

some toughness: The winter winds are so ferocious that empty railroad cars are known to topple over. The local joke is that you can tell when the wind has stopped . . . everyone falls down.

To get some sense of what Paradise Valley was like before its "discovery" in the mid-1990s, turn left onto East River Road about 4 miles south of the park. Follow it along the base of the Absarokas through little Pine Creek and past the junction to Chico Hot Springs until it rejoins US 89 about 20 miles north of Gardiner. For another worthwhile detour, backtrack from the junction of East River Road and US 89 to the bridge across the Yellowstone River and turn left on the gravel Old Yellowstone Trail at a place called Point of Rocks. This scenic route roughly follows the old Park Branch Line Railroad that brought early visitors to Yellowstone. Look for eagles, bighorn sheep, elk, white-tailed deer, and mule deer

Bighorn sheep are commonly seen in the Gardner River Canyon inside the North Entrance. NPS

along this stretch—especially in the spring, before the snows melt in the high country. You can return to US 89 by crossing the iron bridge at the Carbella fishing access site.

The highway then cuts through the narrow Yankee Jim Canyon before emerging into the Gardiner Basin, where another charismatic animal joins the wildlife feast in the winter and spring: the bison. Many Yellowstone bison roam outside of the park in search of forage in the winter. Until the spring of 2011, they were rounded up and put into a corral; those that tested positive for a bacterial illness called brucellosis were herded onto livestock trucks and shipped to slaughter. Others were transferred to one of four quarantine pens on the east side of the highway—readily apparent for their tall double fencing and red-and-white U.S. government warning signs. Today, though, these last remnants of the herds that roamed the Great Plains by the tens of millions—a genetic treasure trove—are allowed to traverse the basin. Their presence demands special attention by drivers, especially at night because their eyes do not reflect headlights.

As you pass through Corwin Springs and by Devils Slide, look west across the Yellowstone River for a row of cottonwood trees making a straight line along a creek bed up to the base of the Gallatins. This is Reese Creek—the Yellowstone National Park boundary. Also here you'll see several large fenced areas across the river where the Park Service is trying to restore vegetation. Soon you'll arrive in Gardiner, which is hard against the park border on the east side of the river, peering at the fabled Roosevelt Arch.

OVERVIEW

For the history buff, the North Entrance—the only entrance station open year-round for automobile traffic—is the place to be. When you make the virtual U-turn out of old-town Gardiner you'll find yourself staring up at the massive stone

Roosevelt Arch, constructed during the summer of 1903—some 31 years after the park's creation. President Theodore Roosevelt laid the cornerstone at what was then the primary place where early well-heeled tourists departed a passenger train and boarded horse-drawn carriages for rides into Yellowstone.

About 5 twisting miles up the road is Mammoth Hot Springs, site of the park's current headquarters and formerly Fort Yellowstone. The stately row of former officers' quarters—now housing park employees—is a reminder of the era (1886–1916) when the military was brought in to establish some order at a time when squatting, vandalism, poaching, and general lawlessness were rampant. Also oozing history here are the Albright Visitor Center and Mammoth Hot Springs Hotel. The centerpiece of this history is Mammoth Hot Springs itself. If there's a close runner-up to Old Faith-

The Roosevelt Arch on the edge of Gardiner is a popular photo op.

ful in terms of natural wonders that define Yellowstone, it's these steamy, bleach-white terraces that shape and reshape the area's geography every day. Nowhere in the world is there a better example of travertine terraces at work.

The Albright Visitor Center at Mammoth has a fascinating wildlife diorama on the second floor. NPS

Mammoth serves as the headquarters for Yellowstone National Park.

At Mammoth, the options are to head east toward Tower Junction or south to Norris. In winter, the road to Norris is open to vehicular traffic only to the upper end of Mammoth Hot Springs; from there, it's a popular snowmobile and snow-coach ride to either Old Faithful or Canyon Village. The road east across the Gardner River—on the second-highest bridge in Wyoming—is open year-round to Tower and the Northeast Entrance to serve the Montana communities of Silver Gate and Cooke City.

The 18 miles to Tower Junction cross the revered Blacktail Deer Plateau, known for one of the most readily spotted wolf packs in the park, numerous bison, a herd of stately bull elk, and dramatic views of the Yellowstone River's Hellroaring Creek drainage. The 21 miles to Norris feature the park's most challenging road-construction achievement at Golden Gate followed by miles of forest and meadows en route to what many believe is the most spectacular geyser basin in the park.

Did You Know? Mammoth once had a geothermal pool in the 1930s open for soaking, but the closest you'll get today is a hot tub on a few of the cabin porches.

GATEWAY COMMUNITIES

Gardiner, Montana

Of all the gateway communities to Yellowstone, Gardiner is the most rugged and raw, a persona befitting its semiarid surroundings. It was created in 1880 entirely for the purposes of serving visitors coming to the park's original entrance, though mining, ranching, and fur trapping certainly have had an influence. The town was laid out on the park's northern border, reputedly by a spiteful local man who was angry with park officials for tossing him out of Mammoth, 5 miles to the south. Today, Gardiner sits on steep benches above the frothy Yellowstone River and in the rain shadow of dramatic Electric Peak. The old part of town faces the park and connects to the newer section by a lone bridge; it is best known as the site of the stone Roosevelt Arch and was the hub of park activity for a half-century after the Park Branch Line of the Northern Pacific Railroad arrived. By 1883, Gardiner had 21 saloons serving about 200 full-time residents. Rail service ended in the 1950s. Today, the town has its share of motels and touristy knickknack shops, but it's also where the majority of the park's employees live. Such wildlife as bison, elk, and deer routinely roam the streets of Gardiner, and the high school football field is the only one in America where bison scat must routinely be shoveled off before spring track meets.

HITTING THE ROAD

North Entrance to Mammoth (5 miles): Lines can get long in the summer at the North Entrance because the station has only one window—though on the busiest days they'll route folks through the employee lane, and an expanded entrance was in the plans in early 2012. Be patient and scan the parched sage and grasslands on either side for bison, elk, and pronghorn. As you idle briefly, you'll notice a gravel road coming in from the west. This is a one-way route that starts behind the hotel at Mammoth Hot Springs and offers a great sense of seclusion along with terrific views of the Gardiner Basin and occasional elk herd.

After a short drive past the Rescue Creek trailhead, the road and Gardner River—yes, the river and town are spelled differently, with the river getting the

Visitors usually see wildlife as soon as they arrive at the North Entrance.

Did You Know? Directly across the Gardner River Valley from Mammoth is the arid 7,841-foot peak of Mount Everts, named for 1870 Washburn-Langford-Doane Expedition member Truman Everts. In September, Everts managed to separate himself from his party, his horse, and all of his supplies—having only two knives and an opera glass. He managed to start a fire with his opera glass, but fell asleep and started a forest blaze that destroyed his knives and singed his hair. Everts survived by eating thistle root and spending nights by thermal features. After 37 days on his own he was rescued by two men looking for him.

proper spelling of Johnson Gardner's name—squeeze together for a serpentine rise through a strikingly arid canyon. Look for bighorn sheep on the sheer pumice slopes on your left. About 3 miles into the drive, you'll pass a sign marking the 45th Parallel, the midway point between the North Pole and the Equator, followed by the border separating Montana and Wyoming.

Just past the second bridge over the river is parking on both sides of the road for the popular **Boiling River** soaking area, one of three places in the park (the Firehole River and Madison Campground Warm Springs are the others) where dipping into hot springs is condoned. It's an easy 0.25-mile walk along the river to the spot where the 140-degree waters of the Boiling River pour out of the ground and race about 100 yards to the 60-degree waters of the Gardner River, creating idyllic pools for soaking. Water temperatures will depend on the river's depth, and the area is typically closed during high water in the spring. Once a rowdy place where locals let off steam with drunken binges and vandalism, tightened Park Service restrictions have made it more family friendly.

The road rises precipitously from the parking area, providing views of the steamy springs and the rugged alluvial cliffs to the east that rise above the lower reaches of the Black Canyon of the Yellowstone River, which is less crowded but only slightly less spectacular than the Grand Canyon of the Yellowstone upstream. You'll pass the Lava Creek trailhead and two barren knolls that were as popular as any site in the park for taking photographs back in the days when visitors arrived via horse and carriage. Soon to come into view amid scraggly juniper and limber pine is the **Mammoth Campground**, the park's lone year-round camping area and, for those who worry about bears, one of the more comfortable places to pitch a soft-sided tent.

Mammoth almost always has a herd of elk grazing on its lawns. It is the place to see single-minded bull elk with giant antlers squaring off with other elk—as well as the occasional vehicle or tourist—during the September rut as they pursue their harems. Most famous was a proud bull simply named Six, which twice had encounters with visitors that cost him his magnificent rack. Six was quite a tourist spectacle for several years until he met an indignant demise after getting his antlers caught in a fence north of Gardiner. Among animal sounds in Yellowstone, there's nothing quite like the bugle of a bull elk.

The first stop to make in Mammoth is the **Albright Visitor Center** (307-344-2263), an old stone building that serves as an anchor for the park's headquarters. Named for the park's superintendent from 1919–29, the center has an engrossing collection of second-floor dioramas of the wildlife for which the park is known. On

This bull elk, known simply as "Six," didn't take kindly to vehicles or people getting too close to him—or his harem.

the first floor is a theater, bookstore, information desk, watercolor paintings by Thomas Moran, and photos from William Henry Jackson; downstairs, accessed from the outside, are basic restrooms. This is a great place to get information before heading deep into the park.

Farther up the road, nowhere in the world is there a better example of travertine terraces at work than **Mammoth Hot Springs.** These ever-evolving springs above park headquarters at Mammoth are split into upper and lower terraces. All have excellent boardwalk access and viewing platforms with interpretive sites. The dominant white rock is the deposits left by the rain and snow runoff that's passed through the fissures in the Earth's surface and reemerged as carbonic acid. The stunning variety of colors, ranging from brown and yellow to azure and teal, are attributed to the dramatic array of microorganisms, temperature variances, and acidity associated with the hot water. The dead pines and firs protruding from pools on the upper terrace are stark evidence of just how rapidly these terraces change. Calcium carbonate (travertine) accumulates rapidly, forming lips that dam the water and kill vegetation. Terraces can grow as much as 8 inches in one year, and about 2 tons of travertine is dispersed throughout the springs each day. Pools that exist today may be gone in five or ten years. If you're short on time, don't miss the New Blue Spring on the upper terrace. Other pools of note are Canary Spring, Angel Terrace, and Palate Spring. Between the terraces and the commercial area, you'll notice an erect hunk of 2,500-year-old dormant travertine called Liberty Cap. It was named by the Hayden exploration party in 1871 for its resemblance to French military caps.

Hot Times in the Old Park

Yellowstone certainly is renowned internationally for its wildlife, but its thermal features are no doubt the reason this fiery region became the world's first national park. With ten thousand geysers, mud pots, fumaroles, hot springs, and travertine terraces, Yellowstone contains more geothermal features on land than the rest of the world combined. Following is a closer look at the four types of thermal features in the park and surrounding areas.

Geysers: The best-known of Yellowstone's thermal attractions are the least common, about 3 percent. Still, the park's 250 geysers (Icelandic for "gush forth") represent more than half of the world's total, and except perhaps for the travertine terraces at Mammoth Hot Springs, no type of thermal feature draws more tourists. Geysers are formed when water and snow seep into the hot rock. As the heated water rises above the cold water and races to the surface, it expands and becomes trapped by steam bubbles in a chamber of resistant rhyolite rock. The pressure eventually forces it skyward violently. Think of your kitchen pressure cooker. Geysers even have distinctions. Fountain geysers spray water widely, while cone geysers, like Old Faithful, are more like an uncorked fire hydrant. Most of Yellowstone's geysers are distributed throughout nine basins, about half in Upper Geyser Basin, where Old Faithful's reliability has lured millions of visitors from the world over. For a geyser treat unfettered by crowds, try the 17-mile round-trip hike into Shoshone Geyser Basin near Grant's Pass.

Hot Springs: They're the same as geysers, without the drama. Most of Yellowstone's hot springs merely spill out of the ground at temperatures nearing 200 degrees, though Crested Pool has been known to explode even though it has no constrictions. The Rockies and Cascade Range of Oregon and Washington are dotted with thousands of hot springs, many offering a welcome respite for the sore muscles of hikers, skiers, boaters, etc. But anyone looking for such relief in Yellowstone will be sorely disappointed. For safety reasons, the park does not allow soaking in thermal pools, even in the backcountry. Tourists have scalded themselves and some springs carry potentially deadly microorganisms. Besides, finding the right temperature mix is a challenge: Most springs are too hot, and the stream water too cold.

Fumaroles: These are geysers without the water, much of which has been vaporized by the time it reaches the surface. Fumaroles are known for their hissing sounds and rotten-egg smell of hydrogen sulfide, most notably at Soda Butte in the Lamar Valley. The appropriately named Roaring Mountain, just north of Norris on the east side of the road, is the most prominent and visible example.

Mud Pots: Take a hot spring, add mud, and subtract a consistent water source. Presto, you've got a mud pot. Mud pots rely on snow and rain for subsistence. The bubbling, which has the look of a witch's brew, is from escaping gasses. Add minerals to the recipe, and you've got a colorful paint pot. Check out the Artist's Paint Pots southwest of Norris, the Fountain Paint Pot Nature Trail in Lower Geyser Basin, and the West Thumb Paint Pots.

Mammoth to Norris (21 miles): Much of what Yellowstone symbolizes is covered in this scenic north-south journey, from mountains and thermal features to wildlife and the Golden Gate, site of one of the more dramatic construction projects in park history. The first mile reaches the upper terraces at Mammoth Hot Springs and then a gate that's closed in the winter except to snowmobile and snowcoach travel. Beyond the gate begins the gradual climb through pine and aspen, and past ghostly shaped hoodoos that provide a sneak peek at similar configurations scattered throughout the backcountry. A short one-way side trip on what was once a stagecoach road provides a close-up look at these funky stone columns.

A 0.5-mile trip past **The Hoodoos** is **Golden Gate**, aka Silver Gate and Kingman Pass. This section was completed in 1883 and required 1,275 pounds of dynamite. The canyon wall is so vertical that a 228-foot wooden trestle was built; today, a concrete bridge wraps around the wall en route to **Swan Lake Flat**. As you reach the top, you'll have dramatic views of Glen Creek tumbling over 47-foot Rustic Falls into the chasm below. The plateau is also known as Gardner's Hole because the river cuts a V-shaped course off the flanks of the Gallatin Range to its speedy meeting with the Yellowstone at Gardiner.

Bison and the occasional grizzly bear are often seen on Swan Lake Flat, which provides panoramic views of mountains in all directions and also serves as the starting point for four worthwhile hikes—including a trek to the top of **Bunsen Peak** to the east. As you continue south through forest, you'll pass the striking columnar basalt of **Sheepeater Cliff**—the Shoshone were also once known as Sheepeaters—and **Indian Creek Campground** before reaching the aptly named

Sheepeater Cliff along the Gardner River was a staging spot for Shoshone Indians.

The Museum of the National Park Ranger honors a storied history. NPS

Willow Park. This is reputedly a good place to spot moose, though we've never seen one there—perhaps because even as large and dark as they are they are easily hidden amid the willows.

Moving southward, with 10,236-foot Mount Holmes and 9,894-foot Dome Mountain looming off to the west, you'll arrive at **Obsidian Cliff**, a nirvana for archaeologists. Because of its sharpness, obsidian was a favored volcanic rock for tools. Pieces from this so-called "Glass Mountain" have been found at archaeological sites as far away as Ohio, Kansas, and Michigan. Collecting or removing any piece from Obsidian Cliff is strictly forbidden; it became a National Historic Landmark in 1996.

Going 4 miles past Obsidian Cliff you will find **Roaring Mountain**. This barren, steamy 400 feet of mountainside just east of the road hisses as you drive by. Named in 1885 by park geologists, Roaring Mountain sends the remnants of 200-degree water into the air as steam. It isn't as effusive as it once was, but it remains a classic example of a fumarole. Beyond Roaring Mountain on the west side of the road is **Twin Lakes**, which are separated by a modest divide that sends the waters of both into different basins. Before arriving at Norris, stop at the **Museum of the National Park Ranger** (307-344-7353, June to September) on the road to the **Norris Campground**. The museum is housed in a rebuilt 1908 cabin that was one of the first soldier stations in the park. Exhibits show the evolution of the park ranger and include the 25-minute movie *An American Legacy*. The museum is mostly staffed by retired Park Service employees.

Mammoth to Tower Junction (18 miles): This stretch offers an eye-pleasing mix of conifer, sage, and high plain, with a dramatic crossing of Gardner River on Wyoming's second-highest bridge and even more dramatic views across the Black

Canyon of the Yellowstone River into the Hellroaring Creek drainage. Nearly all of Yellowstone's wildlife species roam here. Before departing Mammoth, consider a short walk up the Old Gardiner Road behind the hotel. Elk are a common sight here, but perhaps the most interesting attraction is the remnants of an old Shoshone teepee about 0.5 mile up the road to an obvious row of conifers bisecting the gravel road to the west. Walk up the north side of the trees about 100 yards to find a shelter that has weathered remarkably well.

Did You Know? American Western figure Doc Holliday, dentist by day and gunman as needed, was often heard saying "I'm your huckleberry," meaning he was their man. The huckleberry is a coveted wild fruit in the Northern Rockies.

As you depart Mammoth to the east, you'll pass the row of old officers' quarters that house park personnel. Look for cow elk grazing on the lawns and perhaps a wedding taking place at the picturesque stone **Yellowstone National Park Chapel**, where mass is still conducted on weekends. The cloned ranch housing down the hill to your left is home to more employees.

At a dramatic 200 feet high, the Gardner River bridge is one of the most spectacular in the region. Built in 1939, it is second in height in Wyoming only to the span over Sunlight Creek in Sunlight Basin northwest of Cody. From there, the road narrows and begins a notable rise high above Lava Creek toward **Undine Falls**, which is actually a series of three falls totaling about 100 feet high that are named for mythological water spirits. Drive carefully here—bison frequently use this stretch as a migratory route between the Gardiner Basin and higher elevations to the east. About 0.5 mile above the falls is the shady **Lava Creek Picnic Area,** one of the most popular in the park because of its bucolic setting and sparkling waters that beckon trout anglers. This is also the southern terminus of the **Lava Creek Trail,** which begins just north of Mammoth and includes part of an old Bannock Indian hunting trail.

In contrast to Undine Falls, **Wraith Falls** is modest in volume even though its height (90 feet) is about the same—especially in late summer and fall. It's a 0.5-mile walk through a pretty meadow to the falls. At 1 mile past Wraith Falls is the beginning of the **Blacktail Plateau** and the western territorial edge of the often-visible Blacktail Plateau wolf pack, which was created in 2009 by perhaps the most famous and most-photographed wolf since *Canis lupus* was restored to Yellowstone in 1995—302M, aka Casanova. The rogue wolf achieved rock-star status and was the subject of the film *Rise of Black Wolf* (see sidebar). The pack is sometimes seen around the shores of the boggy **Blacktail Ponds**, where bison, coyotes, goldeneye ducks, and sandhill cranes are also common sights.

On the south side of the road is the **Blacktail Deer Trail**, which begins with a short walk to the cabin once inhabited by Mary Meagher, a park biologist and author who could identify and distinguish every individual bison that lived in the area. You'll notice in the plateau's wide-open spaces hundreds of large boulders sprinkled across the landscape. These are glacial "erratics," left over from the last great ice retreat. If you pay close attention, you'll also note that many of these erratics seemingly have single conifer trees seemingly growing out of them. These boulders create their own microclimates, providing just enough shade, water, and protection from the elements to sprout growth otherwise not possible.

302—Yellowstone's Rock-Star Wolf

Nowhere in the world are wolves more visible than in Yellowstone. And none of the several thousand that have traversed the ecosystem since their restoration in 1995 has been more famous—or more extraordinary—than No. 302, aka the Black Wolf and, to his human admirers, Casanova.

Certainly 302's visibility is a key factor of this phenomenon. Born into the Leopold pack in 2000, Black Wolf cajoled his way into the park's most famous group, the Druids, before breaking away with four members of the Agate pack to form the Blacktails. Casanova fascinated droves of wolf watchers by tempting fate with the Druids, somehow earning the affection of the powerful pack's females despite the inherent dangers—solidifying his reputation as a lover-not-a-fighter.

Casanova's legend was further etched in Yellowstone lore by Emmy Award–winning filmmaker Bob Landis, whose *Rise of Black Wolf* chronicling 302's life debuted on National Geographic television on Thanksgiving in 2010. Remarkably, in a place where wolves are fortunate to survive for four years, Black Wolf lived to be 9½, ultimately perishing in a territorial battle with unknown wolves in October 2009.

Before he died, though, he had mated with Agate females, who bore his pups in one of the dens once used by his original pack—the Leopolds. Though the Druids disappeared in 2009, victims of mange and stronger packs that coveted the Lamar Valley elk buffet, Black Wolf's DNA lives on through the Blacktails, which are commonly seen between the Hellroaring Overlook and Tower Junction. Ask any of the devoted "wolfers" about 302 and you're sure to elicit a look of reverence and a misty eye or two.

About 2 miles past the ponds and trailhead is a short walk on an interpretive trail that provides a nice sense of all the turmoil underfoot. In another mile is the **Blacktail Deer Plateau Drive**, a rugged, 7-mile, one-way diversion that rises and falls through dramatic country. More than a century ago, when Yellowstone was toured by the elite, there were many service roads similar to this so staff could bring supplies to hotels and stores without being seen by well-heeled visitors. The remnants of these roads are still visible in places just off the main roads. Perhaps the most remarkable section of this drive is **The Cut**, a canyon that once served as an early Indian trail.

If you choose to save Blacktail Deer Plateau Drive for another day, you'll soon arrive at **Phantom Lake** on the south side of the road. It is so-named because it routinely dries up in the summer. Soon after, you'll notice an alluring panoramic vista opening up on the left side of the road. Be patient—you'll get a chance to pull over at the **Hellroaring Creek Overlook**, a great place to break out the binoculars or spotting scope. In the spring and fall, especially, the distant hillside—split by the rushing waters of Hellroaring Creek—can be blanketed by elk and bison, with the occasional wolf pack or grizzly bear wandering through. Look to the northeast for the **Hellroaring Creek Trail** suspension bridge crossing the Yellowstone River as it plunges through Black Canyon.

At 2 miles past the overlook is **Floating Island Lake,** which for the past decade or so has featured an island of reedy materials on which sandhill cranes have routinely nested. This has become a marvelous viewing area for other wildlife too, including grizzly bears and ducks. As you continue on with more dramatic views, the road will make a sharp right turn and you'll be looking into the wood-cluttered **Elk Creek Valley.** Unlike other areas that were burned in the famous 1988 fires, this one has not recovered as well because the Wolf Lake blaze burned so hot it sterilized the soil here. Vegetation has been slow to return, but that's a boon for wildlife watchers—black bears, moose, wolves, fox, bison, and other megafauna are frequently seen, causing traffic jams.

Did You Know? Though technically it's true that Yellowstone became the world's first national park in 1872, it wasn't the first land set aside by the U.S. government for such protections. In 1864, President Abraham Lincoln created the Yosemite Grant in California. But Yosemite was managed by the state of California and didn't become a national park until 1890.

As the road does a horseshoe across Elk Creek and bends back to the east, you'll reach the turnoff for the **Petrified Tree.** It's a 0.5-mile drive to see the lone remaining entombed redwood remnant in an area that once boasted several; most were removed or destroyed by vandals or artifact hunters, and unfortunately the lone holdout must survive behind bars. Happily, anyone willing to hike off the beaten path a bit can find more impressive examples on Specimen Ridge, where

Entombed remains of redwood trees can be found on Specimen Ridge.

27 forests are stacked on top of one another. Preserved trees there include red-woods, oaks, mangroves, and breadfruit.

Looking north before arriving at **Tower Junction**, you'll notice a broad plain that'll probably include a handful of grazing bison. Though Yellowstone is probably as healthy ecologically as it has been since its creation in 1872, this is a great place to stop and ponder humankind's interventions and their impacts. Called **Yancey's Hole**, the area where Roosevelt Lodge's cookout facility is now located once boasted a hotel and saloon amid a soggy landscape where beavers were hard at work creating valuable wetlands. When wolves were extirpated by the 1920s, eliminating a keystone predator, elk populations rose dramatically and rapidly devastated trees, shrubs, and grasses. Without trees to fell, the beaver disappeared—and so did the wetlands, leaving the arid area you see today. Man isn't completely hands off now, either; Roosevelt Lodge staff often haze black bears away before tourists arrive in horse-drawn wagons for their nightly steak-and-potato cookouts in Yancey's Hole.

Arriving at Tower, you'll notice a ranger station on the right, followed by a Sinclair service station and the entrance to **Roosevelt Lodge**—a rustic setting that's a favorite for locals who want to get away from the madding crowds in the summer (Roosevelt Lodge is covered in Chapter 4).

Pick Your Spot

LODGING INSIDE THE PARK

Mammoth: Welcome to the 1930s, when the North Entrance was Yellowstone's primary traffic corridor and the ✪ ⼻ ⼕ **Mammoth Hot Springs Hotel & Cabins** ($$/$$$, 307-344-7901, May to September/December to March) was the cornerstone of park activity. Built in 1911 and reconstructed in 1937, history adorns the halls in the form of photographs, creaking floorboards give authenticity, and one wing of the original hotel remains. With a little imagination you can picture Calvin Coolidge resting after arriving on the train for a few days of fly-fishing. The no-frills simplicity means clean, glossy-painted rooms with a bed and washbasin—toilet and showers down the hall. Cabins run the gamut from two "luxury" suites (phone, cable, TV, Internet, and a private bedroom)

and cabins with private hot tubs to Frontier cabins with showers and Budget cabins with a sink. A quiet lounge next to the lobby features a grand piano and giant map of the U.S. inlayed with 15 types of wood. Mammoth quiets down early, and don't expect to sleep in: The paper-thin walls reverberate in the morning with the echoes of people eager to take in Yellowstone's treasures. There's a gift shop in the lobby, but one of the best gifts is out the front door, where a large elk herd frequently grazes.

ALTERNATIVE LODGING INSIDE THE PARK
Camping

Mammoth Hot Springs: The most popular campground in Yellowstone is **Mammoth** ($, 1-866-439-7375), which is also the only year-round place in the park to pitch a tent or anchor an RV. There are 85 sites set amid sagebrush, juniper, and limber pine in the driest corner of the park. The campground is

Mammoth Hot Springs disperses tons of travertine daily.

primitively luxurious, with flush toilets and pay showers. Most of the sites are pull-throughs for RVs. Expect to have company from the Mammoth area's ubiquitous elk herd and an occasional pronghorn or black bear that wanders through the fringes.

Norris: Even larger than Mammoth is **Norris Campground** ($, 1-866-439-7375, May to September), another popular location with 100 sites, flush toilets, 2 marked 50-foot pull-through RV sites, and 5 more for 30-footers set amid the pines. Above Golden Gate in the woods is the more primitive **Indian Creek** (June to September), which has 10 sites for 40-foot pull-through RVs and 35 more for 30-footers among 75 slots overall.

BEST LODGING OUTSIDE THE PARK

Gardiner: The **Absaroka Lodge** ($$, 1-800-755-7414 or 406-848-7414) is popular not necessarily for the quality but because all rooms have an attached balcony practically suspended high above the dramatic Yellowstone River Canyon, right next to the high bridge that connects both sides of town. It is also known for making the cover of National Geographic magazine, though the stars of the photo were two bison. Among chain motels, the modern log-sided ❧ ❙❙ **Comfort Inn** ($/$$$, 406-848-7536) on the north end of town stands out; at 77 rooms it isn't overly large, the hot breakfast is better than most, and there are two large indoor hot tubs. In addition, the full-service Antler Pub and Grill is in the front of the property. For a more quaint experience, the 🐾 **Riverside Cottages** ($/$$$, 1-877-774-2836 or 406-848-7719) are a collection of cute yellow cabins, a four-plex, and a family suite perched high above the river and in the center of the business district. The Gardiner Chamber of Commerce gushes that it has "the best views in Gardiner," including Electric Peak in the Gallatin Range. 🏵 **Jim Bridger**

Court ($$/$$$, 1-888-858-7508 or 406-848-7371, May to October) is a tight semicircle of small mountain-style log cabins. In the drive-to-your-door department, the choice is the **Westernaire Motel** ($/$$, 1-888-273-0358 or 406-848-7397), with excellent views of the Gallatin Range to compensate for the lack of in-room amenities. Relatively new on the scene is ⁓ **Cowboy's Lodge and Grill** ($$$, 406-848-9175), which has four beautifully appointed rooms behind the restaurant. Only one has any semblance of views, toward the Yellowstone River, but the interior décor makes up for it.

Less than 4 miles north of Gardiner the **Headwaters of the Yellowstone B&B** ($$/$$$, 406-848-7073) offers four first-floor rooms in a home overlooking the river, plus two cabins open year-round; the Riverview sleeps six and Mountainview sleeps four. Each room includes a private bath, breakfast, and exceptional views. The riverfront property includes a sandy beach with chairs and fire pit. *Note:* The Olsons sometimes close for routine maintenance during the off-season.

Jardine: The **Diamond Bar-D Guest Ranch and Hunting Lodge** ($$$, 406-223-0148, June to September/December to April) 5 miles east of town is a remote mining outpost that puts visitors as close to the Yellowstone backcountry experience as possible without sacrificing comforts. Situated on Crevice Mountain at 8,300 feet and in the migratory route for the famed Northern Range elk herd, the property is itself an old mining town. Hunters, wildlife watchers, and photographers will find nirvana in the traditional Western log cabins (which sleep up to six) and trails out back that lead directly to the park. The Diamond is prized for its unstructured environment, seclusion, healthy meals, and nightly campfires, sometimes including educational talks.

Emigrant: Carol and Pete Reed go the extra river mile to pamper and accommodate their guests at 🌿 🐾 **Paradise Gateway B&B and Guest Cabins** ($$/$$$, 1-800-541-4113 or 406-333-4063). Four rooms in the main log home are bright and cheery, the three cabins on their riverfront acreage private and uniquely Montana. An exceptional breakfast is served to non-cabin guests in their antique-packed country kitchen. For that ultimate experience in Paradise, check into the eco-oriented 🌿 **Rivers Bend Lodge** ($$$$) designed by the Reeds' son, who grew up in the area wishing for his own riverside retreat. He frequently inhabits the home with his TV-star girlfriend, which adds to feeling like one of the rich and famous during your stay. Every detail has been carefully considered, most notably a casting rock embedded into the ground just a few feet above the blue ribbon trout waters. The adjoining **Eagle's Nest Tourist Home** and **Trout Tourist Home** are also available for rent. A long fly cast from the river is a historic Yellowstone park cabin overlooking one of two trout ponds. The Reeds also offer three private log cabins nearby.

The spectacular **Mountain Sky Guest Ranch** ($$$$, 1-800-548-3392 or 406-333-4911, May to October) is a former working ranch tucked into a picturesque Gallatin Range canyon off a gravel road, 4.5 miles from US 89. Thirty guest cabins with one, two, and three bedrooms are sprinkled among pine and fir trees. For a true mountain getaway experience, two cabins are located on remote portions of the ranch, including one on a creek available June, July, and August. Seven-day rates include all meals and the use of tennis courts, heated pool, sauna, horseback riding, the trout pond (with instruction), yoga, a fitness room, and an extensive hiking program. The lodge is a classic log structure, with stone fireplace, log furniture, and a long porch suited for listening to nature. Three-night minimums are OK in May and early June; the rest of the season seven-night stays are required.

Added to the National Register of Historic Places in 1999, 🏅 🍴 🐾 Chico Hot Springs Resort and Day Spa ($$/$$$$, 1-800-468-9232 or 406-333-4933) is as popular with the locals from three surrounding counties as it is for out-of-towners. It is a destination stop in the heart of Paradise Valley for many reasons: the thermal outdoor pool, the five-star dining room, the happening saloon adjacent to the pool with several TV screens, darts, pool, shuffleboard, regular live music, the best pizza and bloody Mary around, and our favorite amenity—poolside window beverage service. The main lodge oozes history, from its uneven floors and huge elk mount to the black and white photos of the late actor Warren Oates, once a

Chico regular. The quaint and simple rooms in the main lodge come with or without bathrooms and are offered at special bargain-basement rates during the off-season. Other choices: Warren's Wing, Lower Lodge, and Fisherman's Lodge vary in style and comfort. For those who want isolation and astounding views of the Absaroka and Gallatin mountains, there are cottages, chalets, and six houses—one can accommodate up to 16. A gift shop, day spa, horseback riding, sled-dog rides, and other activities can be arranged.

BEST ALTERNATIVE LODGING OUTSIDE THE PARK

Camping

Gardiner: Rocky Mountain Campground ($, 1-877-534-6931 or 406-848-7251, April to October) sits on a hill, well above the east side of the Yellowstone River, facing the North Entrance. Tent sites are on grass; there are a few RV pull-throughs and two cabins. Rates are reasonable and fluctuate depending on season, except for tent spaces. For a more intimate view of the Yellowstone

Views of Emigrant Peak fill the picture window at Paradise Gateway B&B along the Yellowstone River north of Gardiner.

River, the **Yellowstone RV Park and Camp** ($, 406-848-7496) is a snug RV campground with 48 sites on a dusty bluff overlooking the river, about a mile from the North Entrance. River access is limited because of the steep embankment, and there are a few tent spaces. If Forest Service campgrounds are more your speed, we suggest the **Tom Miner Basin Campground,** which requires a 12-mile drive on gravel to the end of Tom Miner Road. This secluded spot has 16 sites and abuts Yellowstone's northern boundary. Trailheads lead to petrified forests on the way up to the Devil's Backbone of the Gallation National Forest.

Emigrant: Parallel to US 89 is Yellowstone's Edge RV Park ($, 1-800-865-7322 or 406-333-4036, May to October), with a tidy side-by-side row of full hook-up sites on the west bank of the Yellowstone. The check-in office has a small store with a cabin suite ($$$) above it that sleeps up to six, and there's a detached cabin sleeping up to four. With about a mile of river frontage, **Mallard's Rest** ($) primitive campground and fishing access is a cool spot to camp or just hang out by the river. It also has a much-used boat launch for put-in or take-out on the Yellowstone.

Pine Creek: Diane and Terry Devine run a smooth, family-oriented operation at the ♨ **Livingston/Paradise Valley KOA** ($, 1-800-562-2805 or 406-222-0992, May to September) in the pines literally on the banks of the Yellowstone River. We think it's one of the most appealing KOAs anywhere. A small indoor swimming pool will cool off the kids, there's a small boat launch on the river, and the covered pavilion provides a perfect platform for breakfast cooked by the KOA crew, group picnics, DIY sing-alongs, and even church service on Sunday mornings. Cook your own meals or walk a country mile to the famous Pine Creek Café.

For an even more alternative camping adventure try **Luccock Park Camp** ($, 406-223-8131, May to October), a Methodist church camp that is open to all denominations. A combination of log and 1950s-style wood-plank cabins can hold from 2 to 30, with elbow room to spare. For a modest $45 per person per day you can have a bed, community shower, *and* three square meals prepared on-site. As Beverly likes to say "You can get over a lot of rustic with good, home-cooked food." You may be sharing the grounds with a youth camp, a family reunion, or a retreat, but it just adds to the mix; plus it makes a good jumping-off point, with the park entrance a scenic 45 miles away.

Local Flavors

DINING INSIDE THE PARK

Mammoth Hot Springs: Food choices are limited at this entrance into the park, but we've enjoyed dinners at the **Mammoth Hotel Dining Room** ($$/$$$, 307-344-7311, B/L/D, May to October/December to March) and find that the food usually lives up to its description. A unique mix of casual and formal ambiance blend with the 1930s history oozing from the walls of a large, open dining room. The breakfast buffet will fill you up without emptying your wallet; consider ordering the huckleberry skillet for "dessert." Lunch is a step up from the usual—standouts being grilled sandwiches,

An elk herd spends the entire year in the Mammoth Hot Springs area.

crispy Parmesan-coated goat cheese sliders, a Mediterranean sampler, and bison tacos. Dinners are heavy on meat, but vegetarians will find something to suffice, such as the smoked trout plate. We like selecting from the salad and small-plate menu, priced at under $10. Reservations are accepted and even recommended, but if you're forced to wait, there's a small bar on the main floor to the right of the entrance that serves appetizers only but has a TV. For a quicker and more standard meal, the **Mammoth Terrace Grill** ($/$$, 307-344-7311, B/L/D), in the same building as the dining room, offers an uninspiring but serviceable assortment of burgers, chicken, fries, and the like.

BEST DINING OUTSIDE THE PARK

Gardiner: This raw frontier town often is chided for its homogenous cuisine, but while it has no four-star restaurants the food and prices are

solid. Starting with burger joints, the most famous in the ecosystem is **Steve's Corral** ($, 406-848-7627, L/D, May to September), once home to the "Helen's Hateful Hamburger"—usually prepared by the cantankerous Helen herself. The attitude and flying food are gone with Helen's passing, but the drive-in remains an iconic summer stop for ice cream, shakes, and a burger, of course. The best pizza in town is served at the ❧ **K Bar Club** ($/$$, 406-848-9995, L/D), a well-worn bar that looks as if it has been frequented hard and put to bed wet, with billiards, casino, and a jukebox, but it's still suitable for kids. Fans of barbecue and brisket will appreciate the ❧ **Cowboy's Lodge and Grill** ($/$$, 406-848-9175, B/L/D), whose 2010 opening gave tourists a long-awaited casual alternative to the town's standard fare; the mounts on the wall are all Montana, but the food reflects the tastes of its Georgia owners. The closest you'll find to gourmet is at **Rosie's** ($$/$$$, 406-848-9198, D, May to September), which has retained Italian overtones from its previous identity as Pedalino's. Leased from local character Red Curtis, who also owns the neighboring Blue Goose Saloon, Rosie's is named for his wife of more than five decades, and it's only open for supper. Tip: You can order off Rosie's menu at the Goose. Our recommendations: bison meatloaf or Big Sky pasta, which is penne loaded with Italian sausage, sopprasatta, chicken, and roasted red pepper bound by creamy alfredo sauce and laced with Romano pecorino. If your tastes lean to the healthier green side, the ✿ Tumbleweed Bookstore and Café ($, 406-848-2225, B/L) has great soups, a few sandwiches, espresso drinks, and fair-trade coffee to be savored while perusing new and used books that focus on the Yellowstone region. If you're not picky about *where* you eat, Town Café ($/$$, 406-848-7322, B/L/D) is a family-style steakhouse dishing up three squares a day for a modest price—and for those early risers coffee is brewing by 6 AM. Worth an honorable mention is the aptly named Antler Pub and Grill ($$/$$$, 406-848-7536, D, May to September), where you can find the usual suspects on the menu and a game of cards under the glassy eyes of wildlife mounts. The Yellowstone Mine Restaurant ($$/$$$, 406-848-7336, B/D) seems to lure folks despite a local reputation for overpriced steaks, seafood, and pasta. Maybe it's the old-timey gold-mine decor.

Corwin Springs: At 6 miles outside of Gardiner on the east side of US 89 is the on-again, off-again, on-again ✿ Lighthouse Restaurant ($/$$, 406-848-2138, D, May to September), easily recognized by its namesake replica out front. Victor and Penelope are back and better than ever with fresh, healthy, and Asian-influenced cuisine

served amid a coastal decor. Not to fret: It's still Montana and you can also chow down on a bison burger and side of hand-cut fries. Sherry prefers the chili lime tilapia on fragrant jasmine rice or truffle mac and cheese. And for the quality, you won't believe the pricing. Don't skip dessert of either carrot or warm fudge cake, both laden with cream cheese frosting. Tip: You may BYO wine or beer.

Emigrant: What's not to love about Chico Hot Springs, a uniquely Montana experience? The ✿ Dining Room at Chico ($$$, 1-800-468-9232 or 406-333-4933, B (Sunday)/D) has some of the most exceptional gourmet dining in the Northern Rockies. It is set in a casual and elegantly Western small narrow space, with an additional small lounge in back where drinks and appetizers may be enjoyed; we're addicted to the baked brie with huckleberry coulis. The dinner menu, while not extensive or unusual, is simply intriguing. It changes periodically, but the exceptional mainstays are the Peking duck, bison short ribs, and rack of lamb or pork chops from a local farm. Seasonal produce and herbs are gathered from the garden out back, which is easy to visit. Flanking the outdoor pool is the dark ✿ Chico Saloon ($$, L/D), which has a separate menu highlighted by rockin' ribs and perfect pizza. Patrons come in an array ranging from swimsuit to star-studded garb. Several small TVs mounted amid baseball caps are usually on sports channels, as is the big screen above and behind the shuffleboard. Throw in a few video poker machines and small stage with dancing area and you've got a Montana-style good time. Music on the weekends throughout the year creates an even more entertaining atmosphere; kids under 21 are allowed until

8 PM. One more option for eats is Percie's Poolside Grille ($$, L/D), with lunch and snack fare that can be delivered to soakers through a service window.

The 🏵 Paradise Valley Grill at Yellowstone Valley Ranch ($$$, 406-222-4815, D) is in a league of its own, a small enterprise that we hope succeeds. Young and energetic chef Josh Pastrama brings big-city culinary experience to the valley. Mingle with local or visiting fishermen, the semifamous, or just plain folk in his intimate dining room while enjoying the best of what local farmers and ranchers have to offer in his artfully presented meals. Desserts are not to be missed, especially the gelatos. A good sign: The Pastramas had plans to open at a Livingston location in 2012.

Pine Creek: The best time to be at 🏵 Pine Creek Lodge & Café ($$, 406-222-3628, B (weekends)/L/D) is on a summer night when live music is played from a rickety platform in a small grassy side yard in the shadow of the Absarokas. Oh, and a narrow stream with footbridge trickles by your lawn chair. Brats, burgers, beer, and wine are available from the folks grilling in front of you. Mind you, that's not where the best food is served—that's inside, whether in the dining room or on the screened porch, and reservations are a must. Our pick for dinner: fish tacos or elk stroganoff. Our pick for live music: The Red Elvises, who make an annual appearance in the valley. *Note:* Ned had the lodge and café up for sale in late 2011, and its future was uncertain.

To Do

ATTRACTIONS

Gardiner: The **Heritage and Research Center** (307-344-2664) is a state-of-the-art, 32,000-square-foot facility housing a wide variety of artifacts, photographs, journals, and other items of historical value involving the park. Though mostly for research and storage, visitors are welcome to view displays. Appointments can be made to do research in the archives and museum collections (8 AM to 5 PM, Monday to Friday), and free public tours are Tuesdays and Thursdays at 10 AM from Memorial Day through Labor Day.

RECREATION INSIDE THE PARK
Fishing

The **Yellowstone River** is the longest undammed river in the U.S. OK, there are five diversion dams for agriculture in eastern Montana, but let's not split hairs. One of America's most prolific trout streams, the Yellowstone alternatively meanders, cascades, and tumbles violently through the park, creating prime habitat for threatened Yellowstone cutthroat populations as well as rainbows, German browns, and brook trout. Though technically only the cutthroats are native, the other species have reproduced naturally for so long they are de facto wild—and fight like it. Cutthroats averaging about 16 inches tend to inhabit the river above the Upper Falls of the Grand Canyon; below the falls, rainbows, brookies, and browns dominate. Wading is mandatory in park streams, where float craft aren't allowed. As is the case with most rivers, the most resourceful will prevail. Scramble down into the

Pronghorn favor the grasslands around Gardiner because they are usually free of snow.

canyon or hike into the remote backcountry above Yellowstone Lake; your rewards will be tranquility and less-wary trout. Once the river leaves the park at Gardiner it broadens and braids, but the fishing remains world-class for trout well past Livingston. If you're a parent or grandparent looking to introduce your child to fishing, take the family to the **Gardner River**, a pretty little stream rushing from the northwest corner of the park to its confluence with the Yellowstone. Just upstream from the north entrance, before the river tumbles over Osprey Falls, it is fed by Panther, Obsidian, and Indian creeks in a meadow shadowed by Bunsen Peak. All four streams may be fished with worms by children 12 and under. The rainbows and brook trout are small, but the kids won't care. They'll delight at a trout wriggling on their hook, and any quiet fishing stretches are likely to be punctuated by close proximity to elk, moose, beaver, and other wildlife.

Hiking

Mammoth Area: Get a good overview of the Mammoth area on the 5-mile **Beaver Ponds Loop** hike through pine and aspen forest, past beaver ponds, and into wildflower-rich meadows that belie the stark beauty of the hot springs. Look for elk, pronghorn, beaver, deer, and moose. Keep your eyes and ears open for black and grizzly bears on the trail, which starts between Liberty Gap and the stone house at Mammoth Terraces. **Blacktail Deer Creek** is a memorable and moderate 12.5-mile trail along a creek by the same name that tumbles more than 1,000 feet to the Yellowstone, where a steel suspension bridge leads you to the Yellowstone River Trail. Continue along the river on the dusty trail to Gardiner at the north entrance. Bring a fly rod; you're sure to have some of the Yellowstone's best fishing waters to yourself.

Perhaps the easiest hike with the greatest mountaintop rewards in Yellowstone is **Bunsen Peak**, which can be as few as 2 miles and as many as 10, depending on

Lightning crackles above Mount Everts southwest of Mammoth. NPS

how much time and effort you want to exert. Views include Mammoth Village and the Gallatin, Madison, and Absaroka mountain ranges as well as the Yellowstone River Valley. The 3.5-mile **Lava Creek** Trail follows the Gardner River and then turns east by the towering bridge toward Undine Falls. **Osprey Falls** is a rugged trail in a starkly beautiful area rarely seen by visitors despite its proximity to the Mammoth-Norris Road. You might share the first 3 miles of the Old Bunsen Peak Road with mountain bikers until you reach the actual Osprey Falls Trail. At the rim of Sheepeater Canyon, the trail drops about 700 feet in less than a mile to 150-foot Osprey Falls on the Gardner River. You're in a deep canyon here, looking up at 500 vertical feet of walls. The spray from the falls will offer a refreshing respite from what's likely to be a warm hike in summer, and the fishing can be great. Be especially bear aware on this trail! The first trailhead North Entrance visitors see is for 8-mile **Rescue Creek**, another deceiving hike that includes a dramatic 1,400-foot climb out of the Gardner River Canyon. Another lesser-known hike with great rewards is **Sepulcher Mountain**, which has a strenuous 3,400-foot ascent to 9,652 feet west of Gardiner. Check with rangers for bear activity. The easiest hike in this part of Yellowstone is **Wraith Falls**, an excellent place for families or anyone wanting a quick break from driving. Minutes after leaving the parking area, after a quick 1-mile jaunt through sage and Douglas fir, you'll be at the falls on Lupine Creek.

Norris Area: Though not as popular as the Fountain Paint Pots viewing area, **Artist's Paint Pots** is an easy 1-mile round-trip stroll on a boardwalk and newly cut trail through burned lodgepole pine that brings visitors up close and personal with the two mud pots. Anyone seeking a little solitude will savor the 8-mile round-trip **Cygnet Lakes** hike through marsh and burned lodgepole to a tiny lake; bring mosquito repellent and keep diligent watch for signs of bear. **Grizzly Lake** isn't a grizzly hangout, but few hikes in Yellowstone paint a more vivid portrait of fire history than this 4-mile round-tripper through spires of charred lodgepole. Burns are visible in every direction once you arrive at the rim of the lake—some from the historic 1988 blaze and others from 1976. Like Grizzly Lake, the 0.5-mile **Ice Lake** trail features the ghostly remains of lodgepole burned in 1988; unlike Grizzly, this easy hike ends in a lush green lodgepole forest and is a great jumping-off point for other walks and handicapped-accessible backcountry campsites. If you want geyser viewing without the crowds, try the modestly rugged **Monument Geyser Basin** hike from the Artist's Paint Pots up a steep mile-long trail to gnarled cones, including the Thermos Bottle Geyser. An interesting hike that combines thermal features, lodgepole forest, springs, a creek, and even some park power lines is the moderately easy **Solfatara Creek**, which has a gentle 400-foot gain. The **Wolf Lake Cut-Off** is a 6-mile round-trip hike that starts along the Gibbon River before veering toward Wolf Lake through burned lodgepole forest past Little Gibbon Falls.

Swimming

Generally, the waters of Yellowstone and Grand Teton are either too hot or too cold for a swim, and for the most part soaks are discouraged because of the instability of ground where thermal features and streams converge. It is illegal to swim, bathe, or soak in any of Yellowstone's thermal springs or pools. Damage to the environment can occur, and the thermal areas can be a health hazard because of scalding temperatures, waterborne fungi and bacteria, and the levels of acidity. That mostly leaves streams that have been warmed by thermally heated waters, though it's fine to swim in the frigid lakes of Yellowstone. **Boiling River Hot Springs** is the best and most popular spot in Yellowstone for soaking. The Boiling River emerges from the ground off the North Entrance Road between Gardiner and Mammoth. It sprints about 100 yards to a churning collision with the chilly

Norris Geyser Basin has a staggering array of thermal features. NPS

A wily coyote searches for a winter meal.

Gardner River. The meeting of 140-degree and 60-degree water meshes for a 50-yard stretch on the west bank, where soakers enjoy idyllic pools. Water temperature varies depend on the Gardner's depth, so the ideal spot might change each time you visit. The Park Service has in place enough restrictions on Boiling River to eliminate some of the rowdiness, trash, and car burglaries that once plagued the area. It is against regulations to move rocks or dig in the river to create pools. Swimsuits are required and the only private changing facilities are the parking-lot outhouses. Summers are busy, but you might have the place to yourself on a winter weekday because of the chilly 0.25-mile walk.

RECREATION OUTSIDE THE PARK

Hiking

North of Yellowstone is some of the wildest country in the region, with hiking trails to match. At the end of the 12-mile Tom Miner Basin Road, which leaves US 89 at the northern entrance to Yankee Jim Canyon, is a trailhead for the **Gallatin Petrified Forest**. Much like Specimen Ridge in Yellowstone, this 26,000-acre area has 30-million-old trees that were buried by a lava flow. The trail starts at the Tom Miner campground on the Gallatin National Forest but eventually crosses into the park. Take another trip through more-recent history on the **Yankee Jim Canyon Road** about 5 miles north of Gardiner. You can reach it by turning off US 89 at Tom Miner Basin and hugging the Yellowstone River southward on the old railroad grade until you reach the well-marked interpretive site. Instead of walking on the flat railroad bed through the canyon, take the still-discernible old road up the side of the hill and back down to where it meets the railroad bed. The 120-year-old stone wall to support the road is still there, along with painted signs on rocks advertising other-era businesses in Gardiner; the road became obsolete early in the previous century when the railroad was constructed.

Advertisements from more than a century ago are still visible along the old toll road through Yankee Jim Canyon.

River Running

For a mountain-birthed stream that flows for 678 miles to the Missouri, the **Yellowstone River** has surprisingly little whitewater outside of the park. In fact, there are only two runs, both short: the Gardiner town stretch and Yankee Jim Canyon. Both are Class III at best, but their proximity to Yellowstone's North Entrance and easy access from US 89 makes it possible to spend a half-day in the park and another half on the river. The Yellowstone narrows at Yankee Jim before spilling into Paradise Valley, serving up three modest Class II–III drops; their difficulty depends on the season. By midsummer, they're pretty tame. The town stretch requires hauling boats about 100 yards down a modestly steep trail from town to where the Gardner River thunders into the Yellowstone. Most trips range from 8 miles in a half-day to 17 miles in a full day. You can choose from four companies near Gardiner that offer these floats.

Sled Dogs

Emigrant: **Absaroka Dogsled Treks** (1-800-468-9232 or 406-222-4645) operates out of Chico Hot Springs north of Gardiner and runs primarily Siberian huskies on trails in the Gallatin Range from Thanksgiving until the end of March, snow permitting. Full-day treks, half-day adventures, and two-hour rides are available. Clinics are offered as well.

4

Yellowstone: Northeast Entrance

Northeast Entrance to Tower Junction/Tower Junction to Canyon Village

GETTING HERE

Whoever said "it's not about the destination, it's about the journey" must have had Yellowstone's Northeast Entrance in mind. Aesthetically, you can't go wrong with either of the two approaches. From the north, you'll arrive (in summer) via the dramatic Beartooth Highway (US 212), which rises to nearly 11,000 feet above sea level in a state where the highest point is 12,799 feet. Almost as spectacular, but not nearly as well known, is the route from Cody over Dead Indian Summit through the starkly rugged Sunlight Basin and along the Clarks Fork of the Yellowstone River. Either way, if you're coming by air we suggest Billings's Logan International Airport (BIL), which is served by seven major airlines, including Delta and United. Cody's Yellowstone Regional Airport (COD) is reached by Delta and United regional carriers from Denver and Salt Lake City, but service can be fickle depending on cloud cover and other weather.

From Billings, head west on I-90 to the industrial community of Laurel (exit 434), then drive south past the refinery on US 212/330. In 12 miles, at Rockvale, you'll reach a fork in the road: US 212 veers right to Red Lodge and US 310 continues straight toward Lovell, Wyoming. Slightly more interesting of the two routes is US 310 through Fromberg, Bridger, and, after veering right onto MT 72, the tiny blip of Belfry—home of the fightin' Bats. At Belfry, take County Road 308 (CR 308) over the hill through Bearcreek to Red Lodge or continue south to Cody.

From Cody, it's 12 miles north on WY 120 to the junction of WY 296 and the beginning of the Chief Joseph Scenic Byway. The route traverses the 8,080-foot Dead Indian Pass and continues through Crandall and Pilot Creek—the end of the road in winter—toward a meeting with US 212 and eventually to Cooke City, Montana.

LEFT: Basin Creek plunges toward the West Fork of Rock Creek near Red Lodge.

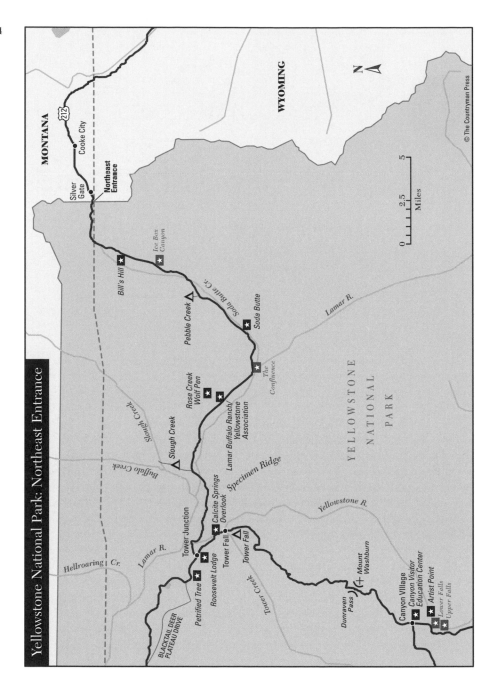

Yellowstone National Park: Northeast Entrance

OVERVIEW

Want to escape the crowds? Spend your time around Yellowstone's least-busy gated entry. Though certainly the Northeast Entrance has its share of visitors, numbers are limited largely by available services in the tiny gateway communities. In addition, there are fewer natural attractions beyond the rugged beauty of the towering Absaroka Mountains and wildlife, which typically scatters to the high country in the warmest months. So while many visitors are clustered around Old Faithful, Yellowstone Lake, and Mammoth Hot Springs, the Northern Range and Lamar Valley remain relatively quiet.

Truth be told, the best time to visit this so-called American Serengeti generally is *anytime* but summer. Elk and bison congregate in the Lamar in the winter, which means wolves are never far behind. Wolves are more visible in the Lamar than anywhere else in the park. Spring is the most spectacular time to visit this corner of Yellowstone because the wildlife are still largely in the valley, accompanied by newborns; bison, wolves, and bears are regularly spotted with their young ones in tow in May, and elk typically drop their calves in June. Autumn is no slouch either, especially in September when the bull elk are in rut, bears are out and about fattening up for winter, and wolves are on the prowl looking for any weak prey.

An area off the road in the Lamar Valley is closed due to its proximity to a wolf den.

Most of the scenes in Yellowstone nature films are shot in the Lamar Valley, in part because of the prolific nature of the wildlife and in part because the road from Mammoth to Cooke City is the only one open to automobile traffic year-round. For much of the year, however, you can access this area only by coming through the North Entrance. The Northeast Entrance isn't manned in winter because Cooke City is the end of the road. The spectacular Beartooth Highway (US 212) has only a brief summer window, from June to October. WY 296,

A pronghorn wanders down the road west of the Buffalo Ranch in the Lamar Valley.

Beartooth Highway: A Scenic and Engineering Wonder

At the turn of the previous century, Yellowstone National Park was becoming an international tourist destination. Such gateway communities as West Yellowstone, Gardiner, Cody, and Bozeman were riding a wave of economic success after automobiles were legally allowed into the park for the first time in 1915. Though separated from Yellowstone by some of the region's most rugged terrain, Red Lodge nevertheless wanted a piece of the action—especially after the nearby coal mine closed in 1924.

A road over the rocky Beartooth Plateau, city fathers surmised, would give tourists direct access to the park's northeast entrance and also enable businesses in Cooke City to tap a mother lode of gold in the New World Mining District about 3 miles from Yellowstone's boundary. They weren't the first to consider travel over the Beartooth—Indians had been doing it for thousands of years—but the task was daunting nonetheless. The grandiose vision was to punch a road into Rock Creek Canyon, carve switchbacks out of the side of a 4,000-foot mountain, lay pavement

The Beartooth Highway was an engineering marvel when completed in the 1930s.

which veers southeast to Cody east of Cooke City, is closed by deep snows on Colter Pass until May—though in 2011 there was a growing movement to plow an 8-mile section that would provide access year-round.

For summer visitors, the Beartooth is unparalleled. They are Montana's highest and brawniest mountains; instead of the craggy peaks associated with the Absarokas and Wyoming's Wind Rivers, this ancient range looks as if a giant decided to take a nap before stepping across the Rockies. You'll feel like you're on top of the world, with precipitous half-dome drops resembling Yosemite's

It may look like winter on the Beartooth Highway, but this photo was actually taken in July.

across the plateau's fragile tundra and 3-billion-year-old rocks, then etch a serpentine route down the back side in Wyoming to Cooke City. It took years of planning.

But in 1931, as the darkness of the Great Depression enveloped a nation, construction began on a road whose difficulty would match the Going-to-the-Sun Road effort still under way in Glacier National Park a decade after it began. Remarkably, construction of the Beartooth Highway took only five years, and opened to great fanfare in 1936. The gold mining at New World never panned out, but by the late 1970s the highway had earned national renown for its incomparable scenic beauty. Answering a letter from a fan inquiring about the most beautiful drives in America, the CBS newsman renowned for his regular "On the Road with Charles Kuralt" features responded "US 212." While atop the plateau, above timberline, it feels as if you can literally reach out and touch the clouds or stars, and you can see many of the nearly one thousand lakes that dot the Beartooth glistening like jewels.

Not surprisingly, keeping the Beartooth Highway open and maintained is a chore unto itself. Wicked weather has wreaked havoc on the road, necessitating renovations that'll require patience from drivers in the coming years. In 2005, a mudslide ruined 13 sections of road and kept it closed all summer, much to the chagrin of businesses in Red Lodge.

The road officially opens Memorial Day and closes after Labor Day, though some years it's possible to drive the route into October. Don't be surprised if you run into snow at any time of year—even on the hottest days of summer the temperature rarely exceeds 65 degrees on the plateau.

El Capitan. Look for mountain goats and maybe even a wayward grizzly bear.

WY 296, dubbed the **Chief Joseph Scenic Route**, is one of Greater Yellowstone's best-kept secrets. Most visitors who reach Cody continue westward up the admittedly beautiful North Fork of the Shoshone River Valley to the East Entrance; those who instead head northwest are in for a treat. The highway traverses the stark and rugged Sunlight Basin. The Clarks Fork of the Yellowstone River cuts a spectacular 1,200-foot canyon as it leaves the mountains and ventures first east and then north. The area is characterized by vast tracts of sage, pine, and

A wall of snow greets a car near the Beartooth Pass in July.

rugged 3.2-billion-year-old rock of many hues. The views west from Dead Indian Pass are beyond striking. Once over the summit coming from Cody, stop at Sunlight Creek and peer over the railing of Wyoming's tallest bridge. Think of the history here, too: Chief Joseph and the Nez Perce came this way on their ill-fated 1877 journey to Canada, knowing they could easily hide from the cavalry in the deep canyons.

GATEWAY COMMUNITIES

Red Lodge, Montana

This alluring town of two thousand at the foot of the mighty Beartooth Mountains is the largest community on the least developed corridor to Yellowstone. Originally a coal-mining town, Red Lodge was best known for years as the starting point for the breathtaking drive on the "Highway to the Sky" into the Beartooths. The influx of tourists helped offset the shutting down of the coal industry and eased the sting of the worst mining disaster (73 died) in Montana history. Red Lodge has moved away from its grimy roots and capitalized on all its outdoor possibilities, the arts, and the Beartooth Highway. Skiing, mountain biking, golfing, fishing, and the town's namesake brewery are favored activities, and Red Lodge offers numerous entertaining events. On the Fourth of July, Red Lodge can get almost as wild and woolly as it did in its days of yore.

Be sure to save at least an afternoon and probably a day or two to explore the rich mining history and trendy boutiques of this Telluride-esque town, which is rapidly losing its distinction as the least-discovered gateway to Yellowstone. Once a raucous blue-collar town with more than 20 saloons and such ethnic neighborhoods as Little Italy, a decidedly tamer but still vibrant Red Lodge was named for a breakaway band of Crow Indians who raised a red teepee. The town is squeezed between grassy benches against the broad eastern shoulder of the Beartooths. For all but the four-plus months of the year that Beartooth Pass is open, Red Lodge is essentially the end of the road. Yet it is still a popular winter destination for its skiing and snowmobiling, and in the shoulder seasons for numerous unique events designed to bolster a year-round economy.

Cooke City, Montana

When they say, "meet me at the end of the road" they really mean it in Cooke City. At least that's true in the winter, when the road really does dead-end in a pile of snow on the east end of town. The plowing from the North Entrance at Mammoth through Yellowstone ends here at this narrow strip town with mostly motels, restaurants, a couple gas stations, and a few homes for the hundred-plus hearty year-round residents. In the late 1800s, Cooke City—named for a Northern Pacific president who never visited the place and refused to build a railroad there, much to the town's chagrin—was a bustling gold-mining town with two smelters, two sawmills, and two hotels. In winter, the main drag is abuzz with snowmobiles, most headed east on the Beartooth Highway. Cooke City typically gets tons of snow, with remnants often lingering until June. In summer, it's more of a traditional gateway tourist community. Evidence of the 1988 fires is starkly evident on the north side of what was then morbidly referred to as "Cooked City," when the old mining town was sure it was destined to meet its maker. Miraculously, the fires skirted the town's northern edge.

Silver Gate, Montana

Silver Gate received its name for the silver haze that seems to hang over the 10,000-foot peaks to the immediate southwest. Peace and proximity are the draws of this tiny hamlet less than a mile from the Northeast Entrance and 3 miles from the hum of Cooke City. Motors aren't endorsed in Silver Gate, except on the cars

Dusk in downtown Red Lodge signals the beginning of an active nightlife.

Cooke City is literally the end of the road on US 212 in winter—unless you have a snow-mobile. NPS

and trucks passing through. The Absaroka Mountains surrounding the town are some of the most dramatic around Yellowstone. Keep your camera handy: It isn't unusual to see moose, bison, or an occasional grizzly bear. The town was barely spared from the 1988 fires, which are evident in the ghostly spires of lodgepole to the north and east. Much of the town today is owned by Henry Finkbeiner, a Southern fellow determined to maintain the rustic quality of the buildings and the surrounding wildness.

HITTING THE ROAD

Northeast Entrance to Tower Junction (29 miles): For those of us who frequent Yellowstone National Park, no road offers more unbridled anticipation than the route going to and from the Northeast Entrance. You are about to enter an incomparable place with more wildlife in the spring and winter than you'll see almost anywhere else. There is so much, in fact, that some visitors have actually asked where the park keeps the animals at night. If it isn't already obvious, the wildness of this area will become self-evident the first time you see a grizzly and wolf sparring over a moose carcass, or a bison cow and her calf suffocating in an icy bog, or a golden eagle slamming into an airborne duck with the force of a missile, or a pack of coyotes herding a frightened pronghorn into submission—all sights we've witnessed in an area that rarely fails to deliver a "gee-whiz" moment.

From the entrance, you'll begin a gradual descent along Soda Butte Creek through thick conifer forests. Soda Butte is unique in that it's the only major head-waters that flow *into* the park. The forest density makes wildlife viewing a challenge, though rest assured there are plenty of grizzlies in this country. Look for moose nibbling on willows along the creek and the occasional mule deer. Slightly more than 4 miles inside the park boundary, you'll notice a dramatic sheer face rising to the north. This is Barronette Peak, named for a gold prospector and early guide named Jack Baronette, who built the first bridge across the Yellowstone River in the park; the misspelling of his name remains to this day. You'll need strong binoculars or a spotting scope, but if you scan the outcroppings closely you might spot a mountain goat. This is the only part of the park that features the goats, an "invasive" species that was transplanted north of the park for hunters and has since moved into the area.

The northeast corner of the park is also the best habitat for the secretive mountain lion. Also in this area is a conspicuous sage knoll just north of the road called "Bill's Hill"—the dramatic place where President Clinton was helicoptered in and put the final nail in the coffin of the controversial New World gold mine in 1996 by declaring, famously, that "Yellowstone is more precious than gold." The mine site, about 2 miles from the northeast corner of Yellowstone, would have included a waste-tailings pond the size of 72 football fields in a seismically sensitive area at the source of streams flowing into Yellowstone and the Absaroka-Beartooth Wilderness. About 3 miles farther west is **Ice Box Canyon**, which quite literally never sees the sunlight of day. Ice lingers well into the summer, and occasionally year-round.

After roughly 10 miles, you'll pass **Pebble Creek Campground** and enter marshy Round Prairie, the first hint of what lies ahead. Though an occasional bull bison will wander into Silver Gate, this is the first place you're likely to spot a few of the shaggy beasts. Wolves are occasionally seen, too. A short drive later you arrive in the eastern end of the Lamar Valley, where the wildlife viewing begins in

A wolf crosses Soda Butte Creek in the Lamar Valley.

earnest. The first landmark is the conical **Soda Butte**, an extinct hot spring recognizable by the unmistakable whiff of sulphur as you drive past. As bison graze on the grasses in the valley, scan the aspens and pines at tree lines for wolves and grizzlies. You might also notice some fenced-in areas on sage hillsides on the north side of the road, with aspen trees growing inside. These are elk exclosures, erected a half-century ago to determine what would happen if the prolific elk herds weren't able to browse relentlessly on grasses and tree shoots.

At 15 miles inside the park you'll reach a place known simply by park regulars as **The Confluence**. Braided channels of Soda Butte Creek and the Lamar River meet here to begin a short run to the Yellowstone. Welcome to the hub of Yellowstone's wildlife-watching universe. In 2009 and 2011, a wolf pack denned in the woods just to the north and regularly crossed the road in search of food in the broad valley. Bighorn sheep are consistently seen on the rocky outcroppings, often within a few feet of the road. Otters often playfully slide in and out of the waters; eagles fish for cutthroat trout here. Bison and elk are common, moose wander into the willow lowlands, and the mighty griz makes regular appearances.

About 3 miles later, the **Lamar Ranger Station/Buffalo Ranch** comes into view. It is here that the bison, which once roamed the prairies by the millions, made their last stand around the turn of the previous century. Wantonly slaughtered for sport and to subdue Indians, the mountain bison was reduced to a meager population of 24—all kept in corrals at the Buffalo Ranch. Some plains bison were transported from Texas to help rebuild the herd. They were fed hay grown and harvested in the valley, and grazed on planted non-native timothy grasses on the benches. For a half-century they lived this way, until in 1968 the park opted for a more natural management system. This treasure trove of genetically pure wild bison—the only significant such herd left in the U.S.—has grown to as much as 5,000. In 2011, they numbered about 3,900.

View east from nearby Buffalo Ranch. NPS

For another taste of history, park at the upper end of the ranch and hike the well-worn trail along **Rose Creek** for about a mile until you reach a dilapidated chain-link enclosure with several large, decaying doghouses inside. This is one of the acclimation pens where the first wolves to be restored to Yellowstone in 1995 were kept for about two months untll their release into a new world. Also at the Buffalo Ranch is the **Yellowstone Association Institute**, where educational classes are frequently conducted by the nonprofit's engaging staff. One of the great advantages of joining a Yellowstone Association field trip is the opportunity to be guided to places park officials might otherwise keep quiet: a remote site where the Shoshone abandoned lodgepoles, the locale of ancient junipers, remnant elk slaughter areas, and abandoned wolf dens. Check out the bookstore in a small cabin; if it's locked a member of the staff generally will be glad to open up. If you stay overnight here during the winter, you're a small island of light amid a sea of darkness and you'll feel as if you have the entire park to yourself.

Chief Ranger Sam Woodring holds wolf pups in 1922, four years before the last wolf in the region was extirpated. NPS

West of the institute, the valley broadens into another extraordinary wildlife area. Bison and coyote are almost always visible here year-round, and the distant foothills frequently have herds of elk keeping a wary eye for wolves and grizzlies. It was here that we last witnessed one of our most awe-inspiring Yellowstone wildlife sights: the famous Druids wolf pack, full-bellied after feasting on a midwinter elk kill, slowly zigging and zagging single file through snow and sage up a south-facing slope to a distant ridge, where all 13 were briefly silhouetted against a bright sky until they vanished into the invisible just beneath the peak for which they were named.

Continuing west, the road slips through the Lamar Canyon, where giant boulders as much as 2.7 billion years old have been exposed by the roiling river waters. The canyon is less than a mile long, and soon you'll enter another open area, marked by the turnoff for **Slough Creek Campground** and trail. Next to the pit toilet is a seemingly out-of-place mailbox. Believe it or not, mail is actually delivered—for the Silver Tip Ranch, which is on the outside edge of the park's northern boundary. Though the 1913 ranch now has an airstrip, guests still arrive and depart via horse-drawn wagon or pack string. Slough Creek itself is a terrific little fly-fishing stream, and the Park Service encourages keeping non-native rainbow and brown trout as it seeks to restore the struggling native cutthroat. As you're looking down the gravel road from the turnoff, the little sage hill just to the right is Dave's

Hill, whose top is worn bare by legions of wolf-watchers. Across the creek valley, in a draw with several dead aspen, is the site of an abandoned wolf den. This turnoff is notable for one other bit of information: In this remote part of the park, it's one of the few spots as of 2011 where you can get cell phone service.

Crossing the new Lamar River Bridge, you will see a sign on the south side of the road that simply says TRAILHEAD. In Yellowstone, these unnamed and unmaintained routes are called "social trails." The conspicuous path upward is the most direct—and steepest—route to Specimen Ridge, famed for entombed trees from several Yellowstone eras. You'll see calcified breadfruit, avocado, sycamore, maple, and other specimens, but the most stunning are the stumps of giant redwoods. The views on top are extraordinary, too.

A member of the now-defunct Silver pack of the Lamar Valley eyes a visitor.

Just beyond the wide parking lot, on the north side of the road, is an area called Little America Flats. A Civilian Conservation Corps camp was constructed here in the 1930s and christened in honor of a similarly named settlement on Antarctica, reputedly because the weather was agonizingly similar. About 3 miles later is the Yellowstone picnic area, in a shaded spot with several glacial "erratic" rocks. Take a few minutes for the

Wolf watchers gather on a small hill near Slough Creek.

short hike above the picnic area to a trail that goes along the rim of the lower end of the Grand Canyon of the Yellowstone. Look for osprey and hawks swooping into the canyon, bighorn sheep on rocky outcroppings, and possibly even a rare sighting of the elusive mountain lion. Black bears are common.

Rising out of the Yellowstone River Canyon, the road comes to a T at Tower Junction. You'll find a gas station, ranger station, and the rustic Roosevelt Lodge, famed for its tiny cabins, Western cookouts, and rocking chairs on the lodge porch. The right fork leads past the gas station toward Mammoth, the left over Dunraven Pass to Canyon Village—the last road in the park to be cleared of snow each spring.

Tower Junction to Canyon Village (19 miles): The gradual climb toward Tower Fall, popular among cross-country skiers for up to six months, rises through a forest to the first breathtaking view, just under 2 miles later, at Calcite Springs Overlook. The view overlooks a part of the canyon called The Narrows and a series of springs famous for their yellowish moonscape appearance. This is a significant place in Yellowstone's history: Thomas Moran's famous paintings of the volcanic upheaval here illustrated the area's incomparable raw beauty, reportedly leading to the park's creation.

Just past Calcite Springs Overlook, the narrow and winding road hugs the columnar basalt en route to 132-foot Tower Fall, likely surpassed only by the Yellowstone Falls as the most photographed in the park. Here you will find a small Yellowstone General Store with the usual treats and trinkets, and a short paved walk to a view of the falls. Look across the gaping Yellowstone Canyon for bighorn sheep.

A few miles past Tower Fall, the road begins a twisting climb toward Dunraven Pass, at 8,873 feet the highest roaded point in the park. This section, which briefly follows Antelope Creek before opening up to a sweeping vista of Antelope Valley, is one of the prettiest in the park. Meadows with wildflowers seem to go

A short trail near Tower Junction leads to a dramatic overlook of the Yellowstone River.

Ancient Tree Making Its Last Stand

On the highest flanks of Greater Yellowstone are gnarled conifer trees, some of the oldest dating to the time of Christ. The whitebark pine scarcely caught the attention of anybody but the most rabid botanist until the past two decades, when they suddenly began dying off in vast tracts. The culprit: a tiny insect called the mountain pine beetle. The reason: Gradually warming temperatures have rendered winters just mild enough to allow the beetle to survive. The little bug has a built-in antifreeze that allows it to live inside the bark of a tree at temperatures down to -30 degrees; anything colder kills them. The problem isn't warming per se; it's that winters simply don't get as cold as they once did. Temperatures have risen 3.8 degrees over the last seven decades at Mammoth Hot Springs.

Whitebark pine experts say the tree will be functionally extinct in Yellowstone by 2020, surviving only in pockets in the highest elevations of the Absaroka-Beartooth front west of Cody. Why the consternation over this seemingly innocuous tree? For starters, the nuts in the whitebark's cones are a primary food source for the grizzly bear, especially for reproduction and hibernation. Furthermore, with whitebarks dying in the park's interior, the bears are pushing outward in search of food, leading to increasing human-bear conflicts. Grizzly mortality in Greater Yellowstone reached record highs in 2008 and 2010. Even more alarming is the ramifications for river flows. Whitebarks grow at the highest elevations and have provided shade for snow. Without the whitebark, runoff is earlier and faster, filling rivers downstream quickly and leaving less water for later in the summer. This in turn is reducing habitat for the native cutthroat trout, which is already being pushed into the region's upper reaches by warming temperatures—proving once again that everything is interconnected.

What to do? Not much. Reforestation plans are under way on some national forests surrounding the parks, but like its cousin, the ancient bristlecone pine, the whitebark grows painfully slowly. Trees won't produce cones for about 50 years. In addition, the parks and surrounding wilderness areas are places where natural processes are allowed to take place. Though some biologists argue that a warming climate is human-induced and thus unnatural, they are still reluctant to intervene.

So, as you drive over Dunraven Pass, mourn the acre upon acre of brown trees, and appreciate the few live ones remaining.

forever to the east and northeast until they hit distant mountains and ridges, most notably the Beartooths and Absarokas but also Specimen Ridge and Mount Washburn. On a warm summer day, the turnout overlooking the valley is a great place to sit in a lawn chair with binoculars, waiting for wildlife to emerge; don't be surprised to see a grizzly or wolf.

As you climb toward Dunraven Pass, you'll note stands of burned timber, remnants of the famous 1988 fires that darkened about ⅓ of the park. You'll also notice vast swaths of brown whitebark pines, the victims of a pine-bark beetle infestation (see sidebar) enabled by a climate that has warmed 4 degrees in Yellowstone since World War II.

Mount Washburn, named for the leader of an 1870 exploratory expedition into the region, is accessed from either side of Dunraven Pass. On the north side is the 1.3-mile Chittenden Road, which ends 3 miles from the fire lookout at the summit. On the south side of the pass is the other end of the Mount Washburn Trail, a steep 2.2-mile jaunt for hikers only. The parking area became well known in 2010 for a camera-indulgent grizzly sow and her two cubs, which delighted visitors almost daily with their hillside antics. The descent from Dunraven offers another breathtaking view of Mirror Plateau, the Absaroka Mountains, and the Grand Canyon of the Yellowstone River to the east. Look for steam rising from Washburn Hot Springs. From there begins a nondescript drive through forests on the approach to Canyon Village.

Pick Your Spot

LODGING INSIDE THE PARK

Tower Junction: Ask any Yellowstone regular or seasonal employee about the best place to get away from it all, and the answer, hands down, is 🐾 🍴 **Roosevelt Lodge Cabins** ($/$$, 307-344-7901, June to September). The tiny cabins are isolated from prime park attractions and close to such wildlife havens as the Lamar and Hayden valleys. The lack of any upscale lodging usually ensures that your neighbors are like-minded. A perfect day at Roosevelt would consist of early-morning wolf watching in the Lamar followed by exceptional fly-fishing on the nearby Yellowstone River, an afternoon horseback ride, an evening wagon ride and cookout, and closing the day from a log rocker on the front porch. The two styles of cabins are primitive and even more primitive—the Frontier has bathrooms with a sink, toilet, and shower, and the Roughrider has no bathroom and is heated by a wood-burning stove. All the cabins are packed close together, and feel a bit like kids' camp, but that's precisely the point. Be sure to book these gems a year in advance, as they fill up quickly.

ALTERNATIVE LODGING INSIDE THE PARK

The **Yellowstone Association Institute** (307-344-2294) has bare-bones cabins at the **Lamar Buffalo Ranch** for an incomparable year-round experience, but you must be signed up for an educational course or tour with the organization. The cabins are heated, but bring your own bedding. A central communal kitchen allows guests to prepare their own food if other arrangements haven't been made, and the immaculate community bathhouse has comfy radiant floor heat for those frigid winter nights.

Camping

The northeast corner of the park features three campgrounds that charge $12 per night—**Pebble Creek, Slough Creek,** and **Tower Fall.** Coming west from the Northeast Entrance, first up is Pebble Creek (June to September), which is just off the road in a pleasant wooded area with 30 sites, including some long pull-throughs. Slough Creek (May to October) is at the end of a 2-mile gravel road and offers 29 sites, including 14 for 30-foot RVs and 14 more for walk-in tenters. Both campgrounds are in grizzly country. Slough Creek is in a prime location for wolf watching, and dinners of fresh-caught rainbow trout are encouraged. Tower

Fall, across the Grand Loop Road from the general store, has 32 sites—all accommodating your 30-foot RV if you can navigate a modest hairpin curve.

BEST LODGING OUTSIDE THE PARK

Silver Gate: The tiny community has a sole mission of being ecofriendly and easy on the ecosystem: For our money, and the sense of getting away, we favor the 🏅 🐾 **Silver Gate and Pine Edge Cabins** ($/$$, 406-838-2371). Twenty-five clean and functional log cabins are tucked into a high (7,400 feet) forested valley where you'll crane your neck to see the jagged top of Republic Mountain towering over the village. Built in the 1930s but recently renovated, the cabins maintain their rustic wilderness character, as mandated by the town's architectural covenants. The seven attached motel rooms are plain and simple; both forms of lodging include kitchenettes with cooking utensils. The managers will eagerly share the story of Silver Gate's rich mining legacy and fix you up with a spotting scope for wolf watching. The Range Rider dance hall in front, once a bordello that was the second-largest free-standing log structure in the country, serves up an eerie assortment of ghostly tales. The small store and check-in provides for general needs, including bear spray. Don't be surprised to find a moose, resident fox, or occasional pine marten wandering past.

Across the highway is **The Grizzly Lodge** ($$, 406-838-2219, June to October), a rowhouse of rooms on the banks of Soda Butte Creek and a good choice if you just need a place to sleep. Another seasonal option: the two pretty-as-a-picture log cabins behind the 🏅 🍴 **Log Cabin Café Bed & Breakfast** ($$, 406-838-2367, May to September) where you can "eat, drink, stay and play." The best part of the deal is the hot breakfast for two at the café included in the low rate.

Cooke City: Amid a sea of typical, small scale motels, the 🍴 🐾 **Antlers Lodge** ($/$$, 1-866-738-2432 or 406-838-2432) fills quickly during the peak summer (June to September) and win-

A young moose grazes on shoots of spring grass outside of Silver Gate's historic Range Rider.

ter (December to March) seasons—for good reason. The 18 log cabins and historic (1913) lodge have a hearty mountain feel, right down to the stone fireplace and elk racks on the walls. Some cabins have full kitchens, some satellite TV. The bar and restaurant can make for late-night loudness. East of town, the **Skyline Guest Ranch** ($$, 1-877-238-8885) is a newer three-story lodge with five spacious guest rooms (each with private bath) and a shared living room, game room, deck, and hot tub. A full hot breakfast is included and dinner is served by reservation. Family outfitters for 50 years, the Jacksons offer trail rides, backcountry camping and hiking, lake and stream fly-fishing, and hunting expeditions operating under permit from the Gallatin and Custer national forests.

Red Lodge: The signature place to stay in town is the redbrick charmer ⬚ ⬚ ⬚ **Pollard Hotel** ($$/$$$, 406-446-0001) taking up the majority of the corner of Broadway and 10th Street. The Pollard has accommodated the likes of Buffalo Bill, John "Liver-Eating" Johnston, and Martha Jane Canary-Burke (aka Calamity Jane) among other frontier celebrities. The building fell into disrepair, then was renovated and reopened in 1994 as a fully modern hotel and dining room that retains much of its former frontier personality but with added touches of elegance. The ⬚ **Beartooth Hideaway Inn & Cabins** ($/$$, 406-446-2288), formerly a Super 8, has a swimming pool and is probably the most appealing of the motor-inn-style lodging, though the newly renovated ⬚ **Yodeler** ($/$$, 406-446-1435) is comfortable and won't disappoint. To feel as if you're in Sun Valley or Aspen, the stylish ⬚ **Rock Creek Resort** ($$$/$$$$, 406-446-1111) 5 miles south of Red Lodge at

the mouth of the mountains is spectacular yet invitingly understated. Townhouses, condos, and standard rooms come in a variety of decors ranging from Guatemalan to Montanan, and you'll be surprised to learn that many rooms have un-Aspen rates.

For upscale-plus B&B lodging, the **Rocky Fork Inn** ($$$, 406-446-2967) has six suites in a sprawling log structure overlooking Rock Creek. **Gallagher's Irish Rose B&B** ($$, 406-446-0303) is a century-old home decorated with original artwork from Leah Gallagher. It has three themed rooms reflecting the town's Irish roots and is closed April/May and October/November.

Beartooth Pass: The ⬚ **Top of the World Resort** ($, 307-587-5368, June to September) is another one of those "gotta try it once" places and is actually more enticing than most of Cooke City's bunking options; however, the four simple rooms with limited electricity are often booked well in advance, so reservations are recommended. Top of the World opens as soon as the Beartooth Highway is clear of snow, usually after Memorial Day; the neighboring store is open three weeks earlier and later than the motel.

BEST ALTERNATIVE LODGING OUTSIDE THE PARK

Crandall: In an area where dude ranches are king, ⬚ ⬚ **Hunter Peak Ranch** ($$/$$$$, 307-587-3711, May to November) is intimate, quiet, and understated. There is a five-unit cabin and two stand-alone cabins, all recently renovated and all on neatly manicured grounds along the Clarks Fork of the Yellowstone River. Meals are priced separately and are by reservation only,

Book your cabins early at the Top of the World Resort near the Beartooth Pass.

and the nearest restaurant is 1 mile away. The **K Bar Z Ranch** ($$, 307-587-4410) offers nightly and all-inclusive lodging during the summer and autumn hunting season. Most of the seven rustic log cabins were built in the 1940s. Family sit-down meals are the norm, along with horseback riding, fishing, and hiking on the activities menu; pack trips into the North Absaroka Wilderness can be arranged. One of the few ranches that isn't in view of a recently burned section of the Shoshone National Forest is the all-inclusive ✪ **Seven D Ranch** ($$$$, 1-888-587-9885 or 307-587-9885, June to September), a 270-acre spread that's home to 10 cabins sleeping anywhere from two to eight for seven nights all-inclusive—three-night stays during off-season. Guests spend time horseback riding, fly-fishing, hiking, engaging in cowboy sing-alongs, line dancing, and purifying in the sweat lodge.

For a truly extraordinary back-to-nature experience coupled with rare modern conveniences, the 1936 ✪ 🐾 Sunlight Ranger's Cabin ($$, 307-527-6291, May to September) is 8 miles from WY 296, with the turnoff just south of the 300-foot-high bridge over the Sunlight Creek Gorge; it has electricity, a phone, range, fridge, shower, a washer and dryer set, a stunning Absaroka setting, and more wolf and grizzly tracks than you can count. It'd be hard to find more plush accommodations in the Forest Service rental program anywhere.

Belfry: In the making-ends-meet department, the ✪ **Beartooth River Ranch** ($$$$, 406-664-3181) is one of a collective of ranches that bring in extra income by giving guests a true ranching experience. Beartooth is a working operation on the Clarks Fork of the Yellowstone River where dudes can opt for all-inclusive or breakfast-only lodging as well as a room or cabin only. The main lodge has 12 guest rooms in three wings with Internet, satellite TV, and private baths, all with either a view of the river or Beartooth Mountains.

Camping

Red Lodge: **Perry's RV Park and Campground** ($, 406-446-2722, May to October) isn't much from the road, but once you get below the office and into the trees you'll see why this oasis 2 miles south of Red Lodge on US 212 is a great spot to pitch a tent. All of the sites are in the cottonwoods and many are on the banks of Rock Creek, which is moving so fast it drowns out any sounds—including the occasional moose and black bear that wanders through. There are 10 tent sites and 20 RV sites at Perry's.

Forest Service Campgrounds: For more primitive adventures, the spectacular Beartooth Plateau has 13 campgrounds with a combined 226 campsites, all within close proximity of the highway. Six are in Wyoming's Shoshone National Forest on the way to Beartooth Pass; there are seven more on the Montana side, managed by the Custer National Forest.

Also on the Wyoming side are three other choices along the Clarks Fork of the Yellowstone River. Crossing into Montana there are three more—Soda Butte, Colter, and Chief

Joseph—outside of Cooke City near Cooke Pass. Expect chilly nights—the higher the elevation, the chillier. It is important to be bear-aware in all of these campgrounds. Of the three near Cooke City, the most alluring is Soda Butte, which has 20 RV/tent sites amid conifers on the edge of the creek; it was closed for much of 2010–11 because of an incident involving a grizzly bear and campers.

Coming out of Red Lodge, there are two good campgrounds: 29-site **Basin** and, 4 miles farther up the gravel road and more secluded amid lodgepole pines, the 35-site **Cascade**. Both are on the West Fork Road southwest of Red Lodge. Cascade is convenient to several trailheads and fishing on the West Fork, and trailers up to 32 feet are OK in either of the two loops. In Rock Creek Canyon, go past **Limber Pine** and **Parkside**—where the paved parking aprons and proximity to the highway entice more people—and settle in at the primitive **M-K Campground**, about 3 miles on gravel off US 212. M-K has 10 intimate sites on a pretty spot overlooking Rock Creek. **Beartooth Lake** on the plateau is a one-of-a-kind experience. At 9,000 feet you'll feel as if you can touch the stars from each of the 21 sites. The campground, which typically opens July 1, has three loops on Beartooth Lake and provides good access to trails into the Absaroka-Beartooth Wilderness.

Local Flavors

DINING INSIDE THE PARK

Tower Junction: Put on your wide-brimmed hat, boots, and spurs for dining at the ✿ **Roosevelt Lodge** ($$/$$$, 307-344-7311, B/L/D, June to September). Start with a rustic log lodge, toss in two stone fireplaces and a corral for aesthetics, and you've got yourself one of the more favored dining spots in the park. Eggs du jour, cowboy burritos, and huevos carnitas will make you think of the ol' chuckwagon. Lunch will have you singing over black bean burgers, bison meatball sandwiches, or our choice—pork carnitas sandwiches. Hold onto your horses, there's a smokin' dinner menu as well: smoked baby-back ribs, smoked chicken, or Teddy's steak all sided by the signature "Rosie" beans. All you'd need to feel like a true-blue ranch hand is a few cattle to herd. For further authenticity, try Roosevelt Lodge's Old West Dinner Cookout, which will take you by horseback or covered wagon across the valley to a full meal deal of steak, potato salad, coleslaw, baked beans, apple crisp, and coffee in picturesque Yancey's Hole, once the site of a bustling hotel. Chances are a fiddle player will come along for the ride. The cookouts are offered each late afternoon in summer and reservations are required; the lodge dining room does not accept reservations, so come early or late or be prepared to wait.

BEST DINING OUTSIDE THE PARK

Silver Gate: The only restaurant in town, 🏵 **Log Cabin Café and B&B** ($$, 1-800-863-2367, B/L/D, May to September), is fortunately a good one, favored for its lightly breaded and grilled Idaho trout that you can get with eggs for breakfast or as an entrée for lunch or dinner. Another signature item is their flown-in Alaskan sockeye, which is either prepared lightly smoked or as a simple filet. They're also proud of their burgers, made from grass-fed beef from Belfry. Save room for the spoon-licking pumpkin-bread pudding.

Cooke City: To hear the best local gossip, hang out at the **Beartooth Café** ($/$$, 406-838-2475, L/D, May to September) and choose from more than 130 beers to go along with traditional Western (burgers, steak, bison)

and slightly exotic (lamb gyros, Mandarin steak salad) and even vegetarian fare. For a bit of gourmet French /American sophistication, it's the 🏵 **Bistro** ($$/$$$, 406-838-2160, B/L/D), which serves well prepared, albeit not speedy, breakfasts, delicious housemade soup, and signature rack of lamb. Their wine offerings are better than their neighbors' and they keep the lights on for you until 10 PM during the summer. **Miner's Saloon** ($$/$$$, 406-838-2214, L/D) is as much an Old West museum as it is an eatery. It has highly rated handmade pizzas, fish tacos, and burgers on which to nibble while playing pool, foosball, or keno; expect an occasional antitourist sentiment.

Crandall: **Painter Outpost** ($$, 307-527-5510, B/L/D) has a deck overlooking the Clarks Fork of the Yellowstone River in Sunlight Basin, 25 miles from Yellowstone's Northeast Entrance. The restaurant, part of an RV park and camping complex, is year-round-ready and usually open. Ditto for the friendly bar sporting a big-screen TV. Home-style cooking comes in the form of soups and stews, cinnamon rolls and pies, and dinner specials that run the gamut from spaghetti to Salisbury steak.

Red Lodge: Plan your trip so that you can dine in Red Lodge more than once, for there are many outstanding choices. Most well-known is the landmark 🏵 **Pollard Hotel Dining Room** ($$/$$$, 406-446-0001, B/D), with a seasonally changing menu, extensive wine list, and full bar that simply deliver classic elegance. New to the hotel is their side-kickin' 🏵 **Pub at the Pollard** ($/$$, L), with a lunch menu specializing in such English pub food as fish and chips, shepherd's pie, and

Bridge Creek Backcountry Kitchen & Wine Bar in Red Lodge is a great place to sip wine and people watch.

Scotch eggs. Evenings bring a lighter menu, small plates, bar specials, and periodic live music to the friendly pub. **⑤ Bridge Creek Backcountry Kitchen & Wine Bar** ($$, 406-446-9900, L/D) best represents the new Red Lodge with its emphasis on fresh, nouveau, and local cuisine—complemented by its extraordinary international wine selection. This is where a clam chowder aficionado can test Bridge Creek's "famous for fourteen+ years" version. Representing the old Red Lodge is the **Carbon County Steakhouse** ($$/$$$, 406-446-4025, L/D), with its upscale "cowboy cuisine" of hormone-free beef, bison, elk, "not from the ranch" seafood, and fresh mussels flown in from the Pacific Northwest on Wednesdays and Fridays. More casual and suited for a late lunch/early dinner or a chips-salsa-margarita break is **Bogart's**

Flowers brighten the backyard at the Café Regis in Red Lodge.

($$, 406-446-1784, L/D), an always-crowded Mexican and pizza watering hole with a rustic Western feel accentuated by its large back bar and mirror.

The 🍲 Café Regis ($, 406-446-1941, B), once an other-era grocery store, is owned by a vegetarian who takes care of fellow health-food fans but also has plenty for the meat lovers. Open until 2 PM, breakfast is served all day and the omelets, tofu scramble, and biscuits and gravy are as delicious as they are filling. The homemade granola is out of this world. To see where the regulars hang out for coffee and conversation, try the historic 🍲 City Bakery ($, 406-446-2100, B/L), which is known for something called *schnecken*—a rich concoction of cinnamon, butter, cream cheese, and nuts in a roll. The tiny hole-in-the-wall became famous for its après ski loaf of French

bread and slab of butter, and many loaves are still made daily. Meals at the **Red Lodge Café** ($$, 406-446-1619, B/L/D), with its almost life-sized historic murals, log furniture, and cool teepee neon sign, is more about tradition and history than memorable food. At printing time, the café had new owners and the grub could improve. The ecoconscious **Sam's Tap Room & Kitchen** ($/$$, 406-446-0243, L/D) on the Red Lodge Ales Brewing Company property has relaxing indoor and outdoor seating for sipping on suds and savoring paninis, chopped salads, baked or cold sandwiches. Cool off with a cone full of soft ice cream or enjoy a burger creekside at Red Lodge's oldest drive-in, the **Red Box Car Drive-In** ($, 406-446-2152, L/D), housed in a hundred-year-old—you guessed it—boxcar.

To Do

RECREATION INSIDE THE PARK

Bicycling

The Northeast Entrance Road is open to road and mountain bicyclists, but like every road in the park it's a safety crapshoot because of its narrowness. Mountain biking opportunities are limited as well, though the 3-mile climb from the **Chittenden** parking area on the Grand Loop Road to the summit of Mount Washburn is sure to set quadriceps ablaze; mountain bikes are not allowed on the trail between Mount Washburn and the Dunraven Pass parking area. For a less-strenuous endeavor, there's the 2-mile ride on the old **Chittenden Service Road** between Tower Fall Campground and the Grand Loop Road just south of Tower Junction. Also OK for mountain bikes is the moderate 1-mile **Rose Creek Service Road** climb behind the Yellowstone Association Institute at the Buffalo Ranch.

Fishing

The **Lamar River** and **Soda Butte Creek** are two of the park's most popular fishing areas, and it's pretty rare in summer to not see fly anglers casting to trout at the confluence. The trout generally aren't big, though park employees report coaxing an occasional 20-incher from under an overhanging bank. Park officials like seeing fishermen ply the waters of **Slough Creek** because they'd like to eliminate rainbow and brown trout to make room for the native cutthroat trout. Lakes are few and small in this region, but 12-acre **Trout Lake's** short-but-steep 0.5-mile proximity to the Northeast Entrance Road and abundance of large cutthroat and rainbow trout

The Lamar Valley is often called the "American Serengeti" for its prolific wildlife. NPS

make it popular. Easily fished from shore as well as from a float tube, Trout Lake, situated on a bench amid Douglas fir southwest of Pebble Creek Campground, once served as an official park hatchery for rainbows. It provides some of the earliest fishing in the park. Look for otters to join in the fishing fun when the trout migrate up the channel.

Hiking

The northeast corner isn't as renowned for its numerous hiking trails as other parts of the park, but they are spectacular nonetheless. Perhaps the most popular is the dusty and often-windy **Specimen Ridge Trail**, a 17-miler that officially begins east of Tower Junction and traverses Specimen Ridge until it connects with the **Lamar River Trail** about 1 mile from the Northeast Entrance Road at Soda Butte. A more direct and much quicker way to reach the ridge is to park at the unofficial 1.4-mile **Specimen Fossil Forest Trail** marker southwest of the new bridge over the Lamar River. This so-called "social" trail is well-worn, easy to follow, slightly steep, and takes you past many of the readily visible specimens—the entombed remains of ancient trees, including a giant redwood stump on the edge of a cliff with spectacular views of the valley. Also still visible on this hike are old teepee rings and the remnants of an elk trap used until the 1970s either for relocating or slaughtering what was then a dramatically overabundant animal. The 12-mile **Pebble Creek Trail** is a full-day adventure that circles around the backside of stately Barronette

Peak in the park's far northeastern corner. If you start at the trailhead 2 miles west of the Northeast Entrance it'll be almost all downhill once you reach the creek. The **Garnet Hill Loop** is a dusty 4-mile sojourn that offers a remote Old West vision of the park, with the Yellowstone River and Yancey's Hole thrown in for good measure. The trail starts less than 100 yards from Tower Junction, traverses sage and pine on the road used for stagecoach cookouts, and then follows Elk Creek to the river.

Hellroaring Trail is a popular 7.5-mile route that veers west from the Garnet Hill Loop at the Yellowstone River. It crosses the river on a suspension bridge, rises to a sage plateau, then drops down into the scenic Hellroaring Creek drainage. Watch for wildlife and bring a fly rod to fish the pools in the creek. In the summer, this is often the warmest area of the park, so bring extra water. The scenic 4-mile **Lost Lake** walk through a pine forest rises 300 feet from Roosevelt Lodge to a pretty little lake where beaver, black bear, and raptors are frequent sights; continue on to the Petrified Tree. A fly angler's favorite, **Slough Creek Trail** rises from one meadow to the next on an old wagon road. The **Yellowstone River Picnic Area** is a rarely used way to see a portion of the Grand Canyon of the Yellowstone River. The 3.7-mile round-trip excursion on the east rim provides exceptional views of the river and canyon, and it's not unusual to see eagles, osprey, and bighorn sheep. Geothermal activity is common here, too. Though not an official route, the 1-mile trail behind the Yellowstone Association Institute along **Rose Creek Service Road** leads to the remains of a chain-link enclosure

Demonstrators in favor of wolf restoration finally got their way in 1995. NPS

Cross-country skiers find bliss against an Absaroka Mountains backdrop in the Lamar Valley.

where some of the first wolves were kept in 1995 during reintroduction. Trees have fallen on the fence and the doghouses-on-steroids are in decay, but the site exudes a strong sense of recent history; give a wide berth to an ornery bull bison that frequents the meadow leading to the enclosure.

Skiing (Nordic)

Thanks to year-round vehicle access, the northeast corner of Yellowstone is a Nordic skier's paradise. Highly popular is the 3.5-mile **Barronette Ski Trail**, which parallels the Northeast Entrance Road and Soda Butte Creek at the base of sheer Barronette Peak. The trail, through mostly forest on an old road, has little elevation gain and is sure to have snow well into the spring. More challenging is the 13-mile **Pebble Creek Trail**, where you'll have solitude and should plan on spending a night if you aim to ski the entire loop between the Northeast Entrance and Pebble Creek Campground. In the same vicinity is the easy Bannock Trail, a 2-mile jaunt that begins south of the road at the Warm Spring Picnic Area and continues east along Soda Butte Creek through a slice of the North Absaroka Wilderness into Silver Gate. If you want a little more exertion, continue 3 more miles on the well-groomed backroad to Cooke City; expect to have company from snowmobiles and perhaps a moose or two.

Four more trails are in the Tower Junction area: **Tower Fall, Chittenden, Lost Lake,** and **Blacktail Plateau.** Park at the closed gate for the gradual 2.5-mile climb through conifer forests from Tower Junction to Tower Fall. Absorb the views of the Yellowstone River far below before embarking on the more challenging Chittenden Trail through the Tower Fall Campground to a meeting with the Grand Loop Road some 5.3 miles later; ski back to Tower Junction to complete a long day. The moderate 4-mile Lost Lake Trail starts at the Petrified Tree and finishes at Tower Junction after traversing the lake, some forest, and meadows. The Blacktail Plateau Trail features 8 miles of gradual climbing and then a modest 2-mile descent back to the main road.

RECREATION OUTSIDE THE PARK

Fishing

The Clarks Fork of the Yellowstone River is a relatively undiscovered treasure with substantial rewards for the trout angler. The Clarks Fork starts near Cooke City, Montana, and makes a wild headlong dash through canyons,

A golden eagle enjoys the view.

forest, and sage country in Wyoming before turning northeast for a more sedate run through the agricultural lands of Montana and a meeting with the Yellowstone at Laurel. Some of the best dry-fly fishing in the Yellowstone region can be had where the Clarks Fork rushes alongside US 212. The river is awash in caddis, drakes, blue-winged olives, pale morning duns, and other dry flies. The region is dotted with private property, but access isn't difficult to find. Given the stunning Beartooth Highway and Sunlight Basin drives nearby, it's a wonder more visitors don't spend more time in this breathtaking area. If you plan to scramble down into the canyon, though, be careful; this is dangerous terrain.

River Running

Not for the faint of heart, the Clarks Fork of the Yellowstone River nevertheless offers an unforgettable experts-only stretch as it thunders through a narrow canyon in Sunlight Basin, not far from the Northeast Entrance. Water ranges from Class IV to the virtually impassible Box Canyon, and more Class IV water is accessible below the canyon. Don't try this river unless you're an experienced kayaker with a reliable roll. A more moderate splash-and-giggle float, the Class II–III Stillwater River from Absarokee to Columbus, Montana, offers reliable summer floating fun a short drive from the Clarks Fork.

Skiing (Alpine)

The Red Lodge Mountain Resort (1-800-444-8977 or 406-255-6973), a family-oriented area at the edge of Montana's Beartooth Mountains, is known for its prolific snows and lack of lift lines. The mountain receives 250 inches of snow on its 1,600 acres and has a 2,500-foot vertical. The resort touts its Lazy M run, a 2.5-mile drop. Despite its small size, there's an equal amount of terrain for each skill level. Snowmaking is possible on nearly ⅓ of the mountain.

Snowmobiling

Though you wouldn't know it by the steady stream of pickup trucks hauling lengthy trailers on the Northeast Entrance Road throughout the winter, snowmobiling is prohibited in this part of the park. These sledders are headed to Cooke City for the miles of trails and more extreme "high-marking" on mountainsides just north and south of the town in the old New World Mining District. **Cooke City** has two service stations with gas and two snowmobile dealerships. The de facto headquarters for snowmobiling in this busy little town at the end of the winter road is the Cooke City Exxon (406-838-2244). Some 100 miles of trails connect with the Beartooth trail system.

5

Yellowstone: East Entrance

East Entrance to Fishing Bridge and Lake Village/Fishing Bridge to Canyon Village

GETTING HERE

Teddy Roosevelt didn't have the nearby Beartooth Highway to wax poetic about more than a century ago, but even if he did it's doubtful he'd have changed his mind about the winding route through the Wapiti Valley along the North Fork Shoshone River west of Cody. US 14/16/20's gradual ascent from Cody begins on the dry side of Yellowstone, where the stark cliffs and rock outcroppings are especially colorful. As the highway hugs the tumbling river into the Shoshone National Forest, high desert eventually gives way to pine and fir, with frothing creeks arriving from rugged drainages.

All routes to this spectacular drive lead to Cody. Visitors arriving from the East Coast or Midwest in a minivan traverse US 14, 16, or 20. The three east-west routes join at Greybull after converging from Dayton, Buffalo, and Casper, respectively. US 14 and 16 traverse the isolated Bighorn Mountains directly to the east—the first Rocky Mountain range many Americans reared east of the Mississippi River ever see, as well as the first dramatic hint of what's ahead. US 14 drivers typically have peeled off I-90 coming south from Montana after crossing North Dakota on I-94. US 16 is for folks exiting I-90 after the long haul across South Dakota. And US 20 is the turn for visitors heading to Cody after driving west on I-80 across Nebraska or even I-70 through Kansas and into Colorado. If you've driven US 20 from the east, though, consider exiting onto WY 120 at the pretty desert hot springs town of Thermopolis and driving northwest along the edge of the riveting Absaroka Front through the little ranching outpost of Meeteetse and on to Cody.

LEFT: A whitebark pine stands guard like a sentinel on the road up to Beartooth Pass.

Pilot and Index peaks serve as prominent gatekeepers to the Northeast Entrance. NPS

If driving across the hot, dry, dusty, and windy Bighorn Basin to Yellowstone's East Entrance doesn't sound all that great, Cody's Yellowstone Regional Airport (COD) is served by United Express from Denver via Mesa and SkyWest airlines. SkyWest has also operated year-round Delta Connection flights out of Salt Lake City, but was trying to bail out in the fall of 2011. Park County was pushing hard to keep the service, and as of press time was successful. Be advised that flying into Cody can come with uncertainty because the airport doesn't have a radar system, meaning flights are sometimes canceled or delayed on those rare cloudy days.

OVERVIEW

Everything you ever imagined the mystical Old West to be—cowboys riding the dramatic open range or bucking broncs on dusty rodeo grounds, iconic ranches extending to the distant horizon and beyond, gunfighters and outlaws terrorizing stagecoaches and robbing trains, lonely outposts with creaky saloons and bustling mercantiles—was manifest in Wyoming's Bighorn Basin.

It was in this thirsty region that the legend of America's most famous cowboy entrepreneur, Buffalo Bill Cody, was birthed and nurtured. John "Liver-Eating" Johnston, the rugged character on which the Robert Redford movie *Jeremiah Johnson* was based, is buried in Cody. Rodeos are staged everywhere from Florida to Oregon, but none capture the dusty essence of the sport like the down-home Cody Nite Rodeo. Also here is the first whiff—literally—of the geothermal fury awaiting visitors 50 miles to the west in Yellowstone, in the aptly named Colter's Hell in the Shoshone River Canyon on Cody's west end. The thermal area emits

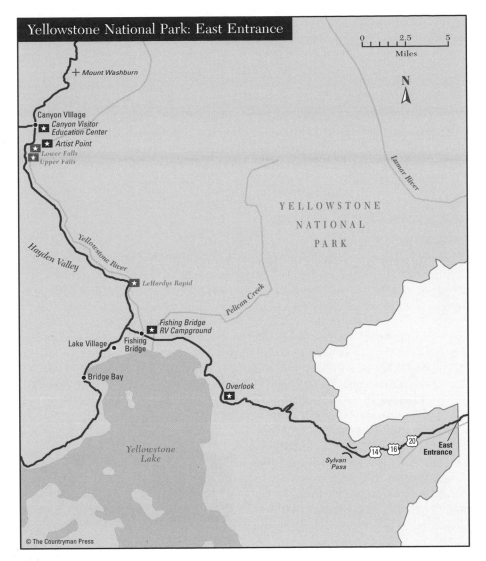

Yellowstone National Park: East Entrance

Mount Washburn

Canyon Village
Canyon Visitor
Education Center
Artist Point
Lower Falls
Upper Falls

Lamar River

YELLOWSTONE

NATIONAL

PARK

Hayden Valley

Yellowstone River

LeHardys Rapid

Pelican Creek

Fishing Bridge
RV Campground

Lake Village   Fishing
Bridge

Bridge Bay

Overlook

Yellowstone
Lake

Sylvan
Pass

14 16 20   East
Entrance

© The Countryman Press

periodic sulphuric odors that spectators at the rodeo and diners at Terraces can't miss. The five-in-one Buffalo Bill Historical Center captures the flavor of the West in each of its mesmerizing museums. And what's not to like about the admittedly hokey yet wonderfully entertaining nightly summer gunfights on historic 12th Street in front of the equally historic Irma Hotel, built by Buffalo Bill?

It is all a consummate prelude for the incomparable wild country so evident in the brawny Absaroka Mountains that rise abruptly from the desert immediately west of Cody. The 52 miles of US 14/16/20 that connect Cody with the park split some of the last great otherwise roadless territory in the lower 48. These mountains and drainages, which contain the largest population of grizzly bears outside national parks, are dotted with dude and guest ranches that emphasize the experience with cookouts and trail rides.

The highway from Cody to the East Entrance was dubbed "the most scenic 52 miles in the United States" by Roosevelt, who loved this country, but the curtain isn't truly pulled back on the wonders of Yellowstone until you reach the summit of 8,530-foot Sylvan Pass, about 7 miles inside the park. There, the beautiful blue waters of Yellowstone Lake, an endless horizon of lodgepole forest, and the distant Teton Range lay out before your eyes like a Thomas Moran painting. All of Yellowstone's wonders are compressed into this section of road: thermal features along the lake's shore just inside the caldera, wandering bison and an acute awareness that you're in grizzly country, the historic Fishing Bridge community with its popular campground, and the riveting Upper and Lower Falls in the Grand Canyon of the Yellowstone River.

GATEWAY COMMUNITIES

Cody, Wyoming

To many Yellowstone visitors, Cody personifies the Old West, starting with the name. Colonel William "Buffalo Bill" Cody first came to this arid region of northwest Wyoming in the 1870s with a professor from Yale University. He quickly became enamored with the area and its development possibilities, vowing to return. A decade later he did, with developers who began constructing the town on the east end of the Shoshone River Canyon (the town was later moved to the present-day west end). Cody built the town's first hotel, the Irma, and named it after his youngest daughter. He also coaxed the Burlington Railroad to build a spur to his new town; persuaded good friend Teddy Roosevelt to build a federal dam on the river west of the city (creating Buffalo Bill Reservoir); orchestrated the construction of the scenic road to what is now Yellowstone's East Entrance; and founded the town's newspaper, the *Enterprise*, which still serves the city. Small wonder that in 1895 the town's fathers voted to name the new settlement Cody. His influence didn't stop at the town's edge: Through Roosevelt, he helped establish the country's first national forest, the Shoshone, and its first ranger station, at Wapiti. Though known as a proud frontiersman on horseback, Buffalo Bill also was an early champion of Indian rights, women's suffrage, and environmental causes. Cody's name lives on throughout the region, including in the famed Cody Nite Rodeo, which began in 1922 and surely is the first rodeo the majority of Americans and foreigners witness. Some of the town's charm has been lost with the arrival of big-box

The Cody Nite Rodeo is a summer staple.
Zach Madison

Cody has a cowboy aura and a spectacular Absaroka Mountains backdrop. NPS

stores, chain restaurants, and motels, but seeing the nightly summer gunfight out-side the Irma is an entertaining reminder of the town's origins.

Among gateway communities, Cody's only downsides are that it's 52 miles from Yellowstone and lodging costs are high even by the exorbitant summer stan-dards in the region. On the flip side, you can almost always count on excellent weather, Cody being one of the driest places surrounding the park. Cody also is scoured by wind for much of the year, which means limited snowpack and early access to wildlife viewing in the spring. This is a great base from which to see ani-mals in April and May, when other high country is buried by snow. Take the paved drives up the North and South Fork of the Shoshone roads or travel 25 miles south to Meeteetse and follow the Greybull River on gravel through the famed Pitchfork Ranch to the eastern edge of the Absaroka-Beartooth Front.

HITTING THE ROAD

East Entrance to Fishing Bridge and Lake Village (30 miles): By the time you've arrived at the East Entrance, it's quite possible that you've already seen a bison, bighorn sheep, or even a grizzly bear. That's how wild the drive between the North Absaroka and Washakie wilderness areas is, and it explains the imposing fence around the elementary school at Wapiti. If you don't see any animals on this stretch, don't fret. Some great scenery and wildlife lie ahead.

It's been uphill all the way from Cody, but the ascent will become even more pronounced once you leave the small entrance station. On the left side of the road, farther and farther below, is meandering Middle Creek; stop at a pullout for a few minutes, especially early in the morning or near dusk, and see if you can spot a bear or moose foraging in the lush surroundings. About 0.5-mile before Sylvan Pass is the overlook for the remnants far below of the innovative **Corkscrew Bridge**, built a century ago on the original East Entrance Road.

Sylvan Pass is the park's second highest, behind Dunraven, and the most challenging to keep open in winter and spring, thanks to the consistent threat of

The Thorofare Region: Yellowstone's Lonely Corner

Few parts of Greater Yellowstone elicit more reverence among wilderness purists than the Thorofare area in Yellowstone's southeast corner. The Thorofare Ranger Station is the farthest inhabited dwelling from a road in the lower 48 states. Eagle Peak, at 11,358 feet the highest point in the park, is rarely scaled. Grizzlies, wolves, moose, mountain lions, and other wild creatures roam without intrusion from man, save for the occasional backcountry hiker. It is 18 miles from the closest road trailhead to Two Ocean Pass, where waters in a high-altitude marsh part ways, some headed for the Atlantic and some for the Pacific. The Thorofare has 15 backcountry campsites for hikers and packers, including a platform at the ranger station. A backcountry permit is required for all overnight stays. Nowhere in Yellowstone is it more important to observe rules regarding storing food away from bears. Anybody who takes the time and effort to traverse this beautiful, remote country will never forget it.

The remote Thorofare Region is one of the wildest places in America. NPS

avalanches. Look up the scree to your left, where you'll see a shack and a cannon. The howitzer represents your taxpayer dollars at work, dislodging snow so a handful of snowmobilers from Pahaska Tepee and Cody can access the park during the winter recreation season. If you're a fiscal conservative, you don't want to know the cost per visit to keep this entrance open. Just below the pass is pretty Sylvan Lake, one of the last roadside lakes in the park to be free of ice each summer.

Slow down for the 20-mph curve that bends around Cub Creek and look for the turnoff to Lake Butte, which offers a picturesque sunset view of Yellowstone Lake and Frank Island, as 10,308-foot Mount Sheridan across the lake in the foreground, and the Tetons some 60 miles in the distance. It's less than a mile through burned timber to the overlook. Back on the East Entrance Road, you'll quickly

The frigid waters of Yellowstone Lake are not for the faint of heart. NPS

arrive at the lake's **Sedge Bay**, named for the nutritious and hardy grass preferred by elk, deer, and bison. Beyond the boat ramp at Sedge Bay another 1.5 miles is **Steamboat Point**, featuring two geothermal features above the lake.

The waters of 132-square-mile **Yellowstone Lake** might look inviting, but they're not for the faint of heart. At 38 degrees, they'll send an instant chill through even the most dedicated water lover; most visitors settle for dabbing their toes. The lake is so big—the largest above 7,000 feet in North America—that its waters lap the shore like an ocean or one of the Great Lakes. Let that be a warning to canoeists or kayakers: Yellowstone Lake is dangerous. If you're in a small craft, stay within striking distance of shore. A spill here could be lethal due to the quick onset of hypothermia.

About 3 miles before Fishing Bridge is the **Pelican Creek** delta. Look for a wide variety of waterfowl here, including geese, ducks, sandhill cranes, and—naturally—the stately pelican. The Pelican Valley just upstream is one of the most extraordinary regions of Yellowstone. It has so much grizzly activity that it is closed to hikers until July, and overnight camping isn't allowed. Also in Pelican Valley is the Mollie's wolf pack, named for the late former head of the U.S. Fish & Wildlife Service, Mollie Beatty, an ardent proponent of restoring *Canis lupus* to Yellowstone. The valley's harsh winter climate is too much for elk, leaving only the hardy bison. The wolves have adapted to bringing down this bigger, stronger, and faster foe; it can take the pack up to eight hours to kill a single bison, at considerable risk to their own health. Thus, Mollie's has become the biggest and strongest pack in the park.

Did You Know? The largest wolf ever collared in the park was a Mollie male weighing in at 142 pounds, though that included 10–15 pounds of freshly consumed meat. Of the 10 largest Yellowstone wolves ever weighed, 5 were Mollies.

Hiking in Pelican Valley is limited to the middle of the day due to grizzly bear activity. NPS

Once in a while they will wander over to the Lamar Valley just to strut their stuff, but they always come home to the Pelican.

After Pelican Creek, the road straightens and enters lodgepole forest for the short run into **Fishing Bridge**, one of the park's most historic settlements. The place itself was named for a bridge built in 1902 (replaced in 1937) where the Yellowstone River emerges after its invisible southeast-to-northwest journey through the depths of Yellowstone Lake. Fishermen would line up shoulder to shoulder in their bid to catch large migrating cutthroat trout, with a predictable mix of large catches and tangled lines. Today, fishing is prohibited from the bridge, and visitors must be content with scanning the crystal-clear waters for dwindling numbers of cutthroat.

Fishing Bridge is also a fulcrum for the evolution of grizzly bear management in the park. When the park ignored biologists and began eliminating open garbage dumps cold turkey in the 1960s, instantly eliminating a prime food source for the grizzly, the great bear had to begin looking elsewhere for sustenance. Campgrounds were the first stop for many, especially at Fishing Bridge, already a popular spot for grizzlies, which congregated around Yellowstone Lake's tributaries to munch on the same migrating cutthroat trout so popular with fishermen. This inevitably led to conflicts that resulted in frightened humans and dead bears. Today, bears have readjusted to new natural food sources and the Park Service has limited conflicts by closing one campground, eliminating some cabins, instituting bear-awareness programs, and requiring hard-sided campers in the remaining camping area north of the East Entrance Road.

Fishing Bridge is a consummate park setting, with its rustic stone and wood buildings blending with lush lodgepole forest. The stone **Fishing Bridge Museum and Visitors Center** (307-242-2450, May to September), built in 1931, is on the

An aerial view of the remote Pelican Valley. NPS

National Register of Historic Places. The general store is classic Yellowstone architecture and a great place to regroup and grab a bite to eat.

Nearly 3 miles past Fishing Bridge, now on the Grand Loop Road headed
toward West Thumb and Grant Village, is Lake Village, which has the famous
Lake Hotel, the Lake Lodge and Cabins, a general store, and a 1923 ranger station
that was recently added to the National Register of Historic Places.

Fishing Bridge to Canyon Village (16 miles): Few routes in Yellowstone pack
more punch than this pretty drive along the meandering Yellowstone River
through the wildlife-rich Hayden Valley. And in a park blessed with spectacular
scenery, there is no more dramatic sight than the Grand Canyon of the Yellowstone. Along the way are some brief stops worth a peek: Mud Volcano, Sulphur
Caldron, and LeHardy Rapids (LeHardys on some park maps).

LeHardy Rapids, named for a topographer whose raft capsized here in 1873,
is slightly less than 3 forested miles from Fishing Bridge junction and considered
the official northern boundary of Yellowstone Lake because it's the first place
where the river drops discernibly. A boardwalk was constructed here in 1984 to
enable viewers to watch cutthroat trout leaping up the rapids like salmon each
spring as they return to the lake from spawning; however, the path is periodically
closed during the spring mating season of resident harlequin ducks.

Below LeHardy, the Yellowstone turns into a broad, lazy river that's building
up a debt that it'll pay with a vengeance downstream. It's an idyllic place for fly-
fishing, though anglers should note the short no-fishing stretch in the channel next
to the road. Keep an eye out for wandering bull bison as you follow the river to the
next attraction, the **Mud Volcano** area. Once volatile, Mud Volcano is relatively
tame but still fascinating with its collection of gurgling mud pots. While you're in

A Yellowstone Native's Fight for Survival

Until the mid-1990s, Yellowstone Lake was one of the finest cutthroat trout fisheries in the world. This was significant for many reasons, most notably that the Yellowstone cutthroat is native to the region—unlike the more sought-after rainbow, brown, and brook trout, which were imported during the settling of the West to enhance fishing opportunities.

The picture literally changed overnight in the summer of 1994, when a fisherman reeled in a lake trout, or mackinaw, another non-native that had been introduced to nearby Shoshone, Lewis, and Heart lakes for the aforementioned reasons. Seems a so-called "bucket biologist" had caught a few lake trout in Lewis Lake and sometime in the late 1980s unilaterally decided to start a population in Yellowstone Lake, regardless of the ramifications. The appearance of one fish sent a shudder through biologists who knew what this moment foretold for the cutthroat.

The lake trout is a voracious eater, consuming more than 40 of the smaller cutthroat apiece per year. They're also prolific breeders. In the quarter-century since their

Cutthroat trout fight LeHardy Rapids in the Yellowstone River as they try to migrate back to Yellowstone Lake.

this small-earthquake-prone area, you might notice the hissing of **Dragon's Mouth Spring** and rumbling of **Black Dragon's Caldron**, which released its fury sometime in the late 1940s with such force that mature trees were flattened nearby. Equally engrossing is **Sulphur Caldron**, albeit from a safe distance. Sulphur Caldron, just north of Mud Volcano and across the road, is more acidic (1.3 pH) than battery acid, according to park literature that cautions visitors from getting too close.

Gillnetters removed nearly 250,000 invasive lake trout from Yellowstone Lake in 2011.

introduction, probably at West Thumb, the lake trout has taken over the waters of Yellowstone Lake. In 1998, more than 18,000 cutthroat trout passed through a weir on Clear Creek en route to their spawning grounds; in 2008, that number had dwindled to a paltry 241. Yellowstone Lake, once the safety-deposit box for this beautiful fish with the telltale red slits just below its gills, is sounding its death knell.

As is always the case in nature, the fallout isn't limited to the trout. Wildlife long reliant on the fish spawning in the lake's tributaries have been impacted as well. Grizzlies, osprey, eagles, otters, and more than forty other creatures have left the lake area in search of food elsewhere; in the case of the grizzly, it has meant pushing into lower elevations where there are more people—and inevitable conflict.

What to do? The Park Service has begun an all-out war, hiring a gillnetting crew from the Great Lakes to catch tens of thousands of lake trout each year. In addition, scientists in 2011 began implanting radio telemetry in so-called "Judas fish" that will lead the researchers to lake trout spawning beds, where they can annihilate the eggs and give the native cutthroat a fighting chance.

Less than 0.5-mile past the caldron the world opens up to the **Hayden Valley**, announced by an ominous white sign with red lettering warning against approaching dangerous wildlife. The sign is more eyesore than helpful reminder, and it's curious why the wildlife-rich Lamar Valley isn't similarly marked. At any rate, the Hayden is unique in that the soil is too thick for trees to take root, and the almost motionless flows of the Yellowstone River along with Trout and Elk Antler creeks form a water wonderland. This in turn provides a wildlife-watching bonanza for

Cyclists take a break in the Hayden Valley. NPS

tourists who routinely see a huge variety of bird and mammal life from elevated perches overlooking the placid river—they don't call one of the viewing sights Grizzly Overlook for nothing.

The road undulates for slightly more than 4 miles across the valley, reentering the forest at Alum Creek. From there, it's another 3 miles to the turnoff across **Chittenden Bridge**—frequently used by wolves and other wildlife as an easy way to cross the river—to **Artist's Point** and the south rim of the 20-mile **Grand Canyon of the Yellowstone**. For ten thousand years, the river has been carving a riveting chasm in the geothermally weakened rhyolite walls, creating a 1,000-foot-deep canyon that's 20 miles long and as much as 4,000 feet wide. It's the one place where visitors stand and stare in awe at the rich hues of sheer orange, pink, tan, and yellow canyon walls, viewed from many different angles. How such a dramatic landscape occurred on a river that mostly meanders isn't entirely clear. Scientists speculate that when glaciers retreated some eleven thousand years ago, they left ice dams at the mouth of Yellowstone Lake. Melting of the ice was like pulling a cork, sending mountains of water northward and scouring the canyon out at the weakest point in the rock. There has likely been more than one such catastrophic flood caused by the melting of glaciers. Today, the river continues to work its erosive magic, digging the canyon deeper for future civilizations. If you have time for only one stop at the Grand Canyon, make it Artist's Point. You'll readily recognize the view of the 308-foot Lower Falls, even though you might have to elbow your way to the stone walls between you and an eye-popping sheer drop to the raging river 1,000 feet below. If you're lucky, the falls will sport a photogenic rainbow. For a more vigorous walk and misty-faced view of the Lower Falls, take the 300-plus steps some 500 breath-stealing feet down **Uncle Tom's Trail** for a closer view of the canyon than most get.

Pick Your Spot

LODGING INSIDE THE PARK

Lake Village: The sisters of lodging options in the village are quite different. Think of the Lake Hotel as the more mature, sophisticated, or stately sister and the sibling Lake Lodge as the more relaxed and playful one. Both have stunning places to sit and contemplate the depths of the frigid blue waters in front of you. Within walking distance of each other, they're separated by a general store and visitors center.

Antebellum meets the Northern Rockies at the ♿ ⚲ ⚏ **Lake Yellowstone Hotel ($$$$) and Cabins ($$$,** 1-866-439-7375 or 307-344-7311, May to September). The face of the Lake Hotel, originally opened in 1891, has changed dramatically with time, and this grand building now looks as if it was plucked from an estate in the Deep South. Lake views are superb from the Sun Room, where music from a grand piano serves as a soothing backdrop for a game of chess or a good book and a glass of wine. Yellowstone's oldest surviving hotel and now the second largest wood-frame building in North America was built by the Northern Pacific Railroad at the popular site of rendezvous between mountain men, trappers, and Indians. Its southern Colonial look was created 12 years later by Robert Reamer, who built the Old Faithful Lodge. Renovations have continued through the years, especially after the hotel began to fall apart in the 1960s. By the 1980s, the hotel had been restored to the elegant, if seemingly out of place, yellow structure visitors see today. It's certainly the most modern hotel in the park. Historical tours are offered at 5:30 PM each day. The hotel has 158 rooms, all charming in their simplicity. The lobby interior furniture even takes a Southern turn with tropical-colored cushions on rattan furniture; it's one of our favorite places to have a cocktail and people/lake

The Lake Hotel, which looks as though it were plucked from a plantation in Mississippi, was scheduled for a new coat of paint in 2012. NPS

watch. For the more economically inclined, the refurbished Lake Yellowstone Hotel Annex doesn't have views but does have comfortable environs that include phones. Even gentler on the budget are the Frontier Cabins, duplex units that were built in the 1920s but remodeled in 2004. Again, simplicity is the theme. ⅙ ⅼ Lake Lodge and Cabins ($$/$$$, 1-866-439-7375 or 307-344-7901, June to September) is a quintessential park-style log lodge, with two stone fireplaces, exposed log beams, and inviting furnishings that make you want to curl up with a good book on the porch or in front of the fire. The cabins, built in the 1920s, are basic, rustic (some downright unattractive), and come in three flavors: the primitive and least-expensive Pioneer, the more traditional log-and-plank Frontier, and the slightly more-spacious Western that are modules of four to six units. Lake Lodge and Cabins do offer a sense of solitude yet are a short walk from the more vibrant happenings at the stylish sister Lake Hotel.

Canyon Village: The ⅙ ⅼ Canyon Lodge and Cabins ($$/$$$, 1-866-439-7375 or 307-344-7901, June to September) compound is spread out among conifer trees. While as unappealing visually as the sprawling Grant Village, it's at least ideally situated for short drives or hikes to the Grand Canyon of the Yellowstone, Mount Washburn, and fishing or wildlife viewing in the Hayden Valley. The two newer Cascade (1992) and Dunraven (1998) lodges are much like motels, but they are at least somewhat attractive with pine furniture and cabin décor. Western Cabins (540 modules) are duplexes or four-plexes, built about a half-century ago during the Mission 66 days and decidedly modular in style. Frontier cabins are

modular and come in clusters of four or eight rooms; all rooms and cabins have private baths. The check-in, dining, and bar area have a definite 1950s and 1960s "mod" style with angular lines and shake-shingle exterior accents considered contemporary chic in the day. A gift shop, cafeteria, restaurant, and deli are part of the village, and the lodge is open a few weeks longer in September than the cabins.

ALTERNATIVE LODGING INSIDE THE PARK

Camping

All three campgrounds listed in this chapter take reservations, making it easier to plan and stylize your national park vacation. **Fishing Bridge RV Park** ($, 1-866-439-7375 or 307-344-7311, May to September), with 325 back-in sites (no pull-throughs), is a hub area, especially for the home-on-wheels crowd. Loaded with activity and a historic general store with lots to choose from, it's one of the few campgrounds offering coin showers, laundry, and a dump station. Entertainment comes in the form of close proximity to the gorgeous lake. And when they say *RV* they mean it, grizzly bear numbers are high in the area and only hard-sided campers are allowed.

More than 400 sites make ⅙ **Bridge Bay Campground** ($, 1-866-439-7375 or 307-344-7311, June to September) a virtual tent city—no surprise given its location next to Yellowstone Lake's only active marina. A store, picnic table at each site, flush toilets, dishwashing stations, ranger presentations, and a nondenominational church service on Sunday provide everything a camper could need. While the exposed lower loops (A–D) offer no privacy and resemble a mini-Woodstock, the upper loops (E–I) are packed just as tightly but have pine trees to provide some separation and make them more desirable. Tent-only loops include food storage boxes to limit bear temptations. *Note:* Some of these loops are closed in early summer due to bear activity.

Preferred for its central location and forested grounds, ♿ **Canyon Campground** ($, 1-866-439-7375 or 307-344-7901, June to September) has 250 tent and RV sites (no hook-ups) with picnic tables and fire grates, coin showers, laundry, amphitheater, Christian Ministry Sunday service, and even an area for hikers and cyclists. Bear boxes are located in the most densely treed areas and serious bear-safety rules are provided at check-in, so be sure you have the proper equipment. *Note:* There are no group sites at this campground.

BEST LODGING OUTSIDE THE PARK

Cody: At the ♊ **Green Gables Inn** ($/$$, 307-587-6886, May to October) Buffalo Bill's great-grandson Kit Carson Cody and wife, Linda, have 15 well-managed, simple rooms with two queen beds and log furniture in each; hanging flower baskets make for a homey splash of color. ♿ 🐾 **Carter Mountain Motel** ($/$$, 307-587-4295) is a small, family-oriented, no-frills motel with 29 clean, reasonably priced, nonsmoking rooms that have microwaves, fridges, and coffeemakers. The large deck makes for great relaxing and views of the sun dropping behind the Absaroka Mountains. Adequate value lodging includes the ♿ 🐾 **Big Bear Motel** ($/$$, 1-800-325-7163 or 307-587-3117), which comprises 47 rooms, including 6 larger rooms, and an outdoor heated swimming pool. The owners are good supporters of the community and horseback rides give it an extra bump. If you're not too picky or a

light sleeper, 🍴 **Sunrise Motor Inn** ($/$$, 1-877-587-5566 or 307-587-5566, May to October) is a drive-to-your-door and economical (by Cody standards) motel within walking distance of the Buffalo Bill Historical Center. And hey, they have a pool to cool down cranky kids (or parents). ♿ **Buffalo Bill's Antlers Inn** ($$, 1-800-388-2084 or 307-587-2084, March to October) has 40 Western-style rooms on two floors with Thomas Molesworth–style burl wood furniture made by the previous owner, along with all the comfort and amenities you would expect from a typical small motel. If your style leans more toward pampering, you'll like the ♿ ♊ **Cody Legacy Inn & Suites** ($$$, 307-587-6067), one Cody's newer lodging options with modern Western-themed rooms, a fitness room, swimming pool, hot tub, and antler-clad lobby accentuated by a huge stone fireplace and black-and-white photos of the town's more famous residents and visitors. Built in 1902, Cody's signature ♊ 🍴 **Irma Hotel** ($$/$$$, 1-800-745-4762 or 307-587-4221) was the first building in town, built by Buffalo Bill Cody himself and named after his youngest daughter. The historic rooms on the bottom floor are furnished much the same as they were in Buffalo Bill's day, minus the TV and Internet access and plus a friendly ghost or two. The newer addition features more contemporary fixtures along with eating options and a small gift shop. If you hear gunshots out front on summer evenings, don't be alarmed: from June to September a gunfight is reenacted at 6 PM in front of the wood-planked veranda.

We admittedly are quite smitten with the stunning ♊ **Chamberlin Inn** ($$$/$$$$, 1-888-587-0202 or 307-587-0202). Ev and Susan Diehl put a ton of sweat and love into restoring and expertly meshing history with modern

A dramatic sunset over the Yellowstone River in Hayden Valley. NPS

amenities in this dreamy charmer. Original brick walls are integrated into the fashionable décor, accented by tile mosaics designed to either emulate or cover a window opening, expertly meshing history with modern conveniences. All rooms but one are accented by Alphonse Mucha tile mosaics. A light rose scent lingers in the halls and small bouquets grace the rooms. The building has had a few personalities but was first a boarding house operated by Agnes Chamberlin, who worked for Buffalo Bill Cody at the Cody *Enterprise* in 1900. Eventually it became a hotel and was expanded to include the Cody courthouse. The hotel's old guest registry includes such names as Marshall Fields and Ernest Hemingway. Hemingway stayed in Room 18 in 1932, finished his *Death in the Afternoon* manuscript, went to fish the Clarks Fork of the Yellowstone River,

returned to mail the manuscript, and then downed a few cold ones at the Irma Bar before heading back to wet a line. The Diehls also offer lodging in Cody's original courthouse, which includes a garden cottage, apartment, and loft apartment.

Jerry and Bette Kinkade are right proud of their unusual bed & breakfast, and have bragging rights to go with 🏵 **K3 Guest Ranch** ($$$, 1-888-587-2080 or 307-587-2080), a 33-acre cattle ranch once listed by NBC-TV as one of the four most unique bed & breakfasts in the world. Some beds are built into actual chuck, hay, or sheepherder wagons, with murals and furniture to match the theme (we're fond of the Teton Room). Guests can keep their own horses in K3's corrals for an extra $15. A hearty ranch-style breakfast is usually cooked outdoors and served family-style. With two fishing streams within 100 feet of the 3,500-square-foot lodge, day trips, outings to see wild horses, a shooting range with gun safety training, and a couple of trick horses, there's plenty to entertain kids of all ages. Call for winter and spring availability. What makes Bill and Dale's 🍴 Mayor's Inn B&B ($$/$$$, 1-888-217-3001 or 307-587-0887) different is that they are also a boutique restaurant serving dinner Thursday to Saturday from May to September. Once the home of Cody's first mayor, Frank Houx, and considered a mansion in 1905, the inn is now four distinct, air-conditioned rooms and a separate carriage house that can sleep up to four with a full kitchen. But honestly, why cook when you can dine on Bill's sourdough flapjacks and buffalo sausage or Devils Tower pork shank and whipped sweet potatoes? Even if you don't stay, have at least one dinner here for their 5, 5, and 5 menu (5 appetizers, 5 entrees, and 5 desserts). "You've never had so much fun in a church" is Barbara and Robert Kelley's motto for their converted **Angel's Keep B&B** ($$, 1-877-320-2800 or 307-587-6205). Each of three rooms has a TV/VCR, air-conditioning, and private bath and a country gourmet breakfast is served—home-baked cookies are always available. About 8 miles southwest from town, **Southfork** ($$, 307-587-8311, June to September) is a large lodgelike home with guest wing, common area, three rooms for rent, and a corral full of rescued Pryor Mountain mustangs. Co-owner Brian Lloyd is a retired chef who cheerfully prepares a made-from-scratch breakfast each morning. Other conveniences include Internet access, a home theater, satellite TV, and huge fireplace. Indian artifacts, Western art, and 360-degree views of the mountains add regional zest.

BEST ALTERNATIVE LODGING OUTSIDE THE PARK

The alternative to motel living while visiting the area mostly comes in the form of guest ranches or bringing your own home and "roughing it." An abundance of dude and guest ranches are tucked into rugged creek valleys between Cody and the East Entrance, none dramatically different than the next but all with their own personalities. We have listed in order from the East Entrance a few standouts for longevity, reputation, hospitality, or slightly superior setting. Be forewarned, most facilities do not have TVs, phones, or Internet, and cell service can be spotty.

Shoshone River Valley: Closest to the park's East Entrance is the historic 🐾 🍴 **Pahaska Tepee** ($$/$$$, 1-800-628-7791 or 307-527-7701, May to October), which is actually in its own category. Not really a guest ranch, motel, or campground, it's all sprawled into one. Built in 1904 by Buffalo Bill and listed on the National Register of Historic Places, Pahaska Tepee has an array of lodging, including the 1903 homesteader cabins with modern amenities, some sure to be well-suited to the budget-minded in your group. Breakfast, lunch, and dinner are served in the knotty-pined dining hall and alcohol is served in the Tepee Tavern. Steeped in history is the pretty **Absaroka Mountain Lodge** ($$, 307-587-3963, May to September), which was once owned by Buffalo Bill's grandson and still sports many of the wildlife mounts that he harvested in the area. Tucked into Gunbarrel Canyon, the 1910 lodge has 18 cabins and a restaurant that serves breakfast and dinner. On the edge of Sheep Mountain and surrounded by 2,500 acres of public lands is ♿ **Red Pole Ranch** ($$, 1-800-587-5929 or 307-587-5929), a hard-working ranch with 8 log cabins dressed in Western motif, some with kitchens—all with fridges, microwaves, bath, and shower. Don and Patty Jo Schmalz are retired outfitters and happily offer advice on activities—and might even disclose some favorite hidey-holes on the Shoshone or other streams.

The historic 🏵 ⊺ **Shoshone Lodge & Guest Ranch** ($$/$$$, 307-587-4044, May to October) is a sweet spot amid forest and consists of 18 uniquely configured golden pine log cabins, each with a bathroom, phone, microwave, and fridge—and a few have kitchenettes. The log and wood dining hall prepares home-style meals, both breakfast and dinner, for an extraordinarily low price. Horseback riding and fishing can be arranged on the Shoshone River and Grinnell Creek; porch sitting requires no advance planning. The family-run, -owned, and -oriented 🏵 ⊺ **Creekside Lodge at Yellowstone** ($$/$$$, 1-800-859-3985 or 307-587-3753, May to October) has 12 compact cabins in a mountain setting along Goff Creek, with 2.5 million acres of Shoshone National Forest in its backyard. A full-service restaurant in the lodge serves breakfast, lunch, and dinner; guided fishing and horseback trips can be arranged to some of the best-kept secret trails on the Shoshone. 🐾 ⊺ **Elephant Head Lodge** ($$$, 307-587-3980, May to October) is a tight half-circle of 15 cabins sleeping 2–15 under the watchful eye of a rock outcropping shaped like—you guessed it—an elephant head. No minimum stay is required and meals are separately charged, which is unusual for a guest ranch. Open to nonguests are the dining room, lounge, and family room in the cozy lodge, which is listed on the

National Register of Historic Places because it was built by Buffalo Bill Cody's niece.

The **UXU Ranch** ($$$$, 1-855-587-2143 or 307-587-2143), with a new owner and management team in 2012, is a village of 10 log cabins with green roofs sprinkled amid Douglas firs. The dining room serves Rocky Mountain cuisine at three meals daily and, now that it has a liquor license, beer, wine, and an array of cocktails complete your meal. Weekly packages are required mid-May to mid-October; nightly rates apply at other times. The UXU, 10 miles from Sleeping Giant Ski Area, makes for a wonderful winter getaway. One-night stays are OK, making for flexible vacationing at ♿ **Bill Cody Ranch** ($$/$$$, 1-800-615-2934 or 307-587-6271, May to September), which has 17 one- and two-bedroom log-cabin duplexes and a few stand-alones. Inclusive packages come with breakfast, dinner, and an afternoon horse ride with sack lunch. Campfires are nightly and chuckwagon cookouts ($14–21) are staged Wednesdays and Saturdays. Individual rock and log cabins straddle Canyon Creek in the heart of the Absaroka Mountains at **Rimrock Dude Ranch** ($$$$, 307-587-3970, May to September), where cowboys and horses roam. Stays are from Sunday to Sunday, and each guest (maximum 36) "owns" a horse for the duration for a variety of daily trail rides. The Cody Nite Rodeo, day trips to Yellowstone, and fishing or float excursions on the Shoshone are included activities. Or you can just enjoy hanging out in the heated pool, hot tub, or game room. Family-oriented fun is the theme at **Rand Creek Ranch** ($$$, 1-888-412-7335 or 307-587-7176, May to October), literally halfway between Cody and Yellowstone's East Entrance. Most of the 8 cabins have kitchenettes and 4 are more like a home. Internet and cell service are available, but it's better to be occupied by kayaking on the pond, fishing, or pack trips through the ranch. Rates include breakfast and BBQ nights every Wednesday and Sunday. Ask about bringing your pet.

Camping

Shoshone River Valley: 🐾 🦌 ¶¶
Yellowstone Valley Inn and RV ($$/$$$, 307-587-3961, May to September) comprises 10 nifty duplex log cabins totaling 20 rooms with modern amenities including wifi, along with 15 motel rooms, most with views of the Shoshone River. Also at the friendly inn are a heated pool (busiest from 8 to 10 PM), indoor hot tub, banquet room, and dance hall where you may be tempted into singing your favorite tune à la Karaoke. Enjoy mountain views in all directions and fishing for trout from their river access. The treeless RV park has 57 sites—19 with full hook-ups, 38 with electric and water, a grassy shaded area for tents, and a dump station. We suggest at least one dinner at the surprisingly excellent and fun restaurant/saloon, even if you're staying elsewhere. 🐾 Green Creek Inn and RV Park ($$, 1-877-587-5004 or 307-587-5004, May to October) is a tidy complex just off the highway with 9 RV sites, 2 cabins, and 15 motel rooms adorned with log furniture. Horseshoe pits, picnic tables, and a playground add to the kid appeal, as does Internet access. The Cody KOA ($$, 1-800-562-8507) is spendy compared to similar campgrounds elsewhere, but that merely reflects the high demand in summer. Located on the far eastern edge of town, it has a pool, a pancake breakfast, and satellite TV access in its deluxe RV pull-throughs among its perks.

National Forest Campgrounds: America's first national forest has 12 primitive public campgrounds in the North Fork of the Shoshone River Valley, all offering varying levels of proximity to the park and fishing. Generally speaking, the closer you are to the park, the more picturesque, forested, and quiet the setting. Three campgrounds— Wapiti, Eagle Creek, and Three Mile—are notable in that no soft-sided tents or pop-up campers are allowed because of grizzly bear activity. And this is definitely bear country, so precautions, preparation, and bear awareness are critical at all campgrounds.

Local Flavors

DINING INSIDE THE PARK

Lake Village: The crème de la crème of Yellowstone restaurants is the 🦌 Lake Yellowstone Hotel Dining Room ($$$, 307-242-3899 or 307-344-7901, B/L/D, May to October), which is notable not just for mesmerizing views of the lake but also for the cuisine. For those seeking a break from typical regional park fare, the hotel adds Asian vegetables and tofu, crab cakes, and lobster ravioli to the mix. The spacious dining area provides a sense of privacy even when crowded; reservations are required in summer. The hotel lobby is dotted with tropical prints, cane furniture, and views of the lake from large windows. It's a terrific place to order a drink and watch people inside and/or bison outside.

There's no getting around the fact that 🦌 Lake Lodge Cafeteria ($$, 307-344-7311, B/L/D, June to

September) is a load-your-tray kind of place, but it does have its advantages: no reservations, no need for a 20 percent tip, and usually no waiting. And the food, for mass-quantity output, is actually well prepared. We had the trout almandine, which was moist, delicately seasoned, and a good-sized portion. A carving station always has roast turkey, one of the cafeteria's signature meals. Entrees come with two sides (starches and veggies) and a roll, and without much damage to your wallet. Tables are cleared quickly, making room for the next batch of hungry customers. We appreciate that you can drink your own wine and views of the lake are free. The front porch is a great place to sip (BYO is acceptable) and absorb nature's finest work while resting in high-back rockers, or order from the small corner bar (slow service).

Canyon Village: You'll find four refueling spots here—**Canyon Dining Room** ($$, 307-344-7901, B/L/D, June to September), **Canyon Cafeteria** ($/$$, B/L/D), **Canyon Deli** ($, B/L), and **Glacier Pit Snack Bar** ($/$$, B/L/D). A rounded rectangular, freestanding fireplace divides the bar area from the eating room at the Canyon Dining Room, the fanciest—but still casual—of the Canyon Village restaurants where no reservations are taken. It's best known for its reasonably priced breakfast buffet (around $10), loaded salad bar with several proteins (also available at dinner), and house specialty prime rib dinner. Other dinner highlights can include: dry rub pork tenderloin, stuffed trout, or veggie farfalle pomodoro. In the cafeteria you might feel as if you're being herded onto an assembly line where a small kitchen serves a large, noisy crowd, but this is best-value dining in the park. A la carte breakfasts are rea-

sonable; lunch and dinner favorites include wraps, salads, hot sandwiches, coconut tilapia, Mediterranean pita, and roasted turkey or chicken. Our suggestion is to start with the black-and-tan onion rings and mustard dip. The Glacier Pit Snack bar in the general store is a perky place because of its 1950s-style soda fountain with classic red round stools perfect for spinning. If you're in a hurry, the Canyon Deli has grab-and-go snacks.

BEST DINING OUTSIDE THE PARK

Cody: Naturally, you won't have any trouble finding a Wyoming-sized steak or megaburger (beef or bison) in Cody. Though not to be confused with Jackson, options aren't merely limited to Western cuisine; you'll find Italian, Mexican, Japanese, and Chinese restaurants. Nothing too fancy, but just about anything a palate desires, especially for families on vacation.

Get your java jolt before taking off on your adventure at ✪ **Beta Coffeehouse** ($, 307-587-7707, B/L), a sporty hole-in-the-wall owned by accomplished area rock climbers. Hot and cold coffee drinks, fruit smoothies, many teas, homemade chai, hot chocolate, and Italian sodas are among a seemingly endless list of choices. Wireless Internet gives it higher marks, but seating is a little cramped. Another happening breakfast and lunch joint is Jim and Caroline's **Our Place** ($, 307-527-4420, B/L), known for good product at good prices. A favorite with the working crowd, ranchers, bikers, and a few tourists in-the-know, Our Place squeezes tables into every possible nook and is always full. Everything is good, but we especially like the rancheros breakfast with green chili, cakelike biscuits, and bottomless 25-

cent coffee. The family-friendly, budget-minded **Sunset House** ($/$$, 307-587-2257, B/L/D) looks much like a Perkins knockoff and has the same kind of menu. It's another place that locals gather for a cup of Joe and traditional egg, bacon, and potatoe breakfast. **Peter's Café Bakery** ($, 307-527-5040, B/L) is a popular spot for locals. Maybe it's the 31 flavors of America's most-consumed guilty pleasure they scoop for you year-round.

The **Irma Hotel Bar Restaurant and Grill** ($/$$, 307-587-4221, B/L/D) is true-blue Western, right down to the gunfight out front every summer evening. The expansive Irma is open early, stays open semilate, and has a serviceable kids' menu. The breakfast and lunch buffet is extensive and holds no surprises—just solid grub for greenhorns. The dinner menu lists seven different steaks, four cuts of their specialty prime rib, and Rocky Mountain oysters to let you know you're in cattle country. They also make room on the menu for bison. The saloon anchors the hotel/dining establishment, sounds and smells like the real deal, and is usually filled with Harley riders (male and female). The outside shaded picnic tables are arranged for optimum viewing of Cody's busy main drag.

One look at Loretta Alexander and you can feel the creative energy and joy she puts into what she does best—cook! Her ❦ **Willow Fence Tea Room** ($, 307-587-0888, L) limits its menu to four handcrafted items daily: a soup, a chef's salad, a sandwich, and an entrée prepared according to her whims. An equal or greater number of tantalizing desserts also tease the palate along with teas too numerous to list. The atmosphere is fun and funky, décor wildly eclectic and oh, BTW, she wove the willow fence surrounding her property. Although ❦ **Geysers on**

the Terrace ($$/$$$, 307-587-5868, D) gets mixed reviews for service, we like this retrofitted, urban-esque place because it isn't just cowboy cuisine. They have an interesting by-the-glass wine menu and a rotating microbrew selection, their dressings and desserts are house-made, and they know what arugula is (culinary standards are low on the frontier). The kids' menu is decent, and sandwich and entrée offerings are intriguing as well as constantly changing depending on availability of quality ingredients. With its proximity to the Cody Nite Rodeo, Geysers can get crowded and loud.

Steakhouses are the norm in the West and Cody doesn't disappoint in the beef's-for-dinner category. **Cassie's Supper Club** ($$, 307-527-5500, L/D) originally was a dance hall and dining club with a history of brothel activity. It was owned by the determined and business-savvy Cassie Walker, who needed income after her husband died. Cassie's is now Cody's iconic steakhouse with its darkened labyrinth of three bars, rooms for eating, a huge dance floor, four pool tables, and a busy museum of mounts on its numerous walls. Live music on weekends adds to the charm or chaos, however you see it. If you're itchin' to extend your rodeo experience, get your dusty boots on over to the ❦ **Proud Cut Saloon** ($$, 307-527-6905, L/D), where you'll find a special area for under 21ers. Owner Pete Crump, one of Cody's former rodeo greats, knows how to get 'er done. Rodeo photos and memorabilia set the mood while handcut steaks, chicken, seafood, or entrée salads will pad your belly and have you sitting right in the saddle. Not wanting steaks, our group was perfectly satisfied with French onion soup, lightly handbattered shrimp, fish and chips, broccoli, and green salad. Service is fast and comes with genuine smiles. At the **Wyoming Rib & Chop House** ($$, 307-527-7731, Br (Sunday)/L (weekdays)/D) award-winning ribs, large Angus steaks, fresh seafood flown in several times a week, and soups and sauces made on the spot mark a few differences in this regional chain. Sunday brunch is unusually flavorful starting with their legendary bananas Foster French toast, followed by a macho burrito and omelets made-to-order, all under $10. Traditional eggs Benedict can be ordered, or better yet, try the New Orleans version with a crabcake instead of the English muffin and crawfish etouffee replacing the hollandaise—*ca c'est bon!* Customary wine, beer, and liquor lists are available, and if you've got a designated driver try their renowned 26-ounce margarita.

A little ethnic diversity goes a long way with the Wrangler set. Cohabitating with the cowboy culture in downtown Cody for more than four years, ❦ **Shiki Japanese Restaurant** ($$, 307-527-7116, L/D) rolls some pretty tight sushi. Not much for ambiance or décor other than the Japanese-style booths in back, it's still welcome relief from meat 'n taters. Under new ownership in 2011, **Adriano's Italian Restaurant** ($$/$$$, 307-527-7320, L/D) is worth an honorable mention for its family orientation and pizza. To satisfy your Mexican cravings, there are two modest choices downtown: **Zapatas** ($, 307-527-7181, L/D) and **La Comida** ($, 307-587-9556, L/D). Zapatas has more authentic homemade cuisine, but the draw to La Comida is the outside seating and a fun bar atmosphere. Locals in the know, though, will tell you the best is **Tacos El Taconazos** ($, 307-587-4045, L/D) for heaping helpings of authentic food, a distinctively Mexican environment, and a bottomless basket of chips with tasty salsa.

Shoshone River Valley: At the ❦ **Yellowstone Valley Inn Restaurant /Saloon** ($$/$$$, 307-587-3961, B/D, May to September) the chefs do it right, starting with the hand-cut rib eye and 8- or 14-ounce tenderloin. Crab legs are a hot item during the tourist season as is the melt-in-your-mouth grilled or pan-fried walleye. An ample breakfast buffet is served from 7 to 9:30 AM and has seen up to 150 hungry customers loading their plates. In the evenings stick around for karaoke with Big Mike.

Meeteetse: If Cody is your home base while visiting the parks, do yourself a huge favor and take the 25-mile drive to visit the ❦ **Meeteetse Chocolatier** ($, 307-868-2567). Yup, a chocolatier—not a sweets shop or candy store, but a true truffle gem in cowboy country. Tim Kellogg happens to be a real cowboy who started making chocolates to fund a saddle purchase and found he's dang good at it. He makes small batches using only high-quality ingredients, organic when possible, and his business is ecoconscious to boot. So many choices, so many calories, but "must haves" include the Taittinger Champagne dark truffle, sea salt caramel wrapped in Belgian dark, sage truffle, pain au chocolat, and the 2-DI-4 hot chocolate—made only by Tim, so hope that he's in. Before savoring the chocolates, have a hearty meal at the **Outlaw Parlor Café and Cowboy Bar** ($/$$, 307-868-2585, L/D), which serves up good chow and is especially interesting for its history lessons. Butch Cassidy was arrested here and pictures of Amelia Earhart with her local ranch-hand friend hang on the walls.

Cody: Few Northern Rockies museums are as engrossing as the **Buffalo Bill Historical Center** (1-800-227-8483 or 307-587-4771), which is open year-round. This impressive collection of Western historical artifacts is five museums under one 300,000-square-foot roof: The Buffalo Bill Museum, Plains Indians Museum, Cody Firearms Museum, Whitney Gallery of Western Art, and Draper Museum of Natural History. It began as the Buffalo Bill Museum across the street, in a log cabin that has since become the Chamber of Commerce offices. Volunteers and docents are especially helpful and friendly. Nearly 250,000 visitors annually pass through what is sometimes called "The Smithsonian of the West." Hunters will appreciate the **Wild Sheep Foundation** (307-587-5508), where exhibits are open to the public from Monday to Friday. The nonprofit organization supports research and education on the bighorn sheep with the goal of increasing populations for conservation and hunting. See living history at the **Harry Jackson Art Museum** (307-587-5508). Harry Jackson was 14 years old when he left his Al Capone–ruled mafia family in Chicago for a new life in the West. His work ranges from World War II paintings to sculptures of Sacajawea. Jackson, who lived part-time in Cody and part-time in Italy, died in 2011 at age 87.

For a glimpse at an unfortunate piece of American history, the **Heart Mountain Center** (307-754-2689) 15 miles northeast of town is the site of an internment camp where 10,700 Japanese-American citizens were relocated during World War II. Today there are a few empty buildings and a brick hospital chimney, but plans for an interpretive center are under way. Heart Mountain is on public land and visitors can view the memorial adjacent to the camp, read the interpretive signs, and explore the area. Fans of the frontier mystique will want to save time for the **Old Trail Town/Museum of the Old West** (1-866-868-2111 or 307-868-2111, May to September) near the Cody Nite Rodeo grounds. The grounds have a collection of 26 Old West buildings from as far back as 1879 and as recent as 1901. You can see horse-drawn carriages, Indian artifacts, and other frontier memorabilia, including a cabin once inhabited by Butch Cassidy and the Sundance Kid. This is where Buffalo Bill Cody originally laid out the town named after him. The small cemetery out back is the resting place of many Western luminaries. People have varying opinions about dams, but either way the **Buffalo Bill Dam and Visitor Center** (307-527-6076, May to October) on the west edge of town is instructive. Originally called the Shoshone Dam and renamed in 1946, 325-foot Buffalo Bill was the tallest dam in the world upon completion in 1910 and was one of the first such concrete structures in the U.S.

RECREATION INSIDE THE PARK

Hiking

Canyon Village Area: Some of the most spectacular vistas in Yellowstone are from the north and south rims of the Grand Canyon of the Yellowstone River. On the south rim, visitors will recognize the view from **Artist's Point** from numerous paintings and photographs. The more adventurous should take **Uncle Tom's Trail** and its 500-foot descent on 328 metal steps to the Lower Falls. On the north rim, if a little vertigo doesn't bother you, hike the paved switchbacks to the **Brink of the Lower Falls**, where you can peek over the railing at the lip of the thundering 308-foot drop and steam from hot springs downstream. A more soothing, but no less inspiring, view is from **Inspiration Point**, probably the second-most popular tourist stop. **Grandview Point** is another worthwhile stop, as is the 0.5-mile descent to **Red Rock Point**, where the mist from the Lower Falls will provide relief on those rare hot summer days. About 1.5 miles north of Canyon Village heading toward Dunraven Pass is the breezy **Cascade Lake Trail**, a jaunt through forests, wildflower-laced meadows, and along small creeks to a pretty lake at the end. About 3.5 miles west of Canyon Village, the moderate 3-mile **Grebe Lake Trail** leads to a lake known for the increasingly rare Arctic grayling, a prized fish that requires exceedingly cold water for survival. Much of the trail winds through the charred remnants of the 1988 fire. The longest trail in the park is the 150-mile **Howard Eaton Trail**, including a moderate 12-mile stretch that hits several small lakes while connecting Canyon Village and Norris. It's often inaccessible until July because of marshy conditions, and while the Howard Eaton certainly is hike-worthy it is no longer maintained by the Park Service. South of Canyon Village in Hayden Valley, a trailhead starts the moderate hike to **Mary Mountain** on the Central Plateau in the heart of the park. Look for bison and elk, and keep a wary eye out for signs of grizzly activity as well. If there's one don't-miss hike in this region, it's **Mount Washburn**, weather permitting. The views of Yellowstone's mountains are terrific, extending to the Tetons on clear days. Two moderately strenuous routes, both 3 miles long, lead to the 10,243-foot summit. Bring a jacket, even if it's warm in the parking lot. Winds howl off the summit, where a fire lookout offers telescopes, water, and a break from sudden squalls. The north trail accessed from Dunraven Pass typically has less traffic and is a slightly more interesting hike. Go in the morning, before the winds blow and thunderstorms arrive.

Observation Peak is a challenging 3-mile hike from Cascade Lake to the top of a 9,397-foot mountain that offers views of the Absarokas to the east, Central Plateau to the south, Prospect Peak to the north, and the Gallatins to the northwest. A terrific six- to eight-hour adventure for fit hikers who want to get off the beaten path is **Seven Mile Hole**, a strenuous 11-mile trek that leaves the south rim of the Grand Canyon of the Yellowstone near Inspiration Point, sneaks past Silver Cord Cascade, and quickly drops 1,400 feet to the Yellowstone River. It's the only real trail to the bottom of the canyon. Watch for dormant and active hot springs. Strap a fly rod to your back and test your casting skills in the river. There are three campsites at the bottom, all requiring a backcountry use permit.

Yellowstone Lake Area: **Avalanche Peak** is a quad-burning 5-mile round-trip climb that's worth the effort once you see the stunning views of the lake and mountains. The switchback trail gains 1,800 feet through forest, whitebark pine, and open scree. **Elephant Back Mountain** is a moderately difficult 3-miler that climbs 800 feet through lodgepole pine to views of the northwest corner of Yellowstone Lake. **Pelican Creek** is a pretty 1-mile loop that traverses lodgepole forest on the lakeshore and a small marsh where bison and birds like to hang out. For views of the lake and its neighboring wildlife, take the easy 2.3-mile **Storm Point Loop**. The route goes through forest to a rocky promontory that juts into the lake. Check the Fishing Bridge Visitor Center for possible closure due to grizzly activity and keep your eyes out for the curious yellow-bellied marmots.

Fishing

It's no longer on any "best-kept secrets" list, but the **North Fork of the Shoshone River** remains an extraordinary experience. Where else can an angler find elbow room on a blue-ribbon trout stream that flows alongside a major highway? Apparently most visitors are in such a hurry to get from Cody to the park's East Entrance that they neglect 50 miles of free-flowing river teeming with native browns, rainbows, and cutthroats averaging about 16 inches. The best fishing, especially with dry flies, is right after runoff ends in early July and again in the fall. Expect smaller fish in August and early September. Study your maps. This is a dude-ranch corridor and much of river flows through private land—which, in Wyoming, includes the bottom of rivers.

Ice Climbing

The Yellowstone ecosystem region also is famed for at least two ice-climbing meccas: the **South Fork of the Shoshone River** west of Cody and **Hyalite Canyon** south of Bozeman. Ice climbers from around the world come to test their mettle on the hundreds of frozen waterfalls along the South Fork. You can check www .codyice.com for updates.

River Running

Sun-kissed trips through Red Rock Canyon and Lower Canyon hover between scenic floats and tumultuous whitewater on the **Shoshone River** near Cody. The rapids are a cushy Class I–II. Guided trips through the dusty canyon are available, but this is an excellent place to try your own hand at entry-level whitewater using a rented raft or inflatable kayak. The popular float starts at Demaris Street west of Cody and goes for 7 to 13 miles, ranging from 1.5 to 3 hours. For more action with a similar pace, at least until water flows are too low in July, put in on the **North Fork of the Shoshone River** for a half-day float. Expert kayakers will find the highly technical Class IV action between Buffalo Bill Dam and DeMaris Springs a thrill. No fewer than five companies will take you down the river or rent equipment.

Skiing (Nordic)

The **North Fork Nordic Trails** (1-800-628-7791 or 307-527-7701) are 25 miles of groomed trails near Pahaska Tepee and the Sleeping Giant Ski Area between Cody and the East Entrance, on the Shoshone National Forest. The trails, supported by the Park County Nordic Ski Association, follow the North Fork of the Shoshone River and are suitable for classic and skate skiing. Equipment rentals are available in Pahaska Tepee.

Snowmobiling

The Cody County Snowmobile Association has 70 miles of groomed trails in the area, though most riders in this neck of the woods like to go to Cooke City and the Beartooth Plateau in Montana. Plenty of rentals are available in Cody. A handful of snowmobilers head up the North Fork of the Shoshone and ride over Sylvan Pass to Fishing Bridge, but the area is avalanche-prone and openings are unpredictable.

6

Yellowstone: South Entrance

*South Entrance to West Thumb/West Thumb to Lake Village
and Fishing Bridge/Grassy Lake Road*

GETTING HERE

The South Entrance is often part of a double-feature: visits to both Yellowstone
and Grand Teton national parks. It's also a common arrival point for tourists
coming diagonally across Wyoming after driving westward on I-80 or I-70
(routes from Jackson are covered in Chapter 7); the other route is via US 26/287
through Dubois. To take this spectacular and stark approach, leave I-80 at Rawl-
ins on US 287/WY 789 and head across the vast Red Desert and Great Divide
Basin to Lander, an active community at the southern foot of the towering
Wind River Range. From there, the road angles to the northwest along the
ever-narrowing Wind River Valley past vivid red rock outcroppings to Dubois—
once called "No Sweat" because of the dry air and relentless winds. Eventually
you'll ascend Togwotee Pass and descend into Moran Junction, slice across the
northeast corner of Grand Teton National Park, reach the John D. Rockefeller
Memorial Parkway through Flagg Ranch, and arrive at the pine- and fir-studded
South Entrance along the Snake River. If you're flying, few airports are as spectacular as Jackson Hole Airport (JAC), the only such commercial facility in the
country located within the confines of a national park. Jackson Hole is served by
American, Delta, Frontier, SkyWest, and United from Denver, Salt Lake City,
Dallas/Fort Worth, Minneapolis, Chicago, Atlanta, and Los Angeles. For a drive
on the wild side, Grassy Lake Road is a rugged 52-mile traverse on pavement,
dirt, and gravel between Ashton, Idaho, and Flagg Ranch, just south of the
South Entrance. Typical sedans can make this road in the summer, but four-
wheel drive is recommended.

LEFT: Black bears aren't as fearsome as grizzlies, but they should be watched from a safe
distance.

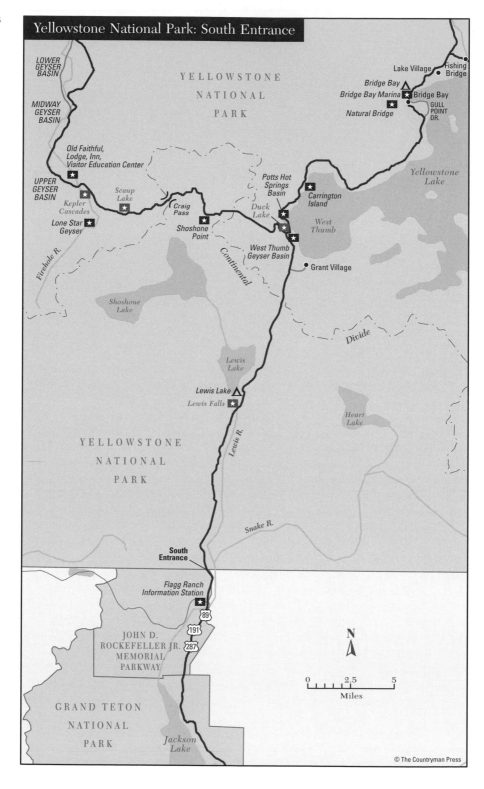

Yellowstone National Park: South Entrance

LOWER GEYSER BASIN

MIDWAY GEYSER BASIN

YELLOWSTONE NATIONAL PARK

Lake Village

Fishing Bridge

Bridge Bay

Bridge Bay Marina

Bridge Bay

Natural Bridge

GULL POINT DR.

Old Faithful, Lodge, Inn, Visitor Education Center

UPPER GEYSER BASIN

Scaup Lake

Kepler Cascades

Craig Pass

Lone Star Geyser

Shoshone Point

Potts Hot Springs Basin

Duck Lake

Carrington Island

West Thumb

Yellowstone Lake

West Thumb Geyser Basin

Grant Village

Firehole R.

Continental

Shoshone Lake

Divide

Lewis Lake

Heart Lake

Lewis Lake

Lewis Falls

YELLOWSTONE NATIONAL PARK

Lewis R.

Snake R.

South Entrance

Flagg Ranch Information Station

89

191

287

JOHN D. ROCKEFELLER JR. MEMORIAL PARKWAY

N

0   2.5   5
Miles

GRAND TETON NATIONAL PARK

Jackson Lake

© The Countryman Press

If there's an entrance where you're most likely to be stuck behind a pickup truck pulling a trailer with a boat, it's probably the South. This is the gateway to Yellowstone's lake region, starting with America's largest high-elevation lake—the clear, cold, and deep Yellowstone Lake. Also here are Lewis Lake and its sister, Shoshone, the largest lake in the country without road access. Another popular lake among anglers is Heart Lake, which requires a 7-mile hike. On either side of the highway is some of the remotest country in the park. To the west is the immense Pitchstone Plateau, a 2,000-foot-high mound of lava that's the birthplace of numerous streams that tumble out of this volcanic region in the park's so-called Cascade Corner. To the east, through territory split by the headwaters of the Snake River, are Two Ocean Plateau, The Trident, and the Thorofare, whose ranger station in the park's southeast corner is the farthest inhabited structure from a road in the U.S.

In part because it is so isolated, the region north of the South Entrance has fewer facilities and activities than any stretch of road in the park. For the 20 miles between the entrance and the once-controversial Grant Village, there is but one campground and picnic area, both at the boat launch for Lewis Lake on the west side of the road about 11 miles inside the park. This route certainly has its share

Yellowstone Lake is the largest high-elevation lake in the lower 48. NPS

Eagle Peak, which rises above the Thorofare in Yellowstone's southeast corner, is the park's highest point. NPS

of spectacular beauty, though. The highway follows a deep gorge carved by the Lewis River as it pours from the caldera beginning roughly on the south end of Lewis Lake. Also notable are the only three crossings of the Continental Divide in Yellowstone.

GATEWAY COMMUNITIES

Flagg Ranch, Wyoming

Flagg Ranch isn't a community per se—it's more of a resort village akin to Colter Bay in Grand Teton National Park and Grant Village in Yellowstone. It does, however, have all the amenities of a gateway community, scaled back: lodging, dining, fuel, some groceries, a gift shop, and a campground. Flagg Ranch is the hub of the 8-mile John D. Rockefeller Memorial Parkway, part of the 24,000 acres dedicated to the philanthropist in 1972 for his devotion to conservation and role in creating Grand Teton National Park. The forested area was a favorite camping site for Indians and then trappers because of its relative flatness and access to extraordinary hunting and fishing.

The U.S. military moved into the region after Yellowstone was created to protect it from the poaching, squatting, and vandalism that was rampant in the park's early days. With its proximity to Jackson, Wyoming, and newly settled parts of southeast Idaho, the southern boundary of Yellowstone seemed particularly vulnerable. For many years after the military left, what became Flagg Ranch was a place much like it is today—a place for travelers to rest and eat between two rugged parts of the Yellowstone region. Flagg Ranch was so remote that at one point it was owned—like many other properties in the region, especially around West Yellowstone—by a mafia don who valued the isolation and security.

Today, Flagg Ranch is the oldest continuously operating resort in the northern part of Jackson Hole, and its immediate future seems assured: Grand Teton Lodge Company, which operates Jenny Lake and Jackson Lake lodges, took over management in late 2011. Though the John D. Rockefeller Memorial Parkway is usually considered to be the 8 miles between Yellowstone and Grand Teton, technically it extends from West Thumb in Yellowstone to the southern boundary of Grand Teton.

HITTING THE ROAD

South Entrance to West Thumb (22 miles): If you hadn't figured it out already while driving the John D. Rockefeller Memorial Parkway, you'll quickly realize you're in wild country upon entering the park. Moose are frequently seen in the marshes along the **Lewis River**. Less than 2 miles inside the park and a 1-mile hike from the road, the waters of **Moose Falls** on Crawfish Creek roar toward a meeting with the Lewis River. Other trails lead into the invisible, toward rugged country infrequently seen by human eyes.

After 4 miles of driving through pine and fir forest, you'll reach the southern end of **Lewis River Canyon**. Everything begins to look starker here, due to the jagged volcanic rocks and remnants of the 1988 fires. Just before the 7-mile marker is an interpretive sign describing those fires and the aftermath; stop for the information as well as some of the best views of the canyon. About 1 mile farther upstream the river is mellow and marshy again just below where the waters of

The Lewis River makes a sharp left turn as it plunges over Lewis Falls. NPS

Bridge Bay is the lone operating marina on Yellowstone Lake. NPS

photogenic **Lewis Falls** plunge 30 feet. The left turn in the river here is so sharp it seems the falls must be part of a tributary. Another mile ahead is the turnoff for **Lewis Lake Campground,** along with a picnic area and boat launch.

The highway hugs the east shore of shimmering Lewis Lake for a couple miles before continuing its ascent through conifer forest to the lowest of the three Continental Divide crossings in the park—this one at 7,988 feet. From here, it's slightly more than a 2-mile descent to **Grant Village,** a small community featuring lodging, a campground, three eateries, a gas station, two Yellowstone General Stores and a Yellowstone Association bookstore, a visitors center/backcountry office, and a picnic area.

Grant Village might be the most controversial of Yellowstone's settlements and, with its completion in the late 1960s, is certainly the newest. The idea under a park master plan was to create a busy hub for a growing number of visitors coming by car and relieve some of the tourist pressure at Old Faithful. In theory, this one-size-fits-all site would eliminate the need for facilities elsewhere, and part of the original deal called for the removal of the Fishing Bridge community because of impacts on grizzly bears. Trouble was, Grant Village was planned in prime grizzly habitat and would dramatically impact no fewer than five cutthroat trout spawning migrations important to the bear's sustenance in the region. Over two decades plenty of folks found plenty of reasons to halt the project, but the Park Service persisted and, like a cat with nine lives, the project finally went forward in the early 1980s.

If the village had been designed to fit Yellowstone's persona, it might've salved some of the wounds of those who couldn't comprehend building such a city in prime wildlife habitat. Instead the lodging could be the original Motel Six: six stark two-story motel-style buildings with 50 rooms each, for a whopping 300 total. Grant Village is for lake lovers who couldn't get a room at Lake Village. It is close to Grand Teton National Park, but otherwise Grant Village is a last resort, so to speak.

About 2 miles beyond Grant Village is **West Thumb**, with the smallish **West Thumb Geyser Basin** perched at the edge of Yellowstone Lake's West Thumb. The area features a Yellowstone Association bookstore and information station, but other facilities once here were all moved to Grant Village by the late 1980s. West Thumb Geyser Basin, once known as Hot Springs Camp, has a short circular boardwalk through colorful pools and geysers. Perhaps the most interesting, or at least best known, is **Fishing Cone**—which juts from the lake and reputedly was a place where anglers could catch a cutthroat trout and cook it at the same time. High water typically submerges much of the cone these days. Also view-worthy: At 53 feet, **Abyss Pool** is the park's deepest, and was one of the most colorful until junk tossed into the pool by visitors altered the rich green hues. For a more detailed look at all of the thermal features, grab a brochure at the information station.

West Thumb to Old Faithful (17 miles): Two crossings of the Continental Divide, a rare roadside view of Shoshone Lake, and Lone Star Geyser are the highlights of this comparatively nondescript section of road connecting lake country with geyser country. Leaving West Thumb, take one last look at the Absaroka Mountains rising above Yellowstone Lake in the distance, with rich blue hues of tiny **Duck Lake** in the foreground. The road soon disappears into the forest while making its initial ascent to the Continental Divide at 8,391 feet. There is a picnic area and plenty of room to pull over for photos at the sign marking the third-highest paved spot in the park.

About 4 miles beyond the first divide is **Shoshone Point**, which offers a fleeting glimpse at Shoshone Lake to the southwest. It's noteworthy because this is the only place where the park's second-largest lake is visible from pavement. Less than a mile past the point are 8,262-foot **Craig Pass** and **Isa Lake**, also known as Two Ocean Lake because waters seeping out of each end of the lily pad–dotted pond

Shoshone Lake is the largest lake in the lower 48 without road access. NPS

flow toward different distant oceans. How is this possible? Like the top of the Two Ocean Plateau in the Thorofare, the divide is so flat that water can accumulate without entirely draining off. Also here are the **DeLacy Creek** picnic area and trailhead.

The next 3 descending miles feature more forest, two trailheads, a picnic area at Spring Creek, tiny Congress Lake, and eventually **Scaup Lake**, named for a duck species and fishless because it has no inlet or outlet. Another 2 miles brings the turnoff to the parking area for **Lone Star Geyser**, formerly Solitary Geyser, which requires a 2.5-mile walk or mountain bike ride on an abandoned service road along the Firehole River. The 10-foot cone-shaped geyser erupts about every three hours, lasts roughly 30 minutes, and reaches heights of 45 feet.

Just downstream of the Lone Star Geyser parking area is **Kepler Cascades**, the beginning of a rugged gorge on the Firehole. The cascades, named for the son of a former Wyoming Territory governor, drop 150 feet in all, including one 50-foot plunge, and they are easily accessed from the road. From Kepler, it's a breezy 4-mile drive into the congestion at Old Faithful, starting with the employee housing area on the south side of the road.

West Thumb to Lake Village and Fishing Bridge (19 miles): For nearly all of this stretch, you'll be hugging the west shore of Yellowstone Lake, much of it along the West Thumb. Bison are frequently seen in these reaches, and are not remorseful about plodding along at their own merry pace down the middle of the road. At 2 miles into the drive is **Potts Hot Springs Basin**, originally considered West Thumb's Upper Group of thermal features. This is an extremely active area that could include as many as 40 geysers. Before 1970, the road bisected the basin, until it was moved to a hillside to the west. The area is unmarked and closed to the public, but it is visible from the road. In another 2 miles, you'll notice a solitary evergreen growing out of a rock reef not far from the lake's shore. This is **Carrington Island,** named after a zoologist who reputedly was the first to sail on Yellowstone Lake. The shallows just off the island have been a primary focus of the lake trout suppression efforts.

Continuing along the shoreline, you'll arrive 2.5 miles later at the first picnic area, called **Hard Road to Travel**. If you have a cooler with snacks and cold drinks, we recommend continuing another mile to the **Park Point** picnic area, with its sweeping views of the lake and 10,305-foot Mount Sheridan to the south. A third picnic area, **Spruce Point**, is nearly 2 miles past and also serves up superior views of Yellowstone Lake. Yet another picnic spot before Bridge Bay is another mile down the pike and features an interpretive sign explaining the history of the area's conifer forest. A mile from Bridge Bay is paved **Gull Point Drive**, a 2-mile detour that hugs the shore before returning to Grand Loop Road; it was closed for parts of 2011 due to high water. This is a good place to fish from the bank, where you get a good glimpse of Stevenson Island, the second largest in Yellowstone Lake.

Just before the entrance to **Bridge Bay Marina** is the turnoff to **Natural Bridge,** a 1-mile walk or mountain bike ride to an arch created by the rush of Bridge Creek. The arch is also accessible from the parking area at Bridge Bay, where boats operated by Xanterra can be rented for fishing and other exploration of Yellowstone Lake. A ranger station assists with boat rentals and a small store services fishing needs. One-hour scenic cruises on the Lake Queen leave the dock

A bison scratches his neck on a hitching post.

periodically during the day. It's **OK** to use such smaller craft as kayaks and canoes here, but heed the sign on the bridge pointing out the dangers of plying cold waters that can turn dangerous in a heartbeat. It is best to use smaller craft in the morning before the winds kick up, and it's always wise to stay within 100 yards of the shore except in motorized craft.

Grassy Lake Road

A side trip worth taking outside of Yellowstone—if you have a four-wheel drive or a high-clearance vehicle—is the little-traveled **Grassy Lake Road**, which splits extraordinary wild country for 52 miles from Flagg Ranch to Ashton, Idaho. It's a unique journey that leads to several great trailheads and fishing access points, but don't embark on it lightly. There are no services, cell phones are mostly useless, rain or snow can turn parts of the road to gumbo, and there are rocks sharp enough to puncture a vulnerable tire or two.

Highlights along the way are the Winegar Hole Wilderness Area to the south, the fishing-rich **Grassy Lake Reservoir**, and hikes into waterfalls—and the scenery in general is wild. An interesting attraction is **Huckleberry Hot Springs**, a short hike north of Flagg Ranch roughly along the Snake River and across the park boundary. Popular among cross-country skiers in winter, Huckleberry is a rock-rimmed pool below a small waterfall known for its seclusion, hot waters (105 degrees), and fearsome signs warning of potential diseases, though many soakers scoff at the alarmism. Agency officials discourage use of the springs and you should enter at your own risk.

The thickly forested gravel and dirt road touches on Yellowstone's southern boundary twice before dipping south and crossing the Idaho-Wyoming state line and eventually emerging into the high-elevation seed-potato country of the Upper Snake River Plain. This is also a popular area for snowmobilers, generally from December to March. Between April 1 and June 1 the road is closed to motorized traffic because of grizzly bear activity. Plan on driving 15–25 mph for a minimum of 90 minutes, and quite likely longer, depending on how recently the road has been graded.

Pick Your Spot

LODGING INSIDE THE PARK

Grant Village: As park lodging goes, perhaps the least exciting is the controversial & **Grant Village** ($$/$$$, 307-344-7901, May to September), a massive commercial endeavor carved out of lodgepole forest as part of the Mission 66 project completed in the 1980s. The idea back then was to create an urban "node" within the park that, in theory, would ease congestion elsewhere, especially at the aging settlements at Fishing Bridge and Old Faithful. In the end, after decades of resistance, the Park Service persevered and got its city. The rooms are basic, small, and often compared to a college dormitory. Still, given how quickly park lodging fills in the summer, "Grant Central Station" provides a base to explore Yellowstone, Shoshone, and Lewis lakes as well as the Old Faithful area. It also has the best proximity to Grand Teton National Park, with fewer crowds.

ALTERNATIVE LODGING INSIDE THE PARK

Camping

With its 400 woodsy campsites, **Grant Village** is a nonstop buzz of activity, and it has all the accompanying amenities, including a dump station, showers, laundry, and generators allowed (until 8 PM). For peace and quiet (no generators allowed), our choice is the 85-site **Lewis Lake** campground on a hill overlooking the lake, a better alternative scenically than Grant Village and Flagg Ranch. Access to the lake, seclusion, and pretty sunsets are the draw here. Because no reservations are taken, check in early; however, if you're coming in late and you've been shut out elsewhere, Lewis Lake is often your last best chance. It is always one of the last campgrounds in the park to fill up.

BEST LODGING OUTSIDE THE PARK

At 2 miles from Yellowstone's southern boundary, & 🐾 ¶ **Flagg Ranch Resort** ($$$, 1-800-443-2311 or 307-543-2356, May to September) is on the west side of the John D. Rockefeller Memorial Parkway, nestled between Yellowstone and Teton in a flat and forested area that almost seamlessly blends the two parks. As for accommodations, the newer four-plex cabins look promising on the outside, but are pretty average and shy on the extras. In recent years a malaise fell over the struggling resort and many visitors left unsatisfied with service, attitude, and cleanliness. Hopes were high in the autumn of 2011 with a takeover by Grand Teton Lodge Company, which now calls it **Headwaters Lodge & Cabins** under the banner of Flagg Ranch Company. Flagg Ranch is the oldest continually running lodge in upper Jackson Hole and makes a dandy jumping-off point for touring both parks. The Steakhouse restaurant presents decent meals, and a deli and gift shop are connected to the main lodge.

BEST ALTERNATIVE LODGING OUTSIDE THE PARK

Camping

Flagg Ranch: Along with the cabins at the 'tweener resort is the **Flagg Ranch Campground** ($, 1-800-443-2311 or 1-800-628-9988, June to October/December to March) in the pines and near the Snake River with 100 pull-through RV sites and 75 tent sites. They aren't cheap—$64 nightly for RVs and $35 for tent sites in 2011—and frankly not particularly alluring, but reservations are nevertheless recommended because it does fill up. The campground is cramped and there isn't much scenery—use it as a base to visit the two parks. In the past there have been complaints about cleanliness, but our hunch is that Grand Teton Lodge Company will clean it up now that it has taken over.

Forest Service Cabins

A unique lodging option common elsewhere in the Rocky Mountains but limited in the Greater Yellowstone area is Forest Service lookouts/cabins. A pleasing selection is the year-round **Squirrel Meadows Guard Station** (208-652-7442) on Grassy Lake Road, about 24 miles east of Ashton, Idaho, and 28 miles west of Flagg Ranch, barely inside the Wyoming border. The historic (1907) two-bedroom cabin is available for rent through the Caribou-Targhee National Forest. As with most forest rentals, propane cooking facilities, bunk beds, and mattresses are provided—but you're on your own for sheets, sleeping bags, pillows, dishes, etc. The cabin does have drinking water from an outdoor hand pump. Winter access is via snowmobile, skis, or snowshoes.

Local Flavors

DINING INSIDE THE PARK

Grant Village: The **Grant Village Dining Room** ($$, 307-242-3499 or 307-344-7311, B/L/D, June to September) has typical park breakfasts and lunches and is seated on a first-come, first-served basis. Breakfast can be ordered from the menu or self-served with a trip or two through the buffet line. Lunches are not much different than any other park offerings, with the exception of the bison sausage, vegetarian Philly roll, and Tuscan bean soup. Sack lunches to go can be ordered. Dinner can offer a surprise or two, for starters a veggie flatbread pizza, followed by bison meatloaf, four-cheese mac and cheese, pistachio chicken, or quinoa cakes. Though cavernous open seating feels nonpersonal, it still ranks high in the ambiance category because of the pine-laced views of Yellowstone Lake. Reservations are strongly recommended; you can cool your heels and wait at the **Seven Stool Saloon**. For a different meal experience with an up-close and personal lake setting, the ✿ **Grant Village Lake House** ($, 307-344-7901, B/D, June to September) is a short walk through the woods to what was once an active marina. Banks of tables lining the windows are the preferred seating, but you can see the lake's West Thumb from most anywhere while you enjoy breakfast or dinner. Breakfast has the typical choices, but the pub-style dinner menu of sliders, sandwiches, burgers, and such has a few twists: Parmesan sweet potato fries, fried green beans, fish sliders, and black bean burgers. Reservations are not taken, so if you're seeking more certainty consider reserving a table and making the short drive to one of the two dining rooms at Old Faithful. Although it's not much different cuisine-wise and tends to be even busier, it's still a good way to experience the "Faithful" happenings.

To Do

BEST DINING OUTSIDE THE PARK

Flagg Ranch: **The Steakhouse** ($$/$$$, 1-800-443-2311, B/L/D, May to September), formerly the Bear's Den Restaurant, certainly has the solid Western style with its elk-antler chandeliers and light-pine accents. What will happen to the menu was uncertain at printing time because Grand Teton Lodge Company took over management in late 2011. Meals were meat heavy with steaks, burgers, and chicken—and a home-style chicken pot pie topped the list. The **Polecat Creek Saloon**, a full bar with some seating, makes up for the lack of "place." We have high hopes that the dining service will improve.

RECREATION INSIDE THE PARK

Fishing

The granddaddy of 'em all is **Yellowstone Lake**, which can seem like an imposing, 87,000-acre body of water—with good reason. Boaters caught off-guard by an afternoon thunderstorm have paid the ultimate price. Anyone pitched into these frigid waters can figure on lasting about 20 minutes before hypothermia sets in. Thus, many fishermen go to the rivers or smaller lakes. The lake has long been known as a repository for the Yellowstone cutthroat trout, which grow to the size of a rugby ball. Fishing for cutthroat is strictly catch-and-release. Anglers are encouraged to fish for lake trout and are required to either keep or kill them. To catch cutthroat, ply some of the areas closer to the shore in a float tube or boat. You'll be glad you did—Yellowstone cutthroat can be seen rising from the lake depths for dry flies or emergers. The best way to do this is early in the morning at Gull Point in Bridge Bay.

The second-largest body of water in the park is secluded **Shoshone Lake**, at 80,000 acres. Shoshone is perhaps the favorite of all two hundred lakes in the park for angling. It is famed for its big brown and rainbow trout, with some scrappy cutthroats and decent-sized brook trout, and lake trout as well. It's fishable all summer, but the best time is fall, when the big fish move into the Lewis River channel. The Shoshone can be fished from trails or by boat, with access from the ramp at **Lewis Lake**—Yellowstone's third largest lake. Lewis also is prized for its browns as well as the occasional brook and lake trout. All of these fish are considered exotic species because they were introduced nearly a century ago in an effort to enhance angling opportunities. Also remote, but as well known

Mount Sheridan rises above Heart Lake. NPS

as Shoshone Lake, is **Heart Lake**, favored by many longtime Yellowstone anglers because it's just far enough off the beaten path to provide some isolation and it offers exceptional fishing for trophy lake trout as well as some cutthroats and whitefish. The journey requires an 8-mile hike on the Heart Lake Trail, which starts just north of Lewis Lake off the road between the South Entrance and West Thumb. Despite the remoteness, don't expect to have the lake to yourself. About 40 percent of Yellowstone's backcountry trips have Heart Lake as the destination.

A wolf paw print is a reminder that you're in wild country.

South of Bridge Bay is **Riddle Lake**, a fun little spot for catch-and-release fishing for native cutthroats. For those who prefer stream angling, the Lewis River has a mellow 2-mile section worth trying just below Lewis Falls. It can produce some solid brown trout. Farther below, the canyon run might look desirable because of limited pressure, but it's dangerous to traverse and those who have tried it report mediocre fishing, at best.

Hiking

West Thumb/Grant Village Area:
For those seeking a short leg-stretcher,

Sandhill cranes have made a great comeback in Greater Yellowstone. NPS

Duck Lake is an easy 1-miler offering views of Yellowstone and Duck lakes, as well as remnants of the 1988 fires. An even breezier walk is on the 0.5-mile boardwalk at **West Thumb Geyser Basin** with its hot springs and dormant geysers on the shores of Yellowstone Lake. For more exertion, the **Lewis River Channel/Shoshone Lake/Dogshead Loop** provides two choices—a moderate 11-mile round-trip that takes in Shoshone and Lewis lakes as well as the pretty channel connecting the two, or a shorter forested hike with a return on the 4-mile Dogshead Trail. Bring a fly rod in the fall because big browns and cutthroats from the lakes head into the channel to spawn. **Riddle Lake** is a moderate 2-mile trek through pretty meadows and marshes to the Continental Divide and a sweet little lake. Whenever you're in willowy marshes, there's a chance to run into an obstinate moose. Because of bear activity, this trail is closed until mid-July. The **Shoshone Lake/DeLacy Creek Trail** is an easy to moderate 6 miles through meadows rife with wildflowers and wildlife possibilities, including sandhill cranes and moose. Hiking the entire circumference of the lake is 28 miles. The **Yellowstone Lake Overlook** walk from the West Thumb Geyser Basin parking area is a popular 2-mile trail with terrific views of the lake, Absaroka Mountains, and West Thumb area after a 400-foot elevation gain.

Hiking

Flagg Ranch Area: The resort offers two quite different hikes that leave from the ranch. The 5-mile **Flagg Canyon** hoof has views of the Snake River as it carves the canyon before spilling out to the south in Jackson Hole. The 2.3-mile **Polecat Creek Loop Trail** encompasses lodgepole forests and marshlands resplendent with wildlife, especially birds, and leads to Huckleberry Hot Springs.

Snowmobiling

Outside of West Yellowstone, the South Entrance is the most popular entrance for snowmobilers and an important part of Jackson's winter economy. Guided trips are available from Flagg Ranch as well as outfitters in Jackson. Preferred destinations are Yellowstone Lake, Canyon Village, and Old Faithful.

Grand Teton National Park and Jackson Hole

North Entrance to Jackson Lake Junction/Jackson Lake Junction to Moran/Jackson Lake Junction to Moose/Moran to Moose/Moose to Gros Ventre Junction/Gros Ventre Junction to Jackson/Antelope Flats Road/Gros Ventre Road/Moose-Wilson Road

GETTING HERE

Few airports offer as rewarding an arrival as Jackson Hole Airport (JAC)—the only commercial airport in America completely within the confines of a national park. For pilots, it's also one of the most challenging. Landings are always north to south, with the approach from the east, so book a window seat on the right side of the aircraft for a bird's-eye view of the Tetons off the right wing (left side for departures!). Seasonal service is provided most prolifically by United from Denver. Delta and SkyWest serve Jackson Hole from Atlanta, Minneapolis, and Salt Lake City; American from Dallas/Fort Worth; Frontier from Denver; and United also from Chicago and Los Angeles.

Once on the ground, it's a brisk 7-mile taxi or rental-car drive south on US 26/89/191 into the town of Jackson. No fewer than 10 taxi and 7 rental-car agencies serve the airport. For drivers, four US highways converge at Jackson, all of them coming from scenic directions. If you're coming south from Yellowstone National Park, the fastest route through is US 26/89/191 on the east side of Jackson Hole—though watch out for moose, bison, and elk on the road. A more relaxing and slightly prettier alternative is to turn south at Jackson Lake Junction and take the well-traveled paved interior road for 10 miles to Moose. If you're arriving from the west, US 26 and ID 31 leave Idaho Falls and eventually fork in different directions—US 26 along the South Fork of the Snake River past Palisades Reservoir and the Grand Canyon of the Snake through Hoback Junction, and ID 31

LEFT: Mesmerizing views come with evening bonfires at the plush Lost Creek Ranch & Spa.

173

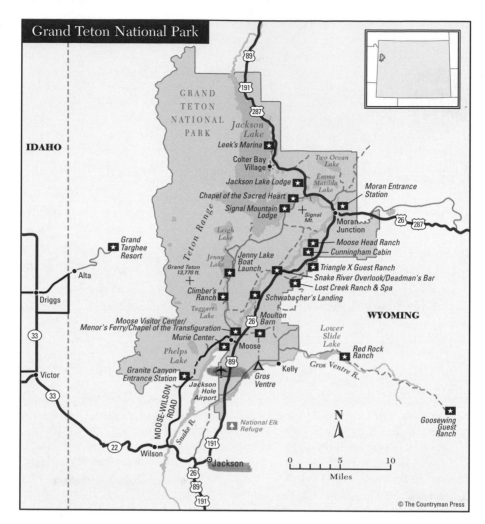

Grand Teton National Park

IDAHO

WYOMING

GRAND TETON NATIONAL PARK

Jackson Lake

Leek's Marina

Colter Bay Village

Two Ocean Lake

Jackson Lake Lodge

Emma Matilda Lake

Moran Entrance Station

Chapel of the Sacred Heart

Signal Mountain Lodge

Signal Mt.

Moran Junction

Teton Range

Leigh Lake

Moose Head Ranch
Cunningham Cabin

Grand Targhee Resort

Jenny Lake

Jenny Lake Boat Launch

Triangle X Guest Ranch

Grand Teton 13,770 ft.

Snake River Overlook/Deadman's Bar
Lost Creek Ranch & Spa

Alta

Climber's Ranch

Schwabacher's Landing

Driggs

Taggart Lake

Moulton Barn

Lower Slide Lake

Moose Visitor Center/
Menor's Ferry/Chapel of the Transfiguration
Murie Center

Moose

Red Rock Ranch

Phelps Lake

Gros Ventre R.

Victor

Granite Canyon Entrance Station

Jackson Hole Airport

Gros Ventre

Kelly

National Elk Refuge

Goosewing Guest Ranch

MOOSE-WILSON ROAD

Snake R.

Wilson

Jackson

N

0   5   10

Miles

© The Countryman Press

over a small pass to the junction of ID 33 in the cozy little community of Victor, and then over steep Teton Pass to a panoramic view punctuated by a wood sign declaring, HOWDY, PARDNER, YOU'RE IN JACKSON HOLE! It's a 6-mile, 10 percent grade to the valley floor at Wilson.

From the east, the choice is the Wyoming Centennial Scenic Byway on US 26/287 up the strikingly colorful Wind River Valley, along the base of the towering Wind River Range, through the arid community of Dubois, and over spectacular Togwotee Pass to Moran Junction. And from the south, there are two options, depending on whether you're coming from the east or west on I-80. US 191 heads due north from Rock Springs and US 189 exits the freeway just east of Evanston. Both knife through the desolate upper Green River Valley to a junction at Daniel, 11 miles west of Pinedale. The highway then eases over a gentle pass near Bondurant and drops along the pretty Hoback River to a meeting with the Snake River at Hoback Junction.

If Yellowstone is a living, breathing example of an ecosystem intact, Grand Teton is its visual alter-ego. Wildlife spillover from the world's first national park is gradually giving Grand Teton a wild flavor, too, but the draw here is obvious: Magnificent views of the most mesmerizing mountains in the lower 48 from nearly every road in the valley. The result is a people-pleasing setting, and pleased they are after a few days of hiking, river running, and picture taking.

First, some definitions. Grand Teton is a part of the larger area known as Jackson Hole. One of the best and most easily accessible places to appreciate how and why this high-altitude valley got its name is atop Teton Pass. At just above 6,000 feet, the southwest corner of Jackson Hole is its lowest part. Though the "hole" appears to be table flat, the northern end is actually about 700 feet higher; thus, it isn't unusual in late spring to be amid patches of snow at Moran Junction and in blossoming wildflowers around Jackson. Also an important part of Jackson Hole is the controversial National Elk Refuge, on the town of Jackson's northern fringe. Several thousand elk congregate here every winter, lured from the mountains and sagebrush steppe by hay and pellets delivered from trucks. The practice began in 1912 to prevent elk from starving during an unusually harsh winter; it continues today largely out of habit and at the behest of outfitters, ranchers, and tourism officials who each have a financial interest in seeing feeding continue.

Bull elk engage each other at the National Elk Refuge outside of Jackson. NPS

The appeal of Jackson Hole is readily apparent—and explains why Teton County consistently flirts with being the most expensive in the nation. Only 3 percent of the county's roughly 2.7 million acres is in private hands, with the remaining ruggedly beautiful 97 percent owned by the American public in the form of the park, elk refuge, and Forest Service lands. South and east of the park, spectacular log trophy homes and dude ranches dominate or mesh with a landscape that has become a destination for the rich and famous as well as the young and active. Ski areas, golf courses, and the town's high-end shopping, lodging, and dining reflect the exclusivity of a county that has a decidedly different personality than any other in Wyoming.

GATEWAY COMMUNITIES

Jackson, Wyoming

One admonition you might hear from anybody who lives in the region is this: Jackson and Jackson Hole are *not* the same. Jackson (population 8,650) is the town; Jackson Hole is the entire valley. You'll hear it from longtime or outlying residents who aren't enamored with the deep-pocketed Eastern influence brought to the town. You'll also hear it from nouveau Jackson-ites who find the outlying areas, and even some of the in-town locales, a bit primitive for their liking. What they have in common is an appreciation for one of the most spectacular settings in the world, even if they might cherish it for different reasons. And they aren't the first. Indians came to Jackson Hole in summers to hunt the bountiful wildlife. It wasn't until 1807, when John Colter veered south from the Lewis and Clark Expedition on its return trip to St. Louis, that the first Anglos saw the region. Fur trappers soon followed to pursue beaver, and many a mountain man converged for regular rendezvous in the "hole" between the Teton and Gros Ventre mountains.

Serious settlement didn't begin until the 1880s, when the creation of Yellowstone National Park sparked interest in the area to the south. Jackson was founded in 1894 as a hub for the cattle ranching industry and a destination for wealthy Eastern hunters. Remnants of a few of the original buildings remain in the town's renowned Town Square, known best for the elk-antler arches at each of the four corners. A first hint that this would be no ordinary town came in 1920, a year after women were given the right to vote nationally, when Jackson democratically picked a woman mayor and an all-woman city council—a first for the country. A rope tow was constructed at Teton Pass in 1937 and Snow King opened a few years later, the first ski area in Wyoming. The movie industry certainly contributed to making Jackson what it is today. *Nanette of the North* was filmed in Jackson Hole in 1921, John Wayne's first speaking part was in Jackson in 1932, and *Shane* was made near Kelly two decades later. Henry Fonda's *Spencer's Mountain* in 1963 is another flick that brought the region to the big screen. Today it's a renowned haven for artists, writers, and other creative types as well as high-powered, deep-pocketed fast-trackers from elsewhere. Celebrities flock to Jackson each summer and winter, grateful that it's one of the few places where their arrival at a restaurant is greeted by little more than a nod. It's part of what's helped Jackson retain some of its charm, even as real estate has exploded off the charts, periodically ranking Teton County as the most expensive in the nation. This phenomenon is due partly to the area's beauty and partly to limited elbowroom. Galleries blend seamlessly with

Antlers arch in Jackson.

curio shops, cosmopolitan restaurants flourish next to busy barbecue joints, and the wealthy mingle comfortably with carefree outdoor lovers with holes in their jeans.

Victor, Idaho

Victor is the first town you'll see after arriving over Teton Pass from Jackson, and the little roadside community of less than one thousand has plenty to offer: two interesting sporting goods stores, a theater, a café, a soda fountain, two microbreweries, and a well-stocked grocery store with hand-cut meats. Once upon a time, when Victor was a major railroad stop between Teton Pass and Swan Valley, the town had more hustle and bustle than it does even today. It had hotels, cafés, and the only bank for miles. The town was a hub for cattle and sheep ranchers, as well as the folks who mined the area stone that can still be seen in some of the architecture.

Driggs, Idaho

A picturesque farming and ranching community in Idaho's seed-potato country, Driggs is now experiencing the benefits and costs of being discovered by the outside world. For that, the town of 1,100 can thank—or blame—the growth over the hill in Jackson and, to a lesser extent, the prolific snows at nearby Grand Targhee Ski Resort. At first, it was an affordable outlying area where service workers could live and commute over Teton Pass without busting their bank accounts. Driggs has now evolved into Jackson, circa the 1970s: a recreation haven for the wealthy and energetic. Driggs and nearby Victor and Tetonia are pastoral little communities on ID 33, in the heart of a largely flat agricultural valley between the Tetons and Big Hole Mountains.

HITTING THE ROAD

North Entrance to Jackson Lake Junction (16 miles): Think of this as the transition zone, which begins 8 miles south of Yellowstone National Park's South Entrance. Much of this forested stretch follows the east shore of Jackson Lake, past Colter Bay Village and a marina. This route is where the glorious Teton Range comes into view, starting with block-shaped 12,605-foot Mount Moran.

You won't find an entrance station coming from this direction because you'll have already paid your fee for Yellowstone (unless you arrived via the rugged Grassy Lake Road from Ashton, Idaho, to Flagg Ranch). However, everything you need to know about Grand Teton is available at the **Flagg Ranch Information Station** (307-543-2327, June to September), which has a bookstore. About 5 miles past Flagg Ranch, the park's border touches the northernmost tip of Jackson Lake, a natural body of water that dramatically increased in size upon completion of the Jackson Lake Dam on the Snake River in 1916. Soon after crossing into the park, you'll see the lake out the passenger side of your vehicle. The first lake access is in another 2.5 miles, at the **Lizard Creek Campground**. In another mile is a lakeside picnic area, followed in short order by Jackson Lake Overlook and three more

A mule deer buck waits to make a safe crossing of the John D. Rockefeller Memorial Parkway north of Grand Teton.

Jackson Lake Lodge: A Controversial Icon

Depending on one's perspective, Jackson Lake Lodge is either an icon of modern construction brilliantly designed to highlight the views of Jackson Lake, Willow Flats, and Grand Teton . . . or an architectural abomination that no more belongs in a Western national park than a fire lookout in Times Square. When it was completed in 1955, many national park enthusiasts accustomed to the rustic and stately elegance of Yellowstone's Old Faithful Inn and Oregon's Crater Lake Lodge were aghast at architect Gilbert Stanley Underwood's creation. Underwood used massive amounts of concrete, and the buildings are mostly oddly shaped rectangles, leaving some to compare it to a bomb shelter. Nevertheless, first-time and annual visitors alike can't help but stop in their tracks after ascending a flight of stairs into a lobby that features 60-foot-high picture windows framing the lake and towering Grand Teton. Over the years there have been occasional calls to tear down the sprawling structure, but it's too late now: Jackson Lake Lodge became a National Historic Landmark in 2003.

picnic sites before the turnoff to **Leek's Marina** (307-543-2494), a must-stop for its excellent pizzeria and accompanying views from the deck.

Another mile south is **Colter Bay Village**, one of the preferred places to hang out for families looking for an economical vacation. Set amid a pretty lodgepole forest, Colter Bay is one of the four park lodges run by the Grand Teton Lodge Company. The picturesque setting on the lakeshore has 166 refurbished homestead cabins that were scattered about Jackson Hole. Also here are a visitors center, store, marina, two restaurants, showers, and a gas station. A number of easy trails through the forest and along several waterways begin here. Unfortunately, for many years visitors were awed by the collection of artifacts in the Indian Arts Museum, but after the 2011 season everything was shipped to a conservation facility for preservation. Back on US 89/191/287, the road makes a sweeping southward bend to the turnoff for **Jackson Lake Lodge**, perhaps the park's signature structure. The lodge is best known for its stunning views of the Tetons through its 60-foot picture window.

The Jackson Lake Lodge has 348 motel-style cottages and 37 rooms in the main lodge. Also here are a medical clinic, a gas station, corrals for horseback adventures, two restaurants, and a view-packed lounge. The grounds unquestionably are the best in the park for wildlife viewing, especially from behind the wall outside the lodge, so bring binoculars or a spotting scope. Elk and moose are almost always visible in Willow Flats, and because of their presence it isn't unusual to see a grizzly.

In recent years, this location has been frequented by what might be the most famous wild bear in the world—a 15-year-old (in 2011) grizzly sow dubbed "399" by researchers. This mama bear and three offspring have delighted tens of thousands of tourists and created dozens of so-called "bear jams" by making regular appearances along the road near Jackson Lake Lodge, Willow Flats, and Oxbow Bend. One of those cubs, dubbed "610," has since grown up and produced her own litter; they are frequently seen together, sometimes having family squabbles over food, with 399's newest kids. *Note:* The frequency of these appearances moved the Park Service to tighten regulations in 2011 regarding proximity to bears. People have always had to stay at least 100 yards away; now, that distance also includes all types of vehicles.

Did You Know? There have been no known attacks by grizzly bears on groups of three or more in the lower 48 states.

Jackson Lake Junction to Moran (5 miles): This short stretch is best known for its proximity to the meandering Snake River downstream from Jackson Lake Dam. Most notable is the Oxbow Bend Turnout, where on a calm day you can see for yourself the often-photographed reflection of Mount Moran in the glassy surface of the river's oxbow. Look here for elk, pelicans, swans, and perhaps grizzly 399 and her family. About 1 mile before the Moran Entrance Station is the left turn on paved Pacific Creek Road, which provides access to trailheads for Emma Matilda and Two Ocean lakes. The paved portion extends to the park's boundary near the Teton Wilderness Area. One gravel road veers north toward Two Ocean Lake; the other fork continues on dirt about 3 miles, also to the boundary between the park and wilderness area. This is Grand Teton's wildest and most wildlife-rich country, and the place where wolves spilling over from Yellowstone first arrived in the park. Though these trails are popular, be sure to carry bear spray.

Jackson Lake Junction to Moose (20 miles): The Teton Park Road winds through the heart of the park and is famed for its many viewpoints and access to all things Grand Teton. The road traverses sagebrush and stands of lodgepole and aspen. Shortly after making the right turn at Jackson Lake Junction, you'll pass through the southern edge of Willow Flats—look for well-camouflaged wildlife in the willows, especially moose—and cross the century-old dam. Fishermen like to congregate below the spillway and also ply the waters of Jackson Lake, which produced the state-record lake trout (50 pounds). Past the dam about a mile is the log **Chapel of the Sacred Heart,** an active Catholic church overlooking the lake where services are conducted each Saturday and Sunday evening in the summer, and weddings are understandably common as well.

About 0.5 mile past the chapel is the turn for **Signal Mountain Lodge** (307-543-2831), which is operated independently from the park's other lodges and touts itself as the only lakeside resort. Begun in the late 1920s with three cabins and three boats, the hillside sprawl features modest motel-lookalike cabins, a campground, a marina with boat rentals, gift and grocery stores, fuel, etc. Ownership has changed several times over its history, but it has had the same operators since 1984 and enhancements have been ongoing.

Signal Mountain Lodge is squeezed between the lake and 7,725-foot Signal Mountain, which is reached via a winding 4.8-mile paved road to the summit. Signal Mountain rises some 800 feet above the valley floor and offers views of the Tetons, Jackson Lake, and a sizable chunk of Jackson Hole. The turnoff is a mile south of Signal Mountain Lodge; no large motor homes or trailers are permitted.

South of Signal Mountain Road is the north junction for the seldom-used River Road—15 miles of paradise for a mountain biker or anyone with a four-wheel-drive vehicle. In about 3 miles River Road turns right, but another stretch of gravel continues down to the edge of the Snake River. River Road, which crosses a sage plain along the west side of the Snake until it rejoins the Teton Park Road, is an excellent place to see Grand Teton's bison herd. Back on the Teton Park Road, nearly 2 miles south of Signal Mountain on the left is the **Potholes Turnout**, so named for its views of glacial depressions, or kettles, carved from the ground as chunks of ice were covered by glacial outwash. About 0.5-mile later on the right is a pullout for the best view anywhere of block-shaped **Mount Moran**, a 12,605-foot mountain that's probably second only to Grand Teton as the most photographed mountain in the range. After snapping a few shots of the seemingly flat-topped peak beyond the southernmost tip of Jackson Lake, look for a gravel turnoff to the right about 2 miles later. This short road leads to the lake's **Spalding Bay**, where boats may be launched and primitive camping with pets is allowed as long as dogs are restrained.

Up next on Teton Park Road is the north Jenny Lake junction, the beginning of a loop that is a slower but more picturesque way to cover the next several miles to the south junction. The road drops to trailheads for String and Leigh lakes for 1.5 miles before becoming one-way and hugging Jenny Lake's wooded east shore past **Jenny Lake Lodge** to the **Jenny Lake Visitor Center** (June to September). Jenny Lake is the one site in Grand Teton that almost nobody skips, whether it's to take the shuttle boat to Cascade Canyon, hike around the lake, or simply marvel at its crystal-clear waters. The visitors center, housed in a log cabin that was once the home of park artist Harrison Crandall, offers exhibits, ranger-led programs, pertinent information, and a fitting stone fireplace.

The roads reconnect a short drive from the visitors center and Teton Park Road meanders through sage and intermittent forest past several scenic turnouts and trailheads for another 8 miles to Moose. Midway through the journey you'll notice the **Climber's Ranch** (307-733-7271, June to September) on the right. Run by the nonprofit American Alpine Club, the ranch is a modestly priced bunking alternative strictly for mountain climbers and their families.

Did You Know? At one time, the Snake River ran through Jackson Lake in much the same way that the Yellowstone River flows through Yellowstone Lake. In 1906–07, Jackson Lake Dam was constructed out of logs, bringing the waters of the lake up about 22 feet. In 1910, the dam collapsed. Seven years later, the old dam was replaced by earth and concrete, bringing the lake's level up another 8–15 feet.

Just before the Moose Entrance Station on the left are the **Menors Ferry Historic District** and **Chapel of the Transfiguration**. The chapel is a log Episcopal church that remains active and the site of an occasional summer wedding. It was built in 1925 through donations from a California family that summered at nearby dude ranches. The chapel is known for exquisite views of the Tetons through small windows in the back. In the same area in the early 1890s, a homesteader named William D. Menor put down roots in the sage soil and built a cable ferry to get back and forth across the

Snake. For some 25 years, it was the only way to cross the river for miles. Menor charged 50 cents for wagons, 25 cents for horses. The store Menor built still stands and is a museum of sorts, housing a collection of artifacts left by early area settlers. A replica of the old ferry is still used to carry tourists across the river, conditions permitting.

Moose is a cluster of buildings, including the park's headquarters and one of Grand Teton's three entrance stations. The sparkling 22,000-square-foot **Craig Thomas Discovery and Visitor Center** (307-739-3399) opened in 2007 after a unique fund-raising effort in which ⅔ of the monies were raised from private donations. The center, open year-round and named after the recently deceased Republican senator from Wyoming who had the foresight to protect such unique landscapes as the Snake River headwaters, has an extraordinary collection of exhibits and videos that'll keep you busy should the occasional rainstorm keep you indoors. Across the Snake River is a busy assortment of commercial endeavors set in a private in-holding within the park, including Dornan's Spur Ranch Cabins, a restaurant and bar with phenomenal views from an upstairs deck, outdoor adventure shops, a gas station, and other businesses. The site has been owned and operated by the Dornan family for six decades.

Did You Know? Grand Teton National Park was not included in the 1995–96 wolf restoration program to Yellowstone, but by 2009 there were six packs created by wolves moving south to carve out new territory. The Teton pack was formed in 1999 with five black pups, but that pack no longer exists. Of the six, only the Huckleberry pack resides almost exclusively within the boundaries of Grand Teton.

Moran to Moose (18 miles): Though less interesting than the Teton Park Road, this largely straight shot on a sagebrush bench above the Snake River is the faster route to Jackson, but not without its share of highlights and great views. Moran is the site of one of Grand Teton's three entrance kiosks, albeit only for traffic headed north after arriving from Dubois or Jackson.

Moran is at the confluence of the braided Buffalo Fork and Snake rivers, amid cottonwoods and conifers. Be especially wary of moose on the road in the first few miles headed south on US 26/89/191 toward Jackson. After a short distance, the road elevates away from the Snake into sage and grasslands where cattle and sometimes bison mingle. About 2.5 miles south of Moran Junction is the **Elk Ranch Flats Turnout**, the first place on this route to absorb the grandeur of the Tetons.

Take a leg stretch 3 miles later at the **Cunningham Cabin**, where John Pierce Cunningham and his wife, Margaret, built sod-roofed log cabins amid the sage in 1890. It is accessible by a short trail at the end of a gravel road. The Cunninghams were early proponents of preserving the area as a national park, though they weren't around to see it come to fruition. They also are known for constructing the trademark buck-and-rail fence that has become a modern fixture in Jackson Hole. The cabin is empty, but a peek inside offers a sense of what it was like to be here a century ago—and the windows form a great frame for a Teton snapshot. Across the highway from the cabin is a gravel road that forms a scenic loop that meanders toward the tree line and makes its way back to the main road after about 5 miles.

The view from Cunningham Cabin.

Less than a mile beyond the Cunningham Cabin on the left is the **Triangle X Ranch**, the only dude-ranch concession in the country within National Park Service jurisdiction lands. The ranch was purchased by the Turner family in 1926 and sold a few years later to a company serving as a front for the Rockefeller family, which was covertly buying Jackson Hole land to set aside for a proposed national park. Many of the Turners moved to other parts of the valley, but one son, John, continued to operate it as a dude and hunting ranch outside of the initial park boundary. When the park was expanded in 1950, it included the Triangle X but the concession was granted. Third- and fourth-generation Turners operate the ranch today, though the park's desire to open the concession to free-market competition leaves the family's future at the Triangle X in doubt.

About 1.5 miles south of the Triangle X is one of those little treats that do not show up on most maps. **Hedrick Pond**, one of many kettles found in this area, is the site where Henry Fonda's 1963 movie *Spencer's Mountain*—the basis for the 1970s television show *The Waltons*—was filmed. Also finding this location appealing is the occasional trumpeter swan.

The remainder of the drive toward Moose is across the sage Antelope Flats, with views that simply won't quit. About 2 miles past the Triangle X is a short gravel descent to **Deadman's Bar**, a popular launching spot for scenic Snake River floats that was named for an 1886 incident in which three men were killed. The turn is just before the famed **Snake River Overlook**, a spot made famous by Ansel Adams's brooding 1942 black-and-white photo from a brief Department of the Interior effort to highlight national parks. Roughly across the highway from the overlook is a gravel road leading toward Shadow Mountain, the upscale Lost Creek Ranch, and some swanky private homes. The ascent to the top of 8,252-foot Shadow Mountain requires some

Did You Know? Looking to the southeast from this vantage point, up the Gros Ventre River Valley, you can see a gash in the side of a mountain. This was created in 1925, when an earthquake sent tons of debris tumbling into the Gros Ventre River, forming a natural dam that backed up what is now Lower Slide Lake. The lake was once much larger than it is now, but in 1927 the rock wall gave way, sending a torrent of water into the valley below and wiping out the town of Kelly, killing six people.

effort—RVs and trailers not recommended—but the reward is broad views across Jackson Hole to the Tetons.

Continuing south on US 26/89/191, you'll pass the **Teton Point Turnout** and arrive 2 miles later at the turn for **Schwabacher's Landing**, one of four boat launches in the park for the Snake River. Even if you don't have a boat, there is a short walk upstream to an exceptional spot to take photos or watch the sun set over the Tetons while scanning the beaver ponds and sage for such wildlife as pronghorn, deer, and elk. Back on the highway, the views continue to be a sumptuous feast for the eyes, first at **Glacier View Turnout** and then at **Blacktail Ponds,** across from the Antelope Flats Road turn.

Moose to Gros Ventre Junction (8 miles): This stretch is more of the same, with a growing sense that you're nearing Jackson. Look for elk and bison on either side of the highway. The route features one stop, the **Albright View Turnout** with yet another glorious photo op of the Tetons, before reaching the junction for the Jackson Hole Airport.

Gros Ventre Junction to Jackson (8 miles): As Jackson nears, posh neighborhoods spring up to the west of the highway, where such symbols of wilderness as elk and moose often browse on rose bushes and other landscaped shrubs. Immediately after the Gros Ventre Junction, the highway crosses the Gros Ventre River. The large fence you'll see angling along the highway and the river's south riparian area epitomize this clash of urban and rural.

The fence represents the northern edge of the **National Elk Refuge,** where the nation's most famous elk herd congregates during the harsh winters after arriving from points afar. In the summer it is almost a barren wasteland, nibbled to the nubs by thousands of elk; in the winter, the ungulates are in easy view feasting on pellets and hay provided by the State of Wyoming and backed by the U.S. Fish & Wildlife Service.

If you're passing through in the summer, don't bother looking for elk. They're almost always in the high country. Do, however, look for moose in the Gros Ventre River bottoms and scan for bison in the wide-open country on either side of the river.

Beyond the Grand Teton National Park boundary, on the east side of the highway along Flat Creek, is the **Jackson National Fish Hatchery** (307-733-2510), which produces Snake River cutthroat trout to replenish populations decimated elsewhere by development. Renovated in 2010, the hatchery has a pond that's an ideal place for kids to learn casting and maybe catch a trout. About 2 miles later, on the flanks of East Gros Ventre Butte overlooking the National Elk Refuge, is the **National Museum of Wildlife Art** (307-733-5771), a treasure trove of nature and wildlife art housed in an extraordinary and expansive rock structure. Visitors are treated to sculptures, painting, photography, and other exhibits that bring the West to life.

Entering Jackson, be sure to stop at one of the finest tourist facilities anywhere—the **Jackson Hole Greater Yellowstone Visitor Center** (307-733-3616), a cooperative effort between seven government agencies and other groups. The impressive wildlife diorama is the highlight of a place where you could spend hours gleaning information about the last great largely intact temperate ecosystem

Elk Refuge: National Treasure or Wildlife Disease Breeding Ground?

In 1912, an unusually harsh winter settled over Jackson Hole and its rapidly growing hub community, Jackson. Until then, elk had migrated into the valley each winter, as they had for thousands of years, and locals paid little attention.

But now, with development eliminating precious forage grounds and snows piling ever deeper, the citizens of Jackson were increasingly witnessing an agonizing sight: starving elk stumbling, staggering, and ultimately collapsing right before their very eyes, a grim image playing out over and over. The well intentioned people of Jackson came to the rescue by tossing hay into the snow, and a wildlife refuge was born.

Ever since, the community has fed the elk each winter, regardless of whether it was necessary, and in the process the herd has increased to well beyond the refuge's capacity. The results have been a mixed blessing. On the one hand, outfitters can promise successful hunts and residents can take out-of-state visitors on sleigh rides amid the "wild" elk. On the other hand, the unnatural congregation of so many animals has wreaked havoc on the ecosystem—the banks of Flat Creek feature hundred-year-old willows an inch tall, hammered each year by elk and bison—and dramatically increased the frequency of disease, some of them now serious enough to threaten the herd's future.

As Jackson commemorated the hundredth anniversary of the feeding in 2012, the community was emotionally divided over whether to continue. Supporters don't want to see elk starve again or lose the economic benefits of such a large herd. Detractors pine for a natural ecosystem that would enhance the health not only of the elk herd but bring back such long-lost species as beaver, moose, wolves, bears, eagles, osprey, songbirds, otters, and other wildlife. In 2011, a court ruled that feeding could continue at least another five years but said in pointed language that such artificial sustenance defeated the purpose of the wildlife-refuge system. Even so, it remains an uphill battle in Wyoming. The Elk Refuge is one of 22 such elk feed grounds in the western part of the state, much to the chagrin of neighboring Montana and Idaho, where such practices are now banned.

on the planet. Be sure to check out the observation deck, which overlooks the southern end of the elk encampment and an example of one of the few natural areas around Flat Creek. To see the refuge from another angle, head east on Pearl Street from downtown and continue for several miles through the refuge until the gravel road begins winding out of the valley toward Curtis Canyon. There are several wonderful viewpoints of the valley floor and Tetons.

Antelope Flats Road (7 miles): This flat paved road heads east near Moose and is the primary route to **Mormon Row,** where remnant homes and barns of early settlements remain. Mormon settlers from Idaho came here in the 1890s and created a cluster of 27 homesteads. The 6 that remain today fell into disrepair until 1990, when the Park Service began preservation. Among the 6 are the **Moulton**

Ranch Cabins, one of the most serene and appealing settings for lodging in all of Jackson Hole. North of the road at the Mormon Row intersection is yet another place you'll recognize from numerous photos of the area—the classic **Moulton Barn** with the Tetons as the backdrop. You'll likely be joining other photographers as they move in and out of the sagebrush looking for the precise spot others have stood to capture the setting's majesty. Bison are a common site among the grasses, wildflowers, and sage, and the pavement is popular among road bicyclists. Antelope Flats Road continues east for nearly 2 miles before making a sharp right down south toward Kelly.

Gros Ventre Road (9 miles): This paved stretch follows the river along the edge of the National Elk Refuge into the Bridger-Teton National Forest. Check out the funky little settlement of Kelly along the way; it's known for its unusual dwellings, including yurts. Keep going past Kelly on Gros Ventre Road to the park boundary, where you

A plaque commemorates the efforts of settlers along Mormon Row.

can still see the decaying cabin used to film the western classic *Shane* with Alan Ladd in 1951. Just outside the park boundary is the **Gros Ventre Slide**, where an entire mountainside slid about 1.5 miles into the river in 1925, forming Slide Lake. Two years later, the natural earthen dam collapsed, sending a wall of water through Kelly and into the Snake River, killing six people. Learn more about this natural phenomenon on the **Gros Ventre Geological Trail**, past what is now Lower Slide Lake.

Moose-Wilson Road (10 miles): This locally popular drive is actually two in one. From Moose to the tiny Granite Canyon Entrance Station, it is a narrow and sometimes winding paved road through picturesque aspen and lodgepole stands, with a mile of bumpy gravel thrown in to keep the traffic and speeds at a minimum. South of the entrance station, the road widens and passes the entrance to Teton Village, where traffic dramatically increases. The road is closed in winter from the entrance station north.

Almost immediately after turning onto the Moose-Wilson Road west of park headquarters, you'll reach the turnoff for the **Murie Center** (307-739-2246). Driving the 0.5 mile of gravel to this collection of cabins is like taking a step back in time, in many ways to the birth of conservation. Free tours are offered at 3 PM Mondays and Wednesdays from May to late October.

Muries: The Consummate Name in Conservation

Few families have done more to protect America's wildlands—from the Northern Rockies to Alaska—than the Muries. Adolph and Louise Murie bought the ranch near Moose in 1945, and they were joined a year later by the more famous Murie duo, Adolph's brother, Olaus, and his wife, Mardy. Olaus was an original founder of The Wilderness Society, and the cabins became the first national headquarters for the environmental group. Less than two decades later, The Wilderness Act of 1964 was forged on this very site. Earlier, the couple pushed for preservation of the Arctic National Wildlife Refuge in their other home state, Alaska, where Mardy had become the first female graduate of the University of Alaska–Fairbanks. The entire Murie Ranch is now a National Historic Landmark, and today the site serves as headquarters for the Murie Center, which promotes science-based understanding of nature and conservation issues through programs that include stays at the ranch.

Take a step back in time at the Murie Ranch outside of Moose.

Back on the Moose-Wilson Road, the pavement bends left onto a bench. A parking area on the left is a popular place to stop and look for wildlife, especially moose, in the wetlands below. Stops are few as the road bends through pretty woods to the turn for the Death Canyon Trailhead. Shortly thereafter is the 1,106-acre **Laurance S. Rockefeller Preserve** (307-739-3654, May to September), an elegant tribute to wildlands and wildlife. The property, fully within the park, has 8 miles of immaculate trails and the 7,500-square-foot building features a sensory feast of nature that reflects the spirit of the Rockefeller family's commitment to conservation. Trucks, RVs, and trailers are prohibited between the Rockefeller Preserve and the Granite Canyon Entrance Station. From the South Entrance to the junction of WY 22 the views of the Tetons return, but the surroundings become increasingly civilized.

Pick Your Spot

LODGING INSIDE THE PARK

Colter Bay: Grand Teton Lodge Company runs the quaint, comfortable, and woodsy **Colter Bay Village** ($$/$$$, 1-800-628-9988 or 307-543-3100, May to September), which is more family-oriented than Jackson and Jenny Lake lodges. This true village is home to 166 comfortable homestead cabins that were brought from the Jackson Hole area and can sleep from two to six people. For a distinctly unique experience, bring your own bedding or sleeping bag, but skip the tent and rent one of 66 tent cabins ($). The encampment almost looks like something out of the Civil War. With two solid log walls, two canvas sides, and a roof, staking a tent was never so easy. If you have a hard-sided camper, you'll find 350 individual dry camping sites and 112 RV spaces. The village is on the north end of the park, making it a great base for also scouting Yellowstone National Park. Its location on the east shore of Jackson Lake makes for ideal boating activity. Tent cabins shut down in early September, before the rest of the village's lodging.

Jackson Lake: On a bench overlooking Jackson Lake, the once-controversial **Jackson Lake Lodge** ($$$/$$$$, 1-800-628-9988 or 307-543-3100, May to October) is also run by Grand Teton Lodge Company. The architecture is decidedly the antithesis of national park themes, but in many respects this is the hub of Grand Teton National Park. Upon climbing the wide stone staircase you are rewarded with the picture window framing "The Grand." In the lodge you will find the Mural Room and Pioneer Grill for food and a cocktail lounge that has regular entertainment, not to mention more views with a thrill from behind the windows or on the outdoor patio. The lounge is for visitors who like to be at the center of the action; there's no better spot for gazing at the lake and the peaks mirrored on the lake or watching moose and elk browse in Willow Flats.

friend liked this

Signal Mountain: **Signal Mountain Lodge** ($$$, 307-543-2831, May to October) is a collection of 1930s rooms, bungalows, cabins, and houses on the south shore of Jackson Lake that run the gamut of amenities, though none would be classified as luxurious. Rooms are motel-style with microwaves and fridges, some with fireplaces. The Lakefront Retreats are snug and somewhat dated but offer terrific views of the lake less than 100 feet away. A marina, store, and other facilities are part of the complex, and in keeping with the park policy there are no TVs in the rooms.

Jenny Lake: If you're not bothered by the steep prices, **Jenny Lake Lodge** ($$$$, 1-800-628-9988 or 307-733-4647, May to October) is a memorable locale. The 37 rustic Western accommodations on the east shore of Jenny Lake provide the consummate Teton vacation and might be the most sought-after lodging in the national park system. The rooms are nondescript log

Jenny Lake Lodge has the most luxurious dining and lodging in either park.

Sitting on the front porch at Jenny Lake Lodge has its privileges.

cabins, but it's the little extras that separate them from ordinary rustic lodging—most notably the remodeled bathrooms and hand-crafted comforters on the beds. Rates include an exceptional breakfast and five-course dinner. Free bicycling and horseback riding are included, and access to Jenny Lake is a few steps away across the road.

Moose: Open mostly year-round with a few short closures, 🐾 🏅 🍴 Dornan's Spur Ranch Cabins ($$/$$$, 307-733-2522) are part of a family-owned, 10-acre spread near the park headquarters and across the Snake River from the historic Menor's Ferry site. Dornan's 8 newish one-bedroom and 4 two-bedroom log cabins with lodgepole pine furniture and modern amenities all sit on the wildflowered banks of the Snake River. Brand new to the rental program in 2011 was the three-bedroom Spur Ranch House. Kitchens are fully

equipped and patios with BBQs face the Tetons, but don't expect to find TVs. A popular restaurant, general store, variety of recreation rental shops, and large wine shop (which holds wine tastings in winter) complete the hospitable village. Minimum stays in the cabins are three nights during the summer and Christmas/New Year's; during shoulder seasons minimums and rates drop.

ALTERNATIVE LODGING INSIDE THE PARK

A number of long-standing guest ranches and operations are technically within park boundaries, grandfathered in as part of the deal to create additional lands for the park in 1950.

Moose: 1 Old Ranch Road is home to 🏅 Lost Creek Ranch & Spa ($$$$, 307-733-3435, May to September), an extraordinary guest ranch with full duplex cabins, living room cabins, and king suites that will host up to 64 guests. Activities included in the rates are horseback riding, trips to both parks, scenic floats on the Snake River, guided hiking in the Tetons, cookouts, skeet shooting, and a trip to a rodeo. Gourmet meals are a staple and the spa is full-service, with facials, manicures, pedicures, and massage by appointment. An outdoor underground pool, hot tub, sauna, steam room, tennis court, basketball court, weight room, workout room, and cardio deck with bicycles facing the Tetons are just examples of unique ways to spend your leisure time.

Full-week stays (Sunday to Sunday) are required. Louise and Kip Davenport have the last privately owned guest ranch—**Moose Head Ranch** (\$\$\$\$, 307-733-3141 or 850-877-1431, June to August)—technically in Grand Teton National Park. Fourteen log cabins, including a two-bedroom that sleeps up to five, are sprinkled among the cottonwood trees and catch-and-release fly-fishing trout ponds. The Davenports take pride in their family-centric vacations; gourmet food prepared by three chefs is served three times daily. Although there are no structured programs, there are plenty of activities for kids and adults, including pure nature appreciation. Credit cards are not accepted.

One of few resorts entirely on national park land, the casual, family-owned & **Triangle X Dude Ranch** (\$\$\$\$, 1-888-860-0005 or 307-733-2183, May to October/December to March) accommodates up to 70 people in a series of log cabins. The all-inclusive rate includes three meals and two horseback rides per day. Elk, fox, pronghorn, moose, and the occasional black bear on the grounds is common, horseback rides are tailored to meet skill levels and interests, and guided fishing and float trips can be arranged. A one-week minimum stay is required from June to August, four nights during the off-seasons, and two nights during winter.

Camping

Grand Teton's five campgrounds are all first-come, first-served except for groups of 10 or more. The maximum stay is seven days and most are open from mid-May to mid-September; group reservations (1-800-628-9988) may be made at Gros Ventre and Colter Bay. RVs are welcome at all but Jenny Lake. **Colter Bay** (\$, May to September) is a sprawling yet surprisingly quiet area set amid lodgepoles with 350 large sites along with a flush toilet, dump station, laundry, showers, groceries, and service station. The separate RV area has 112 sites and spots for tents. The only larger camping area in the park is at **Gros Ventre** (\$, May to October), with 360 sites on the Gros Ventre River about 11 miles southeast of Moose. Happily for procrastinators, even on the busiest summer days you've got a shot of landing a site there. **Jenny Lake** (\$, 1-800-628-9988, May to September) is a wildly popular spot with 49 tent-only sites amid forest and glacial boulders near the shimmering lake; be there well before 11 AM if you want to have any chance of nabbing a spot. Perhaps the least appreciated and definitely least used is **Lizard Creek** (\$, 1-800-672-6012, June to September), with many of its 60 sites on Jackson Lake north of Colter Bay. Lizard doesn't open until mid-June and closes after Labor Day weekend. Spacious **Signal Mountain** (\$, 1-800-672-6012, May to October) has 86 sites, flush toilets, a dump station, service station, and a grocery store, and it's open until early October.

Canvas-sided tents at Colter Bay Village give campers a mix of creature comforts and rustic accommodations.

BEST LODGING OUTSIDE THE PARK

Jackson: For your convenience we have separated our suggestions for the numerous Jackson lodging options into six categories: Budget, Economy, Middle of the Road, High End, B&Bs, and Ultraluxury.

In the *Budget* category, the ⬧ **El Rancho Motel** and **Anvil** ($, 1-800-234-4507 or 307-733-3668) are conveniently town-centered and reasonably priced. The spartan Rancho consists of 25 no-frills rooms–no air-conditioning, no fridge, no microwave. The Anvil has air-conditioning and is a little newer; neither accepts pets. The ⬧ **Alpine Motel** ($$, 307-739-3200) has 20 rooms with micro and fridge. The **Four Winds Motel** ($/$$, 1-800-228-6461 or 307-733-2474) and **Golden Eagle Inn** ($, 1-888-748-6937 or 307-733-2042, May to October) are midsized, standard sleeping joints, family-owned and -operated by Jim and Dood Loose. They come clean and comfy, with a friendly staff. One of Jackson's older motor-court motels is the family-owned **Rawhide Motel** ($, 307-733-1216), a basic 23-room motel on two floors and a fine choice if you're searching for simple and clean.

The iconic 🏵 **Kudar Motel** ($$, 307-733-2823, May to October) was built in 1938 and is certified for preservation. Many repeat customers have been coming to Joe and Ron Kudar's place since the 1950s for the frontier feel of its 14 motel rooms and 17 cabins located less than three blocks from Town Square. A neon sign and a grassy area with picnic tables in the center of a circular driveway give it that *Happy Days* aura. Five blocks south of the town center is a row of 12 western red cedar log cabins with standard rooms that make up the family-owned and-operated **Buckrail Lodge** ($/$$, 307-733-2079, May to October).

In the *Economy* category, the four Town Square Inns are centrally located and within easy walking distance of

Town Square. Closest is the ♿ 🐾 Antler Inn ($/$$, 1-800-522-2406 or 307-733-2535) with its 110 rooms, laundry area, exercise room, and hot tub. ♿ 🐾 🦎 Cowboy Village Resort ($$, 1-800-962-4988 or 307-733-3121) brings the country to the city with 82 individual log cabins, all with kitchenettes and sofa sleepers; decks come with charcoal BBQ grill and picnic table. You'll also find a hot tub, swimming pool, guest laundry, and meeting room. Next door is the ♿ 🐾 Elk Country Inn ($$, 1-800-483-8667 or 307-733-2364), a somewhat orderly mix of 90 units, including 25 stand-alone cabins, hot tub, picnic area with grills, and a playground. The ♿ 🐾 49er Inn & Suites ($$, 1-800-451-2980 or 307-733-7550) consists of 145 rooms and suites, an indoor Roman tub and outdoor hot tub, fitness room and sauna, conference rooms, and continental breakfast.

Also in the reasonably priced category is the 🐾 Jackson Hole Lodge ($/$$, 1-800-604-9404 or 307-733-2992), owned by the Jicarilla Apache Nation but managed by Outrigger Lodging Services. The centrally located two-story log façade building has 60 units, mostly suites with a kitchen, fireplace, eating area, and writing desk. An indoor heated pool, two Jacuzzis, dry sauna, and game room with table tennis, foosball tables, and air hockey complete the "what to do after the park" activities list. Decorated in an early 20th century Victorian fashion with American antiques, Parkway Inn and Spa ($$, 1-800-247-8390 or 307-733-3143) also has an indoor lap pool, two jetted spa tubs, and an expanded continental breakfast. Owned by a former mayor of Jackson, the affordable ♿ Ranch Inn ($$, 1-800-348-5599 or 307-733-6363) has rooms with balconies facing the Snow King ski area and are within easy distance of down-

town. If you're a fan of Branson, Missouri, you'll love the 🍴 Virginian Lodge ($/$$, 1-800-262-4999 or 307-733-2792), a gaudy complex of 170 rooms with a modern Wild West theme, 20 suites with full kitchens, 130 RV sites (May to October), and an outdoor heated pool with hot tub.

Across the highway from the National Elk Refuge and away from the buzz of downtown is the 24-room Elk Refuge Inn ($$, 1-800-544-3582 or 307-733-3582), featuring 10 balcony rooms with kitchenettes, benches for viewing, grills, and a small picnic area. The Miller family also owns the super-friendly Miller Park Lodge ($$, 307-733-4858), less than three blocks from downtown, which has a nice re-do on the rooms, some with Jacuzzi tub and fireplace. ♿ 🐾 Flat Creek Inn & Mart ($$, 1-800-438-9338 or 307-733-5276) is next to the Refuge Inn and comprises three separate two-story buildings with 75 rooms, all facing the refuge; the mart part is a convenience store and gas pump.

For *Middle of the Road* lodging, Nancy Stodala and her sons run the boutique ♿ 🦎 Grand Victorian Lodge ($$$, 1-800-584-0532 or 307-739-2294, May to October), 10 rooms and one suite, all uniquely decorated. Breakfast and afternoon tea (or coffee) with homemade cookies are included; if you're looking for a fall getaway, Nancy offers some terrific deals. The 🐾 Sundance Inn ($$/$$$, 1-888-478-6326 or 307-733-3444, May to October /December to March), a Jackson stalwart, was built in the 1950s and maintains its art deco theme in 25 cozy accommodations. The owners have operated the motel for 21 years and have developed a loyal clientele. The ideal location of the ♿ Lexington at Jackson Hole Hotel & Suites ($$$, 1-888-771-2648 or 307-733-2648), formerly the Trapper Inn, gives the 90 nonsmoking rooms with fridges, microwaves, and expanded continental breakfast an edge; the warm cookies and complimentary beverages are an even bigger edge.

In the *High End* bracket, if you're more accustomed to the conformity of an upscale chain hotel, consider the ♿ ❀ Homewood Suites by Hilton ($$$/$$$$, 1-800-225-5466 or 307-739-0808), offering 41 spacious suites with full kitchen, living room, and fireplace. The usual perks include indoor swimming pool, hot tub and fitness room, complimentary hot breakfast, plus snacks and beverages served from 5:30 to 7:30 PM Mondays to Thursdays in the reception area. Though just three blocks from Town Square, the Pottery Barn-ish elegant ❀ ❦ Inn on the Creek ($$$/$$$$, 1-800-669-9534 or 307-733-1565) feels private and secluded. A variety of tastefully appointed rooms have touches of indulgence ranging from the down bedding and fireplaces to the box of chocolates, terry robes, and tranquil views of Flat Creek. The ❦ Rusty Parrot Lodge and Spa ($$$$, 1-800-458-2004 or 307-733-2000) claims to be the only four-star hotel in Jackson, and does a fine job of maintaining the status. Down comforters and gas fireplaces, a full chef-prepared breakfast at the Wild Sage Restaurant, full concierge service, and an outdoor hot tub overlooking town are just a few of the special touches. Body Sage, the first full-service spa in Jackson, is a part of the lodge and therapeutic treatments can be tailored and arranged.

The English-Tudor, revival-style, brick-and-stucco ♿ ❦ ❦ Wort Hotel ($$$$, 1-800-322-2727 or 307-733-2190) is a National Historic Landmark that takes up an entire city block. Remnants of its years as an illegal gambling hall remain throughout, including an original roulette wheel, blackjack table, and historic photos. Greeting visitors is a lobby filled with locally made log furniture, a large rawhide and iron chandelier, and the original staircase and fireplace that survived a devastating fire in 1980. The full-service hotel's 59 classy rooms range from deluxe to the fit-for-a-king Silver Dollar Suite and are adorned with either two queens or a king bed, granite and marble bathrooms, plush carpet, a fresh rose, valet parking, and luxurious bedding topped with a stuffed bear for company. The Silver Dollar Grill, known for its 2,032 inlaid silver dollars, can be lively and loud with musical entertainment.

There are also European style *B&Bs* in or near town to add to the mix. With 22 rooms just three blocks from Town Square, ♿ Alpine House Lodge & Cottages ($$$, 1-800-753-1421 or 307-739-1570) feels more like a mountain resort but more personal. Amenities include a hot tub amid perennial gardens, Finnish dry sauna and spa, and chef-prepared gourmet breakfast. Five creekside cottages have full living space and kitchens. ♿ The Bentwood Inn ($$$, 307-739-1411) was built in 1995 using 200-year-old logs left over from the 1988 Yellowstone fires, and has five elegantly appointed rooms. Halfway between downtown Jackson and Teton Village on a wooded 3.5 acres with views of the Tetons, *Country Inns Magazine* recently rated it among the top 10 inns in the nation.

For those looking for an *Ultraluxury* experience and money is barely a consideration, the peaceful ♿ ❦ Amangani Hotel ($$$$, 1-877-734-7333 or 307-734-7333) is a discreetly posh 40-suite hotel built mostly from redwood and Oklahoma sandstone with astonishingly close-up views of the Tetons. Part of the exclusive Aman resorts, this spread is on 1,000 acres of wildlife sanctuary and migratory route for mule deer and elk between Jackson and Teton Village. There is a full-service spa, pool, and health center for guests. Their restaurant, The Grill at Amangani, is open to the public. ⛱ ♿ **Spring Creek Ranch** ($$$$, 1-800-443-6139 or 307-733-8833), a complex of villas, executive homes, condos, and rooms (four-plex cabins) with a view is amid a wildlife preserve and next to Amangani. A spectacular home base for horseback riding, tours of the park, nature talks, sleigh rides, or communing with the great outdoors, the ranch has naturalists on staff. The on-site Granary Restaurant and Lounge has "upscale mountain-man cuisine," according to *Bon Appetit* magazine.

Wilson: Climb 95 steps through pine and fir forest to a heavenly hideaway appropriately named ❀ **Teton Treehouse** ($$$/$$$$, 307-733-3233, May to September). Owners Denny and

Sally Becker like it to feel that way. Denny, a former wilderness and river guide, started adding on to his hillside home on Heck of a Hill Road three decades ago, creating plush guest rooms with views of the valley and Sleeping Indian Mountain. Windows extend into the forest, creating a space to read or watch such wildlife as a plethora of birds and the occasional moose or deer. Guests mingle over a heart-smart breakfast served promptly at 8 AM to discuss plans for hiking, fishing, floating, or park touring while the hosts share the wonders of the valley. Sherrie and Ken Jern have created the quintessential B&B at the ❀ **Wildflower Inn** ($$$$, 307-733-4710). This gorgeous log home on three acres has earned rave reviews for reasons that quickly become apparent. The landscaping is so colorful and neatly tended, the wooded grounds so lush, and the four single rooms and two-room suite with private decks and bathrooms so luxurious, they've earned plaudits from *Bon Appetit, Sunset,* and

The Wildflower Inn between Wilson and Teton Village is elegant in every way.

Glamour. The beds are handcrafted and dressed with lofty down comforters and fresh flower bouquets are generously sprinkled throughout.

Carol and Franz Kessler's family-friendly ❄ **Teton View Bed & Breakfast** ($$$, 307-733-7954, May to October) blends mountain hospitality with European flair in the form of a guest room in the house, a two-room suite, and a cabin with a kitchen. A full breakfast, outdoor hot tub, and deck with close-up views of the Tetons add to the appeal. The ❄ **Sassy Moose Inn** ($$/$$$, 307-413-2995), a log inn of five cowboy-cabin rooms in a rural setting west of Jackson, is open year-round. A stay includes a hearty breakfast, an outdoor hot tub screened for privacy yet still providing stunning views of the Tetons, and good proximity to ski slopes.

Teton Village: Teton Village is a compact community at the base and sides of Jackson Hole Mountain Resort. There are several lodging options for all varieties of vacations. The hospitable, traditionally Bavarian ❄ 🍷 ⅼⅼ **Alpenhof Lodge** ($$$/$$$$, 1-800-732-3244 or 307-733-3242, May to October/December to April) is one of the older lodges serving the ski area and follows the opening and closing of the resort. Forty-two welcoming rooms typically include hot and cold European breakfasts, delivered to rooms in the slow season. The outdoor heated pool and hot tub remain open during the winter; an indoor sauna and massage services are also available. A bistro on the second floor serves lunch, casual dinner, and great Après ski fare. Live entertainment often graces the grounds during ski season.

The super-friendly ♿ 🍷 ⅼⅼ **Teton Mountain Lodge & Spa** ($$$/$$$$, 1-800-631-6271 or 307-734-7111) has 145 rooms of several varieties. Lodge rooms are traditional hotel rooms with lots of extras. Alpine suites are studio-style efficiencies with full kitchen. Sundance junior suites have king beds, kitchenettes, whirlpool tubs, and first- or second-floor views of the valley. The lodge's one- and two-bedroom suites come with a full kitchen, and the three-bedroom and penthouse suites are beyond a home away from home. Other perks include concierge services, a fitness center, indoor and outdoor pools, a massage and spa center, steam room, and breakfast-package rates. The Cascade Restaurant offers new Western cuisine, each entrée prepared fresh to order; in summer you can choose to dine al fresco amid views of the Gros Ventres. Another gem on the mountainside, the ♿ ⅼⅼ **Snake River Lodge & Spa** ($$$$, 1-800-445-4655 or 307-732-6090), features 140 rooms and several off-site condominiums. Lodging options range from the standard Lodge Rooms to Residence Suites. There is an indoor-outdoor heated pool and, as the name implies, a full-service spa. The Game Fish Restaurant (B/L/D) serves to guests and the public. With ♿ ❄ ⅼⅼ **Four Seasons Resort Jackson Hole** ($$$$, 1-800-295-5281 or 307-732-5000), the name says it all, and the luxury comes in a wide array of room options and variety of packages, including bed & breakfast. A spa, restaurant, two lounges, and ski-in and -out access to the mountain are a few of the many perks; weddings, business retreats, and other celebrations are common here. Beagle-sized or smaller dogs are allowed.

Victor, Idaho: Shona **Kasper's Kountryside Inn** ($/$$, 208-787-2726) consists of two peaceful and private three-room suites that can sleep up to four, full kitchens, cheery furnishings, and large viewing windows less than a mile from central Victor. At the 🐾 **Fox Creek Inn B&B** ($$/$$$, 208-787-3333 or 307-413-3583) country luxury is inspired by the European inns Julie Boisseau has visited and her gourmet day-starters are from a French cooking course she attended in Avignon. 🐾 **Moose Creek Ranch** ($$/$$$, 208-787 6078 or 208-881-3206) has it all: pavilion canvas tents, cabins, a five-bedroom home, a handful of RV sites, and a place to bunk your horse, all on the banks of a beautiful creek. The heavy cloth camping tents make for nice "roughing it."

Driggs, Idaho: We mention the two chains in town—the ♿ **Best Western Teton West** ($$, 1-800-780-7234 or 208-354-2363, May to September) and the ♿ **Super 8 Teton West** ($$, 1-800-800-8000 or 208-354-8888) because sometimes all you need is a bed and pillow or familiarity. Both are owned by the same company and offer basically the same amenities: indoor pool, hot tub, coffeemakers, micro-fridge, cable TV on flat screens, a laundry facility, and the ubiquitous free continental breakfast. The major difference is that Super 8 is open year-round and a little less expensive while the Best Western, a little more duded up, is only open during the summer season and has a few hot items in the breakfast buffet. They are serious about their no-pets rule.

John and Nancy Nielson welcome you to 🐾 **The Pines Motel Guest Haus** ($, 1-800-354-2778 or 208-354-2774), their year-round European-esque hamlet of seven small rooms—each with fridge, microwave, phone, cable TV, and privileges to the large hot tub. The 🐾 🌸 **Teton Valley Cabins** ($$, 1-866-687-1522 or 208-354-8153) are exceptionally reasonable

lodgettes in a variety of sizes and shapes, 20 units in all, including six standard motel-type rooms and seven log duplexes with kitchenettes that share a porch. It is located on Ski Hill Road 1 mile from "downtown" Driggs, you'll also find an outdoor hot tub, laundry, and homey picnic area with horseshoes, volleyball, and grill.

Alta/Grand Targhee: When you say Alta, you really mean Grand Targhee, the ski area and reason this little mountain community exists. It has no stores, one restaurant/bar/grill, and limited lodging options. You can't beat the location in the undulating pine- and aspen-bathed foothills of the Tetons, about 6 miles east of Driggs, Idaho, barely inside the Wyoming border. **Targhee Lodge Resort** (1-800-827-4433 or 307-353-2300, June to September/November to April) is actually three lodges in one, with check-in at the same desk and outdoor pool and hot tub shared by all three properties. There are four restaurants (at least two are open in the summer) and all three properties are ski-in and ski-out to Targhee's lifts. The Targhee ($$) is suited for the budget-conscious, with 15 standard motel rooms. Sioux Lodge ($$$/$$$$) comprises 32 high-end condominiums that come in three styles: studio, loft, and two-bedroom. And the newest of the three is Teewinot Lodge ($$$), 48 spacious rooms and a small lobby fireplace with comfortable seating. The resort also rents vacation properties off the mountain. *Note:* Rates increase during music festival weekends and rooms book quickly.

The **Alta Lodge B&B** ($$, 1-877-437-2582 or 307-353-2582 or 805-245 8531), owned and run by Dee Cotton, is made up of four large, comfortable bedrooms and unobstructed views of the west side of the Tetons through large picture windows. A full country breakfast will prepare you for the slopes 8 miles away, whether you're skiing or hiking. **Wilson Creekside Inn B&B** ($, 307-353-2409) is a 180-acre working sheep ranch and country farm turned into a four-room B&B on Teton Creek, a mere 5 miles from Grand Targhee. Credit cards are not accepted.

BEST ALTERNATIVE LODGING OUTSIDE THE PARK

Moran: Brad and Joanne Luton own ♿ **Luton's Teton Cabins** ($$$$, 307-543-2489, May to October), 13 attractive, authentic Western log cabins 4 miles east of Moran, near Grand Teton's North Entrance. The cabins, which look like they belong, are surrounded by national forest lands and are renowned for seclusion, quiet, their central location, and views of the Teton Range; horse boarding is available. Credit cards are not accepted.

Three guest ranches on Buffalo Valley Road are listed from closest to farthest from the park beginning with the ♿ **Heart Six Ranch** ($$$$, 1-888-543-2477 or 307-543-2477), open year-round in the Buffalo Valley. It comprises 14 modern, Western cabins and hundreds of horses and mules for packing on thousands of acres of public lands. The family-oriented ranch offers horseback riding, archery, target shooting, float trips, fishing the Buffalo Fork River, backcountry adventures, and campfires with nightly entertainment. In winter, the focus shifts to snowmobiling and hunters come in the fall to trek the nearby Bridger-Teton National Forest and wilderness area. Off-season options are more flexible with reduced rates and meals offered à la carte after August. Owned by the same family, **Buffalo Valley Ranch and Café** ($$$,

1-888-543-2477 or 307-543-2062) has three well-kept, remodeled apartment units on the 1908 homestead site overlooking the Buffalo Fork River. The ranch is designed to get guests outdoors, so there are no phones or TVs, just a washer and dryer for cleaning up after a day in the mountains or on the river. In front of the triplex is the year-round café (307-543-2062), originally a store-home combo known to be frequented by "scalawags, renegades, discharged soldiers, and pre-destined stinkers." A fly shop is next door. **Turpin Meadow Ranch** ($$/$$$$, 1-800-743-2496 or 307-543-2000, June to March) is on 32 acres of seclusion, natural beauty, and serenity. There are 13 charmingly rustic log cabins, a lodge, and a restaurant that serves three meals daily. An activities list includes horseback riding, fly-fishing, snowmobiling, and cross-country skiing. The ranch divides its operations into three seasons: summer, fall (hunting), and winter (snowmobiling packages).

More of a small village, ♿ 🍴 **Togwotee Mountain Lodge** ($$$/$$$$, 1-800-543-2847 or 307-543-2847), 16 miles east of the park, is a full-service resort with a concession permit from the Bridger-Teton National Forest. There are 28 lodge rooms and suites and 54 roomy, detached log cabins with stocked kitchenettes, front porches, and grills—a place to call home while you spend your days playing outdoors. Hiking, fishing, riding, rafting, and cookouts in summer give way to dog sledding, snowcat skiing, and guided snowmobiling tours into Yellowstone in the winter. The Grizzly Grill ($$/$$$, B/L/D) and the Red Fox Saloon ($/$$, L/D) are equipped to satisfy your hunger and thirst; even vegetarians are accommodated. A gas station and convenience store are also part of the village.

Kelly: The ⚔ ⚘ **Flat Creek Ranch** ($$$$, 1-866-522-3344 or 307-733-0603, May to September) is proudly owned by Marcia Kunstel and Joe Albright, a descendant of former Yellowstone National Park superintendent Horace Albright. Five small historic guest cabins, maximum capacity 15, are on 160 acres at the end of a bumpy four-wheel-drive road, remote and surrounded entirely by public lands. Stays can be seven nights beginning on a Friday or Monday, four nights from Monday to Thursday, or a three-night Friday to Sunday getaway. Rates include three meals each day with wine or beer, fly-fishing and gear, trail rides, and shuttles to and from town and the airport. Swimming and canoeing on a nearby lake are options. The Albright family has owned the ranch since the 1920s; they make it a point to ensure that guests enjoy the area as it has been enjoyed since the property's inception. Another rod-and-hoof dude ranch, the ⚘ **Gros Ventre River Ranch** ($$$$, 307-733-4138, May to October), surrounded by wilderness and national forest land, is home to four log cabins and five log lodges along the Gros Ventre River, with 2 miles of private river access and two stocked ponds. Karl and Tina Weber's cabins were brought to the site from the second-oldest dude ranch in the valley and remodeled for a contemporary Western look and feel. Rates include meals, wine, riding, canoeing, fishing, and cookouts. The ranch just missed being buried by the 1925 landslide that created Slide Lake, visible from the lodge. Weeklong stays are required during peak season, three nights are OK early or late season. Credit cards are not accepted.

Another all-inclusive former working ranch reborn into retreat lodging for up to 30 is 🐾 **Goosewing Ranch** ($$$$, 1-888-733-5251 or 307-733-5251, June to September). It's situated on a remote 50 acres in the Gros Ventre Valley, surrounded by wilderness and national forest, with an abundance of wildlife and outdoor play options such as trail rides, archery, hiking, mountain biking, fishing, wagon rides, cookouts, hot tub soaking, and swimming in an outdoor heated pool. The menu is seasonally varied, and meals are complemented by beer, wine, and liquor. Three-night minimum stays begin on Sunday or Thursday, four-night stays on Sunday or Wednesday, and weekly stays are Sunday to Sunday. **Red Rock Ranch** ($$$$, 307-733-6288, June to September), surrounded by national forest and wilderness in the Gros Ventre Mountains, has 10 cabins for groups of up to 25 for six-night all-inclusive stays and two-night minimums in September. David and Debbie McKenzie like to entertain guests with riding, hiking, trout fishing on Crystal Creek, mountain biking, swimming in the ranch's pool, hot tubbing, cookouts, campfires, and nature activities as well as gourmet meals served family-style.

Situated at the south end of Mormon Row are the ⚘ **Moulton Ranch Cabins** ($$/$$$, 307-733-3749, May to September). These are five extremely popular log cabins on prettier-than-a-picture grounds with almost larger-than-life views of the Tetons as background. The 1-acre property, often visited by bison, is at the base of Blacktail Butte and about 100 yards south of the famous Moulton Barn, which can be rented for special events. Fifth-generation Jackson Hole resident Ron Davler owns and runs the **Anne Kent Cabins** ($$$, 307-733-4773), three decidedly rustic log buildings in this tiny and eclectic community. The views are astonishing and the cabins are

The Moulton Barn framed by the Tetons is a Holy Grail for photographers.

difficult to book. Credit cards are not accepted.

Wilson: **Trail Creek Ranch** ($$$, 307-733-2610, June to September) is a working horse ranch with quite a history, hidden away on 260 acres in the mountains yet only 10 miles from Jackson. Betty Woolsey, captain of the first women's Olympic ski team, bought the land for its powdery slope and turned it into a dude ranch for fellow outdoor enthusiasts. When she died in 1977 she put her 270-acre parcel in a conservation easement so that it would remain pristine and wildlife-friendly. There are two distinct stand-alone cabins and five rooms in different buildings. Views from the porches, serenity, trail rides, and a heated swimming pool complete the package.

Teton Village: Sleep on the cheap in bunk or private rooms available in summer, fall, and winter seasons at 🐾 **The Hostel** ($, 307-733-3415) where you can select king rooms for two, quads with four twins, or shared bunk rooms for men, women, and both.

Camping
Jackson: The **Wagon Wheel Village RV Park and Campground** ($, 1-800-562-1878 or 307-733-4588, May to October) is a 40-site campground that's part of a larger lodging facility on the banks of Flat Creek, a short walk from the Town Square. The campground has shower and restroom facilities a short walk from the main village.

Moran: The **Grand Teton Park RV Resort** ($, 1-800-563-6469 or 307-733-1980) east of Moran offers 50-amp pull-through RV sites, a hot tub, seasonal pool, showers, recreation room, grocery store, playground, and various rental equipment for outdoor fun.

Hoback Junction: About 13 miles south of Jackson is the Snake River Park **KOA** ($, 1-800-562-1878 or 307-733-7078, April to October), near the renowned whitewater stretch of the Snake River Canyon. Tent sites are grassy and secluded; rates vary depending on season.

Victor, Idaho: Teton Valley Campground (208-787-2847) has full hook-up pull-throughs, wireless Internet, a heated pool, showers, laundry, and a recreation room. Camping cabins are available.

Forest Service Campgrounds

The Bridger-Teton National Forest has 18 campgrounds in the Jackson Hole area, 12 on the Jackson Ranger District and 6 on the Buffalo Ranger District. Coming south from Yellowstone, top choices in the Buffalo district include the intimate nine-site **Hatchet**, off US 26/287 about 8 miles east of Moran Junction on the Buffalo Fork River—great for fishing and its views of the Tetons. Farther south, on the north shore of Lower Slide Lake and at the end of the pavement on the Gros Ventre Road, is 20-site **Atherton Creek**, on the shores of Slide Lake. Continuing up the Gros Ventre, **Red Hills** has 10 sites along the river. Up next is **Crystal Creek**, a 6-site spot set amid the aspens near Soda Lake and the highest campground along the river, about 25 miles northeast of Jackson. Farther south, after a drive through the National Elk Refuge, is quiet **Curtis Canyon**, a great spot to watch hang gliders shove off from Lookout Point. **Coal Creek**, on the other side of Teton Pass but still in Wyoming, is a primitive campground with great access to Jackson and trails on the pass.

Local Flavors

DINING INSIDE THE PARK

Colter Bay Village: Hearty eaters will appreciate the all-you-can-eat breakfast buffet, and lighter partakers will appreciate the à la carte menu at **John Colter Ranch House** ($$, 307-543-3335, B/L/D, June to September). Lunches are reasonable, and your typical meat choices headline the dinner menu: steaks, prime rib, bison, fish, and chicken. The new Ranch House now has a small full bar attached, with table service as well as bar tables from which you can order bits and bites up to 11 PM. The Southwestern-seasoned buffalo flank steak cooked to order and laid in a black bean cake reportedly is well above average. The restaurant/bar has a cafeteria feel, with plenty of trees and parking lot to view out the glassy exterior.

Jenny Lake: Paradoxically an unpretentious group of cabins surrounding a compact, nothing-fancy log lodge, ❧ Jenny Lake Lodge ($$$$, 307-733-4647, B/L/D, May to October) is undoubtedly the most exquisite dining in either park, giving Jackson chefs a run for their money. Dinners, by reservation only, are also the most expensive in the area, but if it's in your budget you won't be disappointed. Lodging (also on the high end of high) does include a gourmet breakfast and the five-course dinner, but for nonlodge guests there is prix fixe pricing around $23 for breakfast and $77 for dinner. If you are watching your wallet, go for lunch, served from 12 PM to 1:30 PM, when the à la carte menu is more

Huckleberry margaritas add punch to the views at Jackson Lake Lodge.

casual—but reservations are a good idea.

Jackson Lake: At Jackson Lake Lodge you'll find three better-than-park-average eating establishments. The 🍸 **Mural Room** ($$$/$$$$, 1-800-628-9988 or 307-543-3100, B/L/D), named for the early-West work of Carl Roters, who was commissioned by John D. Rockefeller Jr. to adorn his "new lodge," has top-notch continental and regional cuisine that completes the view-with-a-room. Breakfast and lunch are what you would expect while dinner is meat-centric with specialties of buffalo prime rib or rack of lamb. Look for moose, elk, and beaver in Willow Flats below the lodge. An American 1950s-style diner, 🍸 **Pioneer Grill** ($$, 307-543-2811 ex 3463, B/L/D) is a place to perch on a green-vinyl and chrome stool and either look across the U-shaped counter at your neighbor's plate, or into the long aluminum-clad kitchen. You'll find a surprisingly interesting menu that runs the gamut, a separate kid's menu, and a take-out window for convenience. There can be a line during prime dining hours and they don't take reservations; we've

The Buffalo Valley Café near Moran is trying to make a go of it year-round.

Leek's Marina and Pizzeria is famed for its pizza and views of Jackson Lake.

been known to order to go and take it to a table on the deck. The 🏅 **Blue Heron Bar** ($$, L/D) is one of our favorite places to kick back with a huckleberry margarita and contemplate the grandness of the Tetons, either through the expansive windows or on the deck, mosquitoes permitting. The bar menu has finger food and small plates; we like the sushi rolls.

Signal Mountain: We commend and recommend 🏅 **Peaks Restaurant** at Signal Mountain Lodge ($$, 307-543-2831 ex 220, D, May to October) for their healthier, sustainable, or organic ingredients and reasonable pricing. Everything is good, and the menu changes throughout the season depending on available local ingredients. The views of Mount Moran, Jackson Lake, and the Teton Range aren't bad, either. At the **Trapper Grill** ($/$$, 307-543-2831, B/L/D) savor a casual, good-for-you-and-the-environment

meal while sitting on the deck gazing at the Tetons mirrored on Jackson Lake. **Deadman's Bar** ($/$$, L/D) has the same menu as the grill but is more of a hidey-hole, with a fireplace and one of the few TVs in the park—often tuned to sporting events. Their claim to fame: blackberry margaritas and a mountain of nachos (bean, chicken, or beef). If you're not expecting fine dining or even table service, **Leek's Marina and Pizzeria** ($$, 307-543-2494, L/D, May to September) will deliver for the hungry. Located near the lake bank, you can watch all the boat activity from the deck tables or inside while you imbibe. Leek's tends to be busy and it's sometimes difficult to obtain a table.

Moose: For pure unadulterated views of the Tetons, nothing tops the deck at 🏅 **Dornan's Moose Pizza Pasta Company** ($$, 307-733-2415 ex 204, L/D). It's a terrific place to regroup, the food is quite good, and it's especially tasty after a day hike or a scenic float on the Snake River. Indoor quarters can be cramped and the bar stools full, so head for the upstairs outdoor tables with the million-dollar view. Next door is Dornan's Wine Shoppe (307-733-2415 ex 202), which claims the largest wine selection in northwest Wyoming—purchased wine is permitted at tables (no corkage) in the restaurant. It's also allowed at **Dornan's Moose Chuckwagon** (307-733-2415 ex 203, B/L/D, June to October), where they have been serving Western-style meals from an open-air kitchen since 1948. Locals and visitors like to carbo-load on breakfasts of eggs, meat, all-can-you-eat pancakes, biscuits, and French toast. Lunches are quick and dinners are cooked in Dutch ovens over fire (except Fridays and Saturdays, when they have private events). The Dornan's community is open year-round, with the exception of the chuckwagon and bicycle shop.

BEST DINING OUTSIDE THE PARK

Jackson: Does anyone in Jackson Hole have a kitchen? With more than 100 dining choices, a staggering number for a town of 8,650, and more than a few that could blend seamlessly into Portland or San Francisco, it's close to a foodie's nirvana. The competition is good news for diners. Naturally, Jackson has its share of Western-style eateries with meat entrees: grass-fed beef, bison, elk, wild game, etc. Yet many restaurants will make you forget you're in the land of rodeos, ranches, and wild animals. Because of the prolific number, we've broken them into categories: Grab and Go, Best in Breakfast, Best for Lunch, Ethnic Excellence, Formal Fine Dining, Steakhouses, and Spe-

cialty Dining. Our picks aren't entirely based on the best food, some are simply must-eat stops for ambiance, history, and/or reputation. Be aware, however, that few restaurants in Jackson Hole are known for friendly service. Some are better than others, and some are ridiculously rude. We suggest that you overlook the attitudes and enjoy the altitude instead!

For *Grab and Go,* you can find a bounty of healthy choices at **Jackson Whole Grocer** ($, 307-733-0450). **Backcountry Provisions** ($, 307-734-9420, B/L) is good for take-out specialty sandwiches and puts emphasis on prepping for outdoor adventures—when was the last time you saw Braunsweiger on the ingredients list? At ❧ **Pearl Street Meat and Fish** ($, 307-733-1300, B/L) you can BYO (build your own) sandwich of meats—most are natural and without hormones or additives—imported cheeses, and unusual breads. Or you can rely on their tried and true combinations. The Teton Club, Sicilian, and grilled steak are rave-worthy. Three to six house-made soups are prepared daily, and they have a healthy salad bar, sans iceberg lettuce. Picnic lunches can be ordered with 24-hour notice; catering options are also available.

For *Best in Breakfast* class, ❧ **Nora's Fish Creek Inn** ($$/$$$, 307-733-8288, B/L/D) (actually in Wilson) is always near the top of anyone's list, as witnessed by the usually full parking lot. The authentic log interior, colorful lamps, and fireplace provide ambiance and warmth; breakfasts are the real deal and easy on the budget. Dinner specialties include elk tenderloin, free-range organic chicken, rack of lamb and baby back ribs with house BBQ sauce, trout prepared five ways, and the always-popular buffalo burger. Reservations are recommended for six or more. 🎖 **The Bunnery** ($/$$, 855-286-6379 or 307-734-0075, B/L/D) is best-known as the healthy breakfast stop, plating up large servings and exceptional baked goods. Many bakery items are simply made from "O.S.M." (oats, sunflower, and millet), including the bread for their hefty sandwiches. You can't go wrong, but if you ask Jeff his fav, it would be the not-as-healthy coffee cake; Sherry loves their granolas. A go-to for locals and visitors is **Pearl Street Bagels** ($, 307-739-1218 (Jackson) or 307-739-1261 (Wilson), B/L) for espresso, sandwiches, bagels, and their version of schmeers; just don't ask for a toasted bagel. Both locations have limited seating, so expect to stand or lounge outside because this is the first place many go for their first shot of morning java. If you need a big honkin' meal in the morning, **Bubbas Bar-B-Que** ($/$$, 307-733-2288, B/L/D) is the place. It's soooo busy and family-friendly, by supper time it can get messy. Later in the day, if you have a hankerin' for smoked meats and sauce, this will do—don't forget the buttermilk pie. Jackson's original coffeehouse is **Shades Café** ($, 307-733-2015, B/L) in an original log cabin with eclectic, reclaimed furniture and shady seating under the willow tree in warmer weather.

For midday or later, casual, and largely family-friendly places (*Best for Lunch*) we have included several choices. Need Internet access and a pick-me-up? Wander into **Café Boheme** ($, 307-733-5282, B/L) for lattes, crepes, Euro-style sandwiches, and paninis; they also serve wine and beer and have a happy hour from 1 to 3 PM. Trendy 🎖 **Betty Rock** ($, 307-733-0747, L/D) slings sandwiches, salads, and wraps in regular, gluten-free, or veggie style; they offer the same dietary choices on their hand-tossed

pizzas Thursday nights, and recently added beer and wine to the mix. The **Virginian Restaurant** ($/$$, 307-733-4330, B/L/D), or simply the "Virg" to the many locals who frequent it, will do right by ya with heapin' helpings of good 'ol traditional eats.

Mountain High Pizza Pie ($$, 307-733-3646, L/D) makes its own white or whole-wheat dough daily, puts together a substantial deep-dish or thin-crust pizza, and will deliver after 5 PM. Subs, calzones, salads, beer, and wine make for difficult choosing. You'll find limited seating inside and a dozen or so picnic tables outside during warmer weather. Owner Bill Field likes to note that a more famous Bill, former President Clinton, once stopped in for a pie. **Sweetwater Restaurant** ($$/$$$, 307-733-3553, L/D) is another popular spot for lunch in the summer with its outdoor dining on a patio shaded by a large aspen tree and enclosed by a tall hedge for privacy. Housed in a log cabin, the inside is rustically warm and is known for such "cowboy comfort food" as elk medallions, bison New York, and speedgoat (antelope). They don't kick dust on the vegetarians—just vegans—and dinner reservations are helpful. The National Museum of Wildlife Art, a gorgeous museum carved into the hillside north of Jackson overlooking the National Elk Refuge, is home to amazing art exhibits and the **Rising Sage Café** ($, 307-733-8649, L) with its better than you'd expect S-S-S-S menu (sandwiches, soups, salads, specialty items). Rising Sage's Tapa Tuesdays ($$, 307-732-5434, D) are from 5:30 PM to 9 PM year-round, a ton of fun, and reservations are appreciated.

Departing away from the Euro-centric and reaching toward more *Ethnic Excellence* in global cuisine, we offer **Merry Piglets Mexican Grill**

($/$$, 307-733-2966, L/D), which prides itself on serving authentic scratch Mexican in the valley for nearly four decades using no MSGs or lard. Homemade sauces and twisted cowgirl dip are *muy rico;* they have a long list of menu items with a fair number of fish and vegetarian choices. For fresh, fast Mexican/American food, **Pica's Mexican Taqueria** ($/$$, 307-734-4457, B (Sunday)/L/D) is a favorite local hangout. The daily happy hour from 3:30 to 5:30 PM is a good time to check out their famous margaritas. Although there is a ton of cultural diversity on the list (tika masala, curry, veggie pho, somosas, burrito mole, Korean wontons), eat at **Lotus Café** ($$, 307-734-0882, B/L/D) for the delicious and wholesome dietary flexibility: vegan, vegetarian, gluten free, nondairy, organic, etc., and the flatbread pizzas—or for their bowls.

Hip with the insiders and a find for outsiders is **Ignite** ($$/$$$, 307 734-1997, D), which lays claim to fresh fish, sushi, exotic cocktails, and a wine shop with no corkage fee applied to dinner. Reservations are absolutely recommended at casual ❧ **Nikai Sushi** ($$, 307-734-6490, D), the preferred Asian grill for fresh and fabulous food, a full bar, good sake, fish flown in daily, and $6 rolls during the off-season. For not-so-typical Thai dishes, in a brewpub no less, try **Thai Me Up** ($$, 307-733-0005, L (weekdays)/D) with their good tap list and full bar concocting such creations as the Thai Bloody Mary and Thaigaritta. **Bon Appe Thai** ($$, 307-734-0245, L (Monday to Saturday)/D) is a little nook of a coffee shop–type joint dishing up authentic and innovative Thai, and also beer and wine. For Italian, we suggest ❧ **Nani's Cucina Italiana** ($$$, 307-733-3888, D) where the mother-daughter team of Carol and Camille prepare

regional and classic cuisine complemented by a full bar that also serves from the seasonally changing menu. Save some tummy space for the *tiramisu,* three heaps of oozing deliciousness in the shape of Grand, Middle, and South Tetons.

As you might expect, a plethora of *Formal Fine Dining* is available in Jackson Hole. The ❧ **Blue Lion** ($$$$, 307-733-3912, D) excels in rack of lamb, but the eclectic and enticing dinners also rank high for elk, fresh fish, and vegetarian entrees. Patio dining in summer makes it even more popular, and reservations are necessary. Always on the top-10 list is the trendy ❧ **Snake River Grill** ($$$/$$$$, 307-733-0557, D), an intimate, special-occasion restaurant touting an ever-changing, seasonal, and organic menu with an emphasis on local ingredients, careful preparation, and presentation with rustic flair. We like to make a meal of starters at the bar accompanied by their dynamite cocktails. *Note:* Reservations are accepted up to 60 days in advance, and the grill is closed in November and April. **Rendezvous Bistro** ($$$, 307-739-1100, D) is a sophisticated yet comfortable American bistro where locals go to see and be seen. Oysters on the half-shell, shooters, and tuna tartare are popular, as is the meatloaf or daily specials offered by chef Roger Freedman, originally from Snake River Grill; reservations are recommended. ❧ **The Kitchen** ($$/$$$, 307-734-1633, D), formerly Blu' Kitchen, serves American modern cuisine with a crudo (raw) bar and a focus on fish and the freshest seasonal ingredients. Jarrett Schwartz is thought by some to be the most innovative chef in the valley, and we won't argue; reservations are a good idea. A local favorite, ❧ **Koshu Wine Bar** ($$, 307-733-5283, D), has a soothing, metro-friendly décor in shades of slate and steel, and prepares Pan-Asian cuisine. It's a little hard to find in back of the Jackson Hole Wine Company, but it's very vino-friendly due to a wine list consisting of whatever you choose from the shelves, with a $10 corkage fee or many by-the-glass choices. Koshu is also known for sake cocktails integrated with fresh ingredients and outdoor seating in summer. Highly recommended and owned by three passionate-about-food chefs is ⚘ **Trio Bistro** ($$$, 307-734-8038, D), where you'll be tempted by a little bit of everything, even gourmet pizza (speck and fig is a combo that sails). Another not to miss is the pan-seared Idaho trout with a side of bleu cheese fondue waffle fries or the BLT soup.

Reservations are suggested at **The Garage** ($$/$$$, 307-733-8575, D), home to diverse comfort food, with a couple veggie options, friendly servers, and a low-rider (kids) menu. Best bets: baby back ribs bathed in bourbon BBQ sauce, bangers and mash, or spinach and arugula salad. The acclaimed and awarded **Wild Sage Restaurant** ($$/$$$$, 302-733-2000, B/D) is at the Rusty Parrot Lodge near Town Square and is favored for regional and exotic cuisine, fresh seafood selections, and a Spectator's Award of Excellence wine list. With only eight tables and seating for 32, reservations are a must. Always popular, **The Cadillac Grille** ($$/$$$, 307-733-3279, L/D) has four dining options: the Garden Terrace, open in summer and overlooking the busy Town Square; the Grille Dining Room in the center of the complex; Billy's Burgers, a 1950s-style diner and home of the ½-pound burger; and the Lounge, where you can order from Billy's or the Grille. The Cadillac features big-city ambiance mixed with Western appeal, a meat-heavy menu,

wood-fired pizza, and some variety—but service can be sketchy and food sometimes disappointing.

In cowboy country there is no shortage of sizzling slabs of meat, and Jackson is no exception when it comes to *Steakhouses*. A short list of recommended steakhouses includes the historic ⚘ **Silver Dollar Grill** ($$/$$$$, 307-732-3939, B/L/D) in the Wort Hotel. It is famed for 2,032 uncirculated silver dollars from 1921 adorning the bar. History mixes with modern amenities in the form of eight televisions, a 60-inch big-screen, nightly happy hour, and live entertainment. At the grill you'll find more intimate, family-attentive dining with a somewhat innovative slate where even a vegetarian can find satisfaction. Not your run-of-the-mill meat-lovin' eatery, the **Million Dollar Cowboy Steakhouse** ($$$$, 307-733-4790, D) has been around longer than anyone can rightly remember. Currently owned by chef Kevin Gries and his wife, Stacy, the team makes the most of regionally purveyed ingredients such as wild game and Wagyu beef. The atmosphere is elegantly Western casual and kid friendly; remember to make a reservation and leave your cell phone behind. If you are into old guns, dead-head mounts, and exceptionally crafted log structures, you might really like the kinda-pricey, carnivoristic **Gun Barrel Steak and Game House** ($$$, 307-733-3287, D). Look for the famous bugling elk atop the building, if nothing else.

Looking for dinner *and* a show that's definitely frontier-centric? *Specialty Dining* starts with the **Jackson Hole Playhouse and Saddle Rock Family Saloon** ($$$$, 307-733-6994, L/D), which entertains you with gunslinging, a singing waitstaff, and gourmet Western cuisine at their rowdy playhouse. Open seasonally, each production has a menu to match, and it's mostly PG-rated fun. The **Saddle Rock Saloon** ($, 307-733-6994, L/D), nick-named the Million Penny Bar, is a great place to lift your sore feet and soak in some suds. Saddle Rock has a lovingly used, horseshoe-shaped bar with saddles for seats, a singing bar-tender, and live entertainment from 12 to 3:30 PM to boot. For a modest imita-tion of a Wild West experience, you'll find two choices: **Bar J Chuckwagon** ($$$$, 307-733-3370, D, May to Sep-tember) (reservations recommended) and **Bar-T-5 Covered Wagon Cookout** ($$$, 1-800-772-5386 or 307-733-5386, May to September) (reservations required). Bar J is a Western show fea-turing stories, poetry, yodeling, music, and an all-you-can-eat chuckwagon buffet, if you don't mind eating on speed dial. Legend has it that Bar J once served five hundred patrons in nine minutes. No alcohol is served and there is additional cost for chicken, ribs, and steak. Bar-T-5 uses horse-drawn wagons to take guests 2 miles into the Cache Creek Canyon for an all-you-can-eat Dutch-oven cookout of chicken, roast beef, potatoes, corn on the cob, Bar-T-5 beans, rolls, and brownies along with entertainment from a four-piece band. Along the way, you'll likely run into Indians, cowboys, and a yarn-spinning mountain man—entertainment well-suited to younger children and families.

Wilson Area: 🎖 Stieglers ($$$, 307-733-1071, D), back after a year's hiatus, is better than ever with true-to-life Austrian cuisine so authentic that Peter provides a mini-German lesson on the menu. Look for it at the front edge of The Aspens (formerly Jackson Hole Racquet Club) business complex between Wilson and Teton Village.

Calico Italian Restaurant & Bar ($$/$$$, 307-733-2460, L (summers) /D) is a family friendly, casual estab-lishment serving Italian and American entrees, pizza, and other tasty tidbits (citrus halibut over lobster ravioli). Fireside and deck dining, specialty cocktails, a solid wine list, micro-brews, and hearty portions give Calico a knowing nod. Next door is the **Q Roadhouse Barbeque** ($$/$$$, 307-739-0700, D), where you will find grilled meats, steaks and seafood, a full bar, and 50 wines for less than $50. (Look in *Best in Breakfast* for Nora's Fish Creek Inn, also a great dinner choice.)

Teton Village: Another fine Italian option in Jackson Hole is 🎖 Osteria ($$$, 307-739-4100, D), which bakes wood-oven pizza in front of diners. It has a great variety of entrees, a solid wine list, and amazing fried Brussels sprouts that even Jeff will eat. We like to split a pizza and antipasti at the bar, but the formal dining is quite nice. At the Alpenhof's 🎖 **Dietrich's Bar & Bistro** ($/$$, 307-733-3242, L/D), the house specialty is cheese and dark chocolate fondue. Swiss ambiance right down to the wooden cutout panels and unusually friendly hospitality fit the old-fashioned, Euro ski resort model, without the high prices. Swiss special-ties such as schnitzels and strudels plus lively music on weekends in winter make for memorable feasting. For more intimate fine dining at the Alpen-hof, look into a reservation at **Alpen-rose Restaurant** ($$$, 307-733-3242, B/D). Japan native Masa Kitami deftly plates authentic nigiri, tight rolls, sashimi, tempura, and soups at **Masa Sushi** ($$, 307-732-2962, D), on the bottom floor of the Inn at Jackson Hole. Popularity and limited seating make reservations necessary; both the

Traditional steaks are the mainstay fare at the Knotty Pine in Victor.

inn and restaurant are closed during the shoulder seasons (fall and spring).

Heading up the side of the mountain, ✪ **Cascade Grill House and Spirits** ($$$, 307-732-6932, B/L/D) at Teton Mountain Lodge is on our list for nouveau Western cuisine supported by regional ingredients that encourage you to "gather, savor and celebrate." Breakfasts and lunch are not only reasonably priced, but a bit reflective of dining out as a special occasion. Dinner will have you choosing between wild game, steak, and seafood as well as inside seating or mountainside views of the Gros Ventres from the heated outdoor patio. Lunch suggestion: a twisted reuben made with grilled wild Alaskan salmon, pickled onion and fennel, dill havarti, and smeared with tomato aioli. Though some locals say it's lost its touch, the **Mangy Moose Restaurant and Saloon** ($$/$$$, 307-733-4913,

L/D) is definitely a mainstay and the saloon a favorite après ski stop. The food is better at dinner than lunch; summer deck seating with views of village activity is a lure.

High-altitude scenery, panoramic views of Jackson Hole, and exquisite dining at 9,000 feet after a seven-minute ride on the Bridger Gondola are the draw at **Couloir** ($$$$, 307-739-2675, D) and **The Deck** ($$, 307-739-2675, D, June to September). Drink specials and an outdoor grill at The Deck make for sit-back-and-enjoy-the-views imbibing; Couloir is peak fine dining for a high price. To get to **Corbet's Cabin** ($, 307-739-2654, B/L) take the nine-minute Aerial Tram ride to the summit for good grab 'n go snacks or a fresh-off-the-griddle waffle with an assortment of toppings; the views of Grand Teton from the deck are exceptional. Be sure to make a reservation and dress smartly casual for **The Grill at Amangani** ($$$$, 307-734-7333, B/L/D) in the ultraluxury resort, where regional cuisine is in complete harmony with its surroundings. Menu selections change seasonally, utilizing fresh produce and regionally produced organic foods, and are accompanied by an award-winning wine list.

Victor, Idaho: For a tiny village, Victor has a remarkable assortment of excellent dining establishments. An institution in town is the **Knotty Pine Supper Club** ($$, 208-787-2866, D), famed for its steaks, Kansas City BBQ, fresh seafood, and house-smoked meats with large sides of potatoes and salad. The rickety Western ambiance

Few restaurants have more unique descriptions of food-making than Spoons Bistro in Victor.

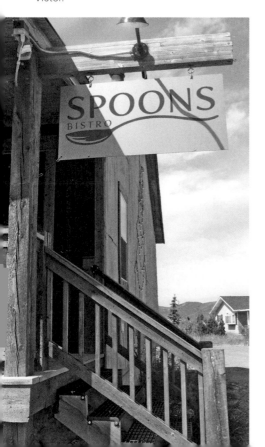

make you feel as if you've stepped into a frontier movie—though the lively bands brought in from across the country certainly give it a more contemporary country feel. At ◉ **Spoons Bistro** ($$/$$$, 208-787-2478, D) local transplant Travis and wife, Nicole, don't merely have creative American/French cuisine, they push the envelope with "molecular gastronomical experiments": champagne caviar vinaigrette with a tiny invisible membrane that tastes just like caviar, fried mayonnaise that emulsifies for a tasty sauce base, or basil "fried" in liquid nitro that is more intensely flavored than just picked. A family-friendly, scribble-on-the-table, kid's menu, deck-dining kind of place, they try to stick to the true definition of bistro. Check their Facebook page for current seasonal hours; reservations are highly recommended during peak times. Not just for breakfast, ◉ **Scratch** ($$, 208-787-5678, B/D), open Wednesday to Sunday, will keep you coming so you can try everything at least once. The cheery colors and kitschy Formica and chrome tables will brighten any mood or clear away the cobwebs, as will the homemade chai. Go to **Grumpy's Goat Shack** ($, 208-787-2092, L/D) just for the experience. If you're a hot dog hound, theirs come from Chicago—home of the best—and are topped with an array of taste bud teasing combinations. And, yes, there are live goats out back to pet. Walk on the wild side at **Wildlife Brewing and Pizza** ($/$$, 208-787-2623, L [Thursday to Sunday]/D), a pizza joint and more with their own respectable microbrews.

If we're staying in to cook or need food on the run, we love the ◉ **Victor Valley Market** (208-787-2230), which is open year round and late. It's our fav stop for stocking up on prepared goodies (baked in the backroom by the

Colorful tables and chairs brighten the morning at Scratch restaurant in Victor.

valley elves), DIY sustenance for the oven or grill, and bottles of wine or premium beer. There is a remarkable amount of food in a small space and the congenial owner makes the visit even more fun.

Driggs, Idaho: From the main strip of ID 33, Driggs looks like a disjointed collection of barely inhabited buildings with limited options for good eats. *Au contraire.* Call it Jackson envy or spillover, renegades who wanted out of the cluster, or just plain fiscal prudence. Whatever you call it, hungry consumers win in this town at the base of something grand!

Sun Dog Café ($, 208-787-3354, B/L) is a tiny, happening place, with squeezed-together tables inside and a handful of four-tops outdoors. They specialize in breakfasts ranging from granola yogurt parfaits to outa-the-pan chorizo 'n eggs, and lunches from blackened tuna Caesar to beef brisket

on Texas toast. House-baked goods in the glass case are especially tempting. Miso Hungry Café ($/$$, 208-354-8015, L) is now *only* open for lunch, so try to plan accordingly—or get the goods to go. He's from South America, she's Greek, so their menu is creative, healthy, and full of worldly flavors. Forage and Lounge ($$/$$$, 208-354-2852, D) opens with happy hour from 4 to 6 PM, which means $1 off glass pours and drafts; beef or veggie burgers come with a free beer and a complimentary glass of house wine comes with the cheese plate. A short menu is long on the unusual and has seasonal change-abouts, with vegans and special diets considered prominently. It's remarkable how many hot dishes come out of that one oven/cooktop, and without clatter. The groovy vibes, metro soothing colors, and Zen-like service make you forget you're in Idaho—as does the ginger mojito.

Coming off the slopes, try your

Irish luck at **O'Rourke's Sports Bar and Grill** ($$, 208-354-8115, B/L/D) to whet your whistle ($3 drafts) and stave off hunger pangs (fried pickles) with typical, extensive pub grub or pizza; they're also known for Sunday eggs Benedict that can be ordered with a bellini, mimosa, or bloody Mary. If you're in the mood for Thai, and don't want to drive into Jackson, give **Teton Thai** ($$, 208-787-8424, L/D) downtown a try. They're open late and have that somewhere-else feeling. For your south of the border cravings, **Hacienda Cuajimalpa** ($, 208-354-0121, L/D) will more than suffice with a typical Mexican menu. We suggest the shrimp tostada loaded with avocado, but don't expect atmosphere unless a flat-screen playing cartoon movies does it for you.

At Driggs-Reed Memorial Airport, commonly referred to as Teton Valley Airport, you'll find small jets and prop planes to watch from the windows or patio at **Warbirds Café** ($$/$$$, 208-354-2550, B (Saturday to Sunday)/L (daily)/D (Wednesday to Sunday)). One of the most highly regarded dining spots in the region, Warbirds has a seasonally changing menu known for elk and buffalo entrees as well as the chef's skilled preparation of fresh fish flown in daily. Steaks, pork porterhouse, and shrimp linguine are popular dinner choices; for breakfast, it's crab cakes Benedict and smoked trout hash. All dishes can be prepared for vegetarians. The full bar, small but thoughtful wine list, and locally produced beers on draft complete the deal. But wait, there's more: free admission to the museum of warbirds (restored and operable military planes). *Note:* 'Birds closes after Targhee Ski Hill shuts down and reopens Mother's Day weekend.

Alta/Grand Targhee, Wyoming: Alta means Grand Targhee Ski Resort, a friendly, fun, less chaotic miniature ski village at 8,000 feet, and though your options are limited they aren't less

Victor's Emporium is famous for its milkshakes.

favorable. Worth the drive up the mountain, the ❧ **Branding Iron Grill's** ($$$, 307-353-2300 ex 1368, B/L/D) menu is not extensive, but balanced. Start your day with the ample breakfast buffet (free to lodging guests) and take a break for lunch offerings of salads, wraps, grass-fed beef burgers, and hot or cold sandwiches. Dinner entrees of steak, pork, chicken, fish, or pasta will satisfy your activity-driven hunger. Seasonal specials on Friday, Saturday, and Sunday nights are screamin' deals, especially the slow-smoked Kobe prime rib din-

ner for $24. At the **Trap Bar & Grille** ($, 307-353-2300 ex 1360, L/D) "an Apre institution," check out the Teton (traditional) or Wydaho (on a bed of waffle fries) nachos or Baja fish tacos as well as your team's game on one of eight high-def flat screens. During the ski season you can grab a burger, brat, or slice of pizza at **Wild Bill's Grill** ($, 307-353-2300, B/L). Be sure to watch for special events at Targhee, such as live music in the bar, concerts on the grounds, and the brew master's dinner (recently $50 all-inclusive).

To Do

ATTRACTIONS

Jackson: Snow King Mountain's 2,500-foot **Alpine Slide** (1-800-522-5464, June to August) starts with a ride up the mountain on a chairlift, followed by 0.5 mile of twists and turns through forest and sage. Speeds are controlled by riders, so it's suitable for all ages. The slide is reached via the **Snow King Chairlift**, which takes riders to stunning views of Jackson Hole and the Tetons as well as a network of trails. Nearby **Amaze'n Jackson Hole** (307-734-0455) offers a race against the clock as well as your friends in a large maze. Squirt guns allowed by day and flashlights by night, and there's a candy store and shaved ice. **Ripley's Believe It or Not** (307-734-0000) has everything zany and wacky, much of it connected to the region, including the Flip-Flop Lodge and Bizarre Forest. The nonprofit **Jackson Hole Museum** (307-733-9605, May to October) was founded in 1958 and features local artifacts dating back to the first humans to walk the area. They offer walking tours of Jackson four days a week in the summer. Exhibits at the free **Jackson Hole Historical Society** (307-733-2414, June to September) range from the history of Plains Indians to the creation of Grand Teton National Park, along with a research library. The beautiful **National Museum of Wildlife Art** (1-800-313-9553 or 307-733-5771) overlooking the National Elk Refuge features 12 galleries with more than four thousand works of wildlife art, including paintings and sculptures. The stone and wood building was carefully constructed to fit into the sage hillside above the refuge and embody the countryside. With its rounded corners, it has the feel of an Indian kiva. In a concerted effort to avoid being known only as a tourist stop, the museum allows residents of Jackson free admission on Sundays. The museum also has the Rising Sage Café.

Teton Village: The Teton Village area has three lifts involving the dramatic inclines out the backdoor. The **Aerial Tram** (May to October) is a 10-minute enclosed ride for up to 60 people that rises more than 4,100 feet to Corbet Cabin at the summit of 10,450-foot Rendezvous Mountain. Needless to say, the views are spectacular. Only slightly less riveting and definitely more intimate is the free **Bridger Gondola** (June to September), which seats 8 and lands at the Couloir Restaurant and The Deck after climbing 2,784 feet in 7 minutes. The final option is geared to mountain bikers who want to feel the wind in their faces as they race down the hill on a trail. The **Teewinot Highspeed Quad Lift** (307-739-2654, June to September) carries 4 riders and bicycles from the Bridger Center more than 400 feet in 3 minutes to six trailheads.

RECREATION INSIDE THE PARK

Bicycling

Road Cycling: Grand Teton features 100 miles of paved roads and tremendous views for the thin-tire crowd. There isn't much variation in terrain, so don't expect a great workout. The best ride is the new 8-mile path along **Teton Park Road** from Moose to Jenny Lake. (*Note:* In late 2011 the park was considering making it mandatory for cyclists to use the path instead of the road.) From Moose, you can pedal the winding Moose-Wilson Road through aspen and pine, keeping an eye out for wildlife. Expect some teeth-rattling on the unpaved portion, but it's usually manageable with thin tires. The 3-mile **Jenny Lake Scenic Drive** is worth a side trip and the **Antelope Flats/Gros Ventre Road** loop has limited traffic and unlimited views.

Mountain Biking: If you're on fat tires, options are limited because hiking trails are off-limits. The 3-mile **Two Ocean Lake Road** ride and the 15-mile **River Road** along the Snake are outstanding experiences. For a true muscle-grinder, ride to the summit of **Shadow Mountain**, so named because the Tetons shadow it at sunset; much of the ride is outside the park, but it starts and ends inside the east boundary.

Fishing

Rivers: Exceptional fishing exists right in the heart of Grand Teton National Park on the **South Fork of the Snake River**, typically referred to simply as "the Snake" until it reaches Palisades Reservoir. Guides are at the ready to lead you to big cutthroats on the entire 80 miles from Jackson Lake to the reservoir. A beautiful tributary of the Snake that receives waters from the highest drainage in the park, the **Buffalo Fork River** in the northeast corner offers great dry-fly trout fishing for those willing to make the effort. The river is braided, flows through grizzly country, and traverses a great deal of private land outside the park, but pressure is light and the cool waters mean the fish are active during the dog days of summer.

Lakes: You name the trout, the deep and cold waters of **Jackson Lake** have it. A state-record 50-pound lake trout (actually a char called a mackinaw) was coaxed from these depths. Cutthroat, brook, and brown trout also inhabit these rich waters, best accessed by boat except in May when bank anglers have a crack at trophy trout that cruise the shores for bait fish. In summer, you'll have to drop line as deep as 200 feet to catch fish. A few coves or inlets can be fished with a fly rod from float tubes. Note that Jackson Lake is closed in October so mackinaw can spawn undisturbed. **Jenny Lake**, the most beautiful body of water in Wyoming, also has its fair share of mackinaws, cutthroats, and browns. Fish from a canoe or kayak around the edges, where the fish will lurk for insects, including a renowned flying black ant "hatch" in late June or early July. Try streamers, woolly buggers, or other submerged flies. Cutthroats will occasionally rise for a dry. Jenny Lake is an excellent choice in October when Jackson Lake is closed. **Leigh Lake** is a remote lake north of Jenny and String lakes famed for its views and solitude. Fish it the same as Jenny—with flashy streamers, woolly buggers, or other deep wet flies. A canoe will provide the best serenity; fish the inlets where waters pour off the flanks of the Tetons.

Hiking

Jackson Lake Lodge/Colter Bay Area: Colter Bay is a leisurely 8.8-mile round-trip walk through lodgepole forest and meadows along streams and past ponds. Several trails branch from the trailhead, all returning to the same place. Look for waterfowl, moose, and trumpeter swans in marshy areas. The end is Hermitage Point, which juts into Jackson Lake. **Jackson Lake Lodge** offers a popular 0.5-mile stroll that ends at a perch overlooking Jackson Lake, with Willow Flats and the Tetons in the distance. Interpretive signs are at the top of the hill.

Teton Park Road Area: **Cascade Canyon** is Grand Teton's most popular hiking area, with most visitors taking the Jenny Lake boat ride to the base of the mountains for moderate to strenuous hikes. Nearly everyone hikes the 1.1 miles to 200-foot Hidden Falls. The majority continue another 1.8 miles to Inspiration Point, which features a busy collection of yellow-bellied marmots, an occasional pika, and stirring views of the lake, Jackson Hole, and the Gros Ventre Mountains. From there, the more adventurous folks turn left and continue another 3.4 miles to Lake Solitude and the rest of the way to Hurricane Pass and views of Schoolroom Glacier, a 19-mile round-trip. The trail forks right toward **Paintbrush Canyon** and Leigh Lake, then back to Jenny Lake. Moose are common in the canyon and black bears are frequently spotted. Self-guiding maps and information are at the trailhead, and there's a fee for the boat trip across the lake.

Another breezy walk is at **Leigh Lake**, where two options are available—a 2-mile round-trip walk to the lake along the channel connecting Leigh to String Lake or a 7.4-mile adventure along Leigh's east shore northward to Bearpaw Lake. On the latter hike, Mount Moran will constantly be in view across the lake. Mosquitoes can be brutal here and bears of both types are known to frequent the area. Many visitors miss the 3.3-mile hike around skinny **String Lake** because of its proximity to Jenny and Leigh lakes, but locals like it for the solitude. This trail also serves as the starting point for the hike up Paintbrush Canyon, a 12.4-mile round-trip sojourn that encircles Holly Lake and returns. If you're looking for more, keep going on a strenuous trail to Lake Solitude and a return down Cascade Canyon for an arduous 19.2-mile affair.

Just before Moose, one of the park's most rugged trails is **Lupine Meadows**, which leads to **Garnet Canyon** and Amphitheater Lake. It's 8.2 miles to the canyon and another 1.4 to a series of glacial lakes on switchbacks. **Taggart Lake** is a popular choice for those wanting to skip the crowds at Jenny Lake. The moderate 4-mile round-trip rises on glacial moraines to Taggart and then Bradley lakes, both surrounded by burns from a 1985 fire. Several loop options are available,

A golden eagle rides thermals in Grand Teton National Park.

including along tumbling Beaver Creek. **Chapel of the Transfiguration** is a breezy 0.5-mile round-trip walk to century-old buildings on the Snake River at Menor's Ferry and a log church built in 1925. Sunday services are conducted in the summer. Other buildings include Bill Menor's old cabin and store.

Moose-Wilson Road Area: At **Death Canyon**, take your pick between the brisk 1.8-mile round-trip to the Phelps Lake overlook on a glacial moraine or the muscle-wrenching 8-mile trek into the wilderness to Static Peak Divide. From the overlook, it's another fairly steep mile down to the lake—remember that you'll have to return this way—and then 2 strenuous miles up into Death Canyon. Here the trail forks at the Death Canyon Patrol Cabin toward Static Peak Divide on steep switchbacks through whitebark pine. It's a challenging up, down, and up to the cabin built in the 1930s by the Civilian Conservation Corps for trail maintenance. A 0.5-mile distance beyond the cabin is another overlook of Death Canyon. Unlike Cascade and Death canyons, **Granite Canyon** doesn't have natural stopping points on the way to the Teton Crest. It is 10 strenuous miles along Granite Creek into subalpine meadows at Marion Lake. About ⅔ of the way up, you can backtrack to the south to where the tramway at Jackson Hole Ski Area drops off riders or head down Open Canyon to Phelps Lake. Of course, at any point you can always turn around and return to the trailhead.

Moran Junction Area: In the northeast corner of the park is **Two Ocean Lake**, where you'll get an entirely different perspective on Grand Teton than from any other trails. While most head up canyons into the Tetons, these wrap around Two Ocean and **Emma Matilda** lakes just outside the Teton Wilderness Area. The hikes range from 6.4 miles round-trip to a 13-mile journey that encompasses both lakes. The focus is lakes, forests, and wildflowers, as opposed to mountain views— though Grand View Point between the two lakes offers vistas of Mount Moran and its siblings. Black bears are common here and grizzlies have moved into the area as well.

West Side: **Teton Canyon** is a rugged 11-mile round-trip scramble up the back side of the Tetons that begins outside the park at the Teton Canyon Campground southeast of Grand Targhee Ski Resort. The trail rises to within 0.5 mile of the summit, where it becomes talus. Go the extra 0.5 mile for splendid views. Above it all is **Teton Crest**, the king of all Teton hikes. Plan to spend at least four days to cover the entire 40 miles on the west side of the Tetons. Only a portion of the trail actually enters the park, and once you're on the trail, it's moderately challenging compared to the canyon hikes that intersect the route. The southernmost terminus is Teton Village, and the trail goes to Paintbrush Canyon. Most hikers wanting to walk the entire trail start either at Teton Village in the south or Paintbrush Canyon in the north, though there are numerous entry and exit points.

Rock Climbing/Mountaineering

Few experiences can match the thrill of standing atop 13,770-foot **Grand Teton** on a cloudless day, and especially on one of those rare windless days. The world stretches forever in every direction. Combined with the different challenges each peak presents, it's no wonder that climbers from around the globe bring their ropes, ice axes, and climbing bolts. More than four thousand people climb Grand Teton each year, usually in July and early August. Novices can get training and go with trained guides. Expect to pay anywhere from $750–1,000.

For less-technical climbs, hikers can reach the summits of **South and Middle Teton** in a day after spending a night at one of four campsites. Mount Moran's isolation from the others often renders it a forgotten peak, but it has several memorable routes to its 12,605-foot summit. Registration isn't necessary to climb any of the Tetons, but overnight camping requires a backcountry-use permit. As with most climbing, it's best to go early, before afternoon winds and frequent lightning storms arrive. By mid-August, anything is possible with the weather. Check with the **Jenny Lake Ranger Station** (307-739-3343) from 8 AM to 6 PM for advice, guidebooks, and information on the availability of campsites. Climbers also have an inexpensive option for lodging before making their assault: The American Alpine Club's **Grand Teton Climbers' Ranch** (307-733-7271) charges $10 per night for bunks in small cabins, cooking facilities, and hot showers; bring your own bedding and food. Reservations are recommended, and the ranch is limited to climbers only.

RECREATION OUTSIDE THE PARK

Bicycling

Road Cycling: On a clear, calm morning, visitors to Jackson will readily notice a steady stream of cyclists heading west on WY 22 through Wilson, where they begin the arduous 10 percent grade 6 miles up to **Teton Pass**. A breezier ride is to go south from Wilson on **Fish Creek Road** or from Wilson to Teton Village on a recently constructed bike path. Jackson also is in the process of developing a paved trail system.

Mountain Biking: For the fat-tire crowd, Jackson Hole is heaven. It doesn't have Moab's slickrock, but neither does it have the crowds. Black Canyon Creek is an 11-miler that's either an all lactic-burning uphill (3 miles) or hair-raising descent (8 miles), starting near the top of Teton Pass at Old Pass Road and finishing in Wilson. The views of Jackson Hole would be spectacular—if you dare look up long enough from this technical trail. Cache Creek is a 23-miler starting at the base of Snow King and winding through aspen and pine high into a meadow, where cyclists are rewarded with a sweet descent toward US 191. Those looking for something more serene will like **Dog Creek**, a relatively flat single-track that starts near Hoback Junction and continues through grasses and spruce to the base of Indian Peak. **Monument Ridge Loop** is one of the area's most popular rides, a

21-miler featuring a heady ascent and screaming descent that's all too short. Catch your breath at the fire lookout at the crest. The climb is on a paved and then gravel Forest Service road about 15 miles south of Hoback Junction; the return descent is mostly on single track. **Phillips Canyon** is an arduous and technical 14.6-miler mostly on single track with stream crossings and tough turns. For a less-strenuous version, i.e., avoiding the ascent, drive to the Phillips Pass parking lot about halfway up Teton Pass. The trailhead is 1 mile up Trail Creek Road from WY 22 at Wilson.

Fishing

Many learned anglers consider the **South Fork of the Snake River** tailwater fishery below Palisades Dam in Idaho, southwest of Jackson, to be the finest for trout in the nation. The water is big, broad, and braided, providing excellent habitat for huge fine-spotted cutthroat and brown trout, and a smattering of rainbows. One reason it doesn't receive as much publicity as the Madison and Henry's Fork is that not everyone has access to a raft or driftboat, easily the best way to fish the swift and treacherous stream. The river isn't famed for its hatches, though they do occur. The **Gros Ventre River** northeast of Jackson is a pretty freestone stream that enters the Snake just north of Jackson. Most of the best fishing for cutthroat and the occasional rainbow is downstream from Kelly to the confluence. The fish range from about 8 to 15 inches and aren't too fussy, even about dry flies. Though swift, it's suitable for wading and much of the river can be fished from the banks. Floating is not recommended. Only 15 miles long, the **Hoback River** south of Jackson nevertheless will produce—and is a solid place for the novice fly angler to experience success. Most of this meandering little freestone river is easily accessed from US 189/191. Don't let its small stature scare you off. The Hoback has many scrappy cutthroat that'll reach 13 inches, with the occasional larger trout that cruises up from the confluence with the Snake. Toss an attractor dry fly and get ready for action. Be sure to ask permission if you want to bank fish from private property.

Hang Gliding

Jackson: **Cowboy Up Hang Gliding** (307-413-4164) in Wilson offers two introductory flights in tandem with a flight instructor over Jackson Hole. The "Great" flight is taken at 2,000–2,500 feet and the "Grand" flight is at 3,000–4,000 feet. Training is offered for beginners and advanced pilots. Rental equipment also is available.

Teton Village: For an adrenaline rush try paragliding or hang gliding with a professional partner through **Jackson Hole Mountain Resort** (307-690-8726) off Rendezvous Mountain, one of 15 places in the valley where gliders ride the thermals. No experience is necessary.

Hiking

Jackson Area: **Snow King** is a 0.5-mile trail at the top of Jackson's local ski hill offering panoramic views of Jackson Hole, the Tetons, and Gros Ventres. It's around $10 to take the chairlift to the summit, or you can give your legs a workout by hiking the entire distance. Enjoy Snake River scenery, as well as rafters plying the whitewater, from **Cabin Creek**, a moderate trail that follows a Snake tributary to a low pass that offers great views of the river's drainage. **Cache Creek** is a pleasant 6-mile stroll on a forested road that follows a gurgling creek of the same name. Even though it is close to town, it has a wilderness feel. Add a few extra miles to a Cache Creek hike on the breezy **Putt-Putt** trail just outside of Jackson. **Ski Lake** is an excellent 4.6-mile hike near Teton Pass that's suitable for families looking for more than a walk around town. The reward is spectacular views of Jackson Hole and a pretty alpine lake. The elevation gain is modest and evenly spread.

Hoback Junction Area: Soak weary muscles in one of two hot springs after an easy 2-mile hike in a lush valley on the **Granite Creek Falls** trail, east of Hoback Junction. Granite Falls has a primitive rock-and-sand natural hot springs where it's possible to soak under warm falls, though most prefer the 104-degree developed pool at Granite Hot Springs up the trail.

River Running

About 25 miles south of Jackson, the mighty **Snake River** quickens its pulse in a headlong rush for Idaho. For 8 miles, the river roils and boils in a series of Class III and Class IV drops, most notably Big Kahuna and Lunch Counter rapids. The popular journey starts swiftly at West Table Creek Campground with the soon-to-follow Station Creek Drop, S-Turns, and Cutbanks. It mellows in the middle and then collects its debt with Big Kahuna, Lunch Counter, Rope, and Champagne rapids. The river puts on its best show of force in June before becoming more sedate in August. The 3.5-hour trips range from $40–85, depending on such amenities as food. Do-it-yourselfers who want isolation might consider the challenging Class III Southgate stretch where the river leaves Yellowstone and hurries toward Flagg Ranch.

Skiing (Alpine)

Think Utah has the best deep powder? Try a day at **Grand Targhee Ski Resort** (1-800-827-4433 or 307-353-2300) on the west side of the Tetons. It's possible to ski in powder up to your eyebrows after a storm rolls in and hits the mountains. Grand Targhee receives more than 500 inches of snow annually on 3,000 acres of terrain on Fred's Mountain and Peaked Mountain. Fred's has 1,600 acres, 400 of which are groomed. The rest is for powder hounds that savor the 2,000 vertical feet of descent. Peaked Mountain piques the interest of more skilled skiers with 2,419-foot vertical and 1,500 skiable acres, most of which are served exclusively by snowcat. Rentals and instruction are available. **Jackson Hole Mountain Resort** (1-888-333-7766 or 307-733-2292) at Teton Village is as known for the Bridger Gondola as its snow. The resort includes Rendezvous and Après Vous mountains, with more than 4,100 feet of vertical and access to more than 3,000 acres of terrain. The mountain receives about 450 inches a year and has snowmaking capability on 160 acres; snowboarding is allowed on all runs. **Snow King Resort** (1-800-522-5464 or 307-733-5200) was Wyoming's first ski area when it opened in 1939 and is known fondly as Jackson's in-town ski hill. With 1,571 feet of vertical on 400 acres, it's surprisingly steep and challenging; 60 percent of the runs are suited for advanced skiers. About ¼ of the skiable terrain is open to night skiing. The resort also has a snow-tubing park.

Skiing (Heli-skiing)

If backcountry adventure is your bag and lift lines aren't, go for the gusto in untracked country with **High Mountain Heli-Skiing** in Teton Village (307-733-3274). This outfit accesses some 305,000 acres south of the Jackson Hole Mountain Resort with helicopters. Each day features six runs spread between the Snake River, Palisades, Hoback, Gros Ventre, and Teton ranges. The six runs range from 12,000–15,000 vertical feet and are for expert skiers and snowboarders only.

Skiing (Nordic)

The **Jackson Hole Nordic Center** (1-800-443-6139 or 307-739-2629) on Village Road in Teton Village has 12 miles of mostly flat professionally groomed track and skating lines. Guided nature trips are offered.

Sled Dogs/Snowmobiles

Togwotee Snowmobile Adventures (1-877-864-9683 or 307-733-8800) features full-day treks and half-day adventures, with snowmobile/sled-dog combination packages also available. The company offers lodging at Togwotee Mountain Lodge southeast of Yellowstone National Park.

Swimming

Granite Hot Springs (307-734-7400) is a pretty mineral pool in a forested valley about 35 miles southeast of Jackson, near Hoback Junction. A maintained gravel road follows Granite Creek to the pool, which has changing rooms and a deck for sunning. Water temperatures typically are in the low 90s in the summer and about 110 in winter. From December to March you'll have to use cross-country skis or snowmobiles to access the pool. You can pitch a tent at the nearby campground and hike into the canyon, where 50-foot Granite Falls is the highlight. Granite Creek also features some primitive hot pools worth checking out.

Practical Information

CLIMATE AND WEATHER

The old axiom about weather changing every five minutes never rang truer than in the Greater Yellowstone ecosystem, where 7,500-foot-plus elevations mean it can snow in July and undulating terrain is the perfect recipe for lightning storms. Warm and sunny summer mornings can turn to rain, sleet, or even snow by afternoon. Average summer highs are in the upper 70s with lows in the mid-40s. Winter highs are in the 30s, lows below 10. Subzero weather is not uncommon. Warm jackets and rain gear are a must even in July if you're planning to leave your car, lodging, or campsite. Remember: You can always remove layers of clothing, but you can't add what you don't have. If you're caught in lightning, get away from water or beaches and leave ridges, exposed spots, and isolated trees. If that isn't possible, lay flat on the ground, preferably in a low-lying ravine. The varied topography also means weather could be dramatically different from Jackson Hole to Yellowstone. The sun can be shining in one area and a downpour occurring in another. Along with cold-weather gear, be sure to bring sunscreen and/or a hat. Don't let the cool temperatures fool you: It doesn't take long to burn under the intense sun at such high elevations.

FEES

Yellowstone and Grand Teton National Parks

Private, noncommercial automobiles: $25 (seven days, good for Yellowstone and Grand Teton)

Individual motorcycle: $20 (seven days, both parks)

Single entry (foot, bike, ski, etc.): $12 (seven days, both parks)

Yellowstone–Grand Teton Pass: $50 (valid for one year from month of purchase)

LEFT: Few locations in Yellowstone are more photographed than the Lower Falls on the Yellowstone River.

America the Beautiful Pass: $80 (valid for one year from month of purchase for all national parks and federal recreation lands)

Senior Pass: $10 (for U.S. citizens 62 and older)

Access Pass: Free for U.S. citizens and permanent residents who are legally blind or disabled; documentation required

Note: All current valid passes are accepted until expired, including the National Parks Pass, Golden Eagle Pass, Golden Age Passport, and Golden Access Passport.

Backcountry permits: $20, required for any overnight stay at the 300 backcountry campsites in Yellowstone National Park (307-344-2160); Grand Teton has 16 backcountry camping "zones" that require a $25 nonrefundable deposit for reservations (307-739-3309), which are strongly recommended and, in truth, absolutely necessary due to popularity of backcountry camping.

VISITORS CENTERS

Yellowstone National Park

Canyon Village (307-242-2550) traditionally features natural history and geology exhibits, with book sales in the lobby. The Canyon Visitors Education Center has two floors of interactive exhibits about Yellowstone's supervolcano. Open Memorial weekend to early October.

Fishing Bridge (307-242-2450) is famous for its "parkitecture" as the prototype for national park buildings. It offers animal and geological exhibits, and has books for sale. Open Memorial weekend to late September.

The bottom sign is sound advice for just about anywhere in the Parks.

Grant Village (307-242-2650) sheds insight on Yellowstone's fire history, most notably the massive 1988 blazes that burned ⅓ of the park. A film called *Ten Years after the Fire* is the highlight. Open late Memorial weekend to late September.

Madison Junction Information Station (307-344-2821) has information and a bookstore. Included is a junior ranger station with programs for children ages 5–12. Open early June to late September.

Mammoth is home to the Albright Visitor Center (307-344-2263)—the park's headquarters, named after the first superintendent, Horace Albright. This old stone building features a theater and animal exhibits. Open year-round.

Norris Geyser Basin Museum (307-344-2812) has a bookstore and exhibits about thermal features. Open Memorial weekend to late September.

Norris Museum of the National Park Ranger shows the history of rangers in the park. Watch a video and hobnob with former rangers who volunteer here. Open Memorial weekend to late September.

Old Faithful (307-545-2750) has an expansive new visitors center that showcases books, maps, videos, and the clock forecasting its namesake geyser's next eruption. Open late April to early November, then mid-December until March.

Grand Teton National Park

Colter Bay (307-739-3594) opens from 8 AM to 7 PM during peak time from early May to early September, changing to from 8 AM to 5 PM in late spring and early fall. Demonstrations, tours, and crafts are exhibited for much of the summer.

Flagg Ranch (307-543-2372) is open from 9 AM to 5:30 PM from June to August and has irregular hours from mid-December to mid-March. It is between the two parks, along the John D. Rockefeller Memorial Parkway, 16 miles north of Colter Bay.

Moose (307-739-3399) is open from 8 AM to 7 PM in the summer and from 8 AM to 5 PM spring, fall, and winter. The Craig Thomas Discovery and Visitor Center is at the south end of the park and serves as headquarters. It is home to exhibits, a relief map of the park, and a close look at the area's endangered species. The only day it closes is Christmas.

Jenny Lake (307-739-3343) stays open from 8 AM to 7 PM all summer, then from 8 AM to 5 PM in September. It's 8 miles north of Moose at the junction of Teton Park Road and is also the location of a ranger station.

SPECIAL PROGRAMS

Park-sponsored programs range from short ranger-led talks each evening to weeklong adventures into the backcountry guided by the Yellowstone Association Institute. Even if you're a regular visitor, they are worth checking out.

Road Construction

About 80 percent of Yellowstone's roads were deemed structurally deficient and in need of repair in 2012. Call the park's 24-hour Current Road Report hotline at 307-344-2117 for the latest information. In Grand Teton, call 307-739-3614.

Yellowstone National Park

Yellowstone Association Institute (307-344-2294, www.yellowstoneassociation.org) in the heart of the Lamar Valley is a nonprofit that offers classes that have turned first-time visitors into lifelong supporters. Since 1933, the institute has partnered with the Park Service to help visitors gain an understanding of the park's flora, fauna, and geology. Offerings range from in-depth field seminars to private day tours and backpacking adventures. Membership levels range from $35–5,000. Some 22,000 people worldwide belong to the organization.

Ranger-led activities (www.nps.gov/yell/planyourvisit/rangerprog.htm) take place at Bridge Bay, Canyon Village, Fishing Bridge, Gardiner, Grant Village, Lake,

Madison, Mammoth, Norris, Old Faithful, West Thumb, and West Yellowstone. In addition, a Stars Over Yellowstone program is offered on weekends at the Madison Campground amphitheater. Also check out the Ranger Adventure Hikes at Canyon Village, Fishing Bridge, Mammoth, Old Faithful, and Tower Junction. Reservations are required for many activities. Check the *Yellowstone Today* newspaper for updates on activities.

Junior Ranger Programs (www.nps.gov/yell/forkids/beajuniorranger.htm) are for children ages 5–12 and their families. Activities include geyser monitoring, wildlife observation, hiking, skiing, snowshoeing, and exploring. Programs are offered in summer and winter.

Grand Teton National Park

Ranger-led activities (www.nps.gov/grte/planyourvisit/ranger-programs.htm) start in late spring and continue into late fall. Activities take place at Colter Bay, Jackson Lake Lodge, Gros Ventre campground, Signal Mountain Lodge, Lizard Creek campground, and Flagg Ranch. Guided hikes are available at Jenny Lake and Colter Bay. **Junior Ranger Programs** (www.nps.gov/grte/forkids/index.htm) are offered for $1, which covers the cost of a ranger patch.

Teton Science School (307-733-4765, www.tetonscience.org) is a long-standing program that has its original campus in Kelly and a sprawling 900-acre campus between Jackson and Wilson. Learn about nearly every aspect of the natural processes taking place in the Greater Yellowstone ecosystem. The classes are geared to kids and young adults in their college years. Seminars ranging from one to five days are offered during the summer tourist season, and simple lectures are available for a nominal fee. The Murie Natural History Museum is on-site.

HEALTH/SAFETY

Hospitals

Yellowstone National Park: Mammoth Hot Springs Clinic (weekdays, year-round), 307-344-7965; Old Faithful Clinic (early May to mid-October), 307-545-7325; Lake Hospital (summer), 307-242-7241

Grand Teton National Park: Grand Teton Medical Clinic at Jackson Lake Lodge (mid-May to mid-October), 307-543-2514 (9 AM–5 PM) and 307-733-8002 (after hours)

Cody: West Park Hospital, 707 Sheridan Ave. (307-527-7501)

Jackson: St. John's Medical Center, 625 E. Broadway St. (307-733-3636)

West Yellowstone: Yellowstone Family Medical Clinic, 11 S. Electric St. (406-646-0200)

Staying Healthy in Greater Yellowstone

Altitude Sickness: If you're coming from near sea level, it's possible that spending time in the thin air of higher elevations in Grand Teton and the Beartooth Plateau could bring on altitude sickness. Symptoms include shortness of breath, headaches, disorientation, nausea, and nosebleeds. The best antidote is to move to a lower elevation until the symptoms disappear.

Pelicans come in for a landing on the Gallatin River in Montana.

Giardia: When they say don't drink the lake/stream water, they mean it. Even in the pristine waters of Yellowstone and Grand Teton, this protozoa lives, thanks to its spreading by humans and animals through waste. Always purify lake or stream water before drinking by boiling, using special tablets, or water purifiers. Giardia won't ruin your vacation because it takes weeks to appear, but when it does, the intestinal pain is unforgettable.

Hantavirus: Another rare disease, but not one to mess around with. Hantavirus is spread by rodents, mostly deer mice and voles, through their droppings. A handful of residents in Wyoming and Montana have been killed by the disease while cleaning out old buildings contaminated with rodent waste. Avoid contact with mouse, rat, or vole droppings, and make a quick check of rustic cabins. It's extremely unlikely that you'll contract hantavirus, even if you do come in contact with rodent feces, but better safe than sorry.

Hypothermia: This is the greatest health threat in the parks, far more than bears, lightning, or any sickness. Even on the warmest days of summer, the right combination of wind, cold, and wet can quickly drop your body temperature to dangerous levels where even death is possible. It isn't limited to flipping a kayak or canoe in Lake Yellowstone, either—though that's an almost certain recipe for disaster. A soaking from a sudden storm can turn the trick as well. It begins with uncontrollable shivering, followed by disorientation, unconsciousness, and death. The way to avoid it is to dress for all occasions, avoiding cotton and denim if you plan to venture far from your car or room. Always bring a waterproof raincoat, windbreaker, or shell. Dress in layers. Wool and polypropylene are terrific because they insulate, retain heat, and dry quickly. In a worst-case scenario, where a hiking partner is showing signs of hypothermia, strip them of their wet clothes and wrap yourself around them, preferably skin to skin, so you're transferring your body heat.

Sun: Don't let the comfortable days, cool nights, and even the presence of snow fool you. Altitudes in Yellowstone and Jackson Hole are well over 5,000 feet, and the air is dry. It doesn't take much to get a severe burn, even on hazy days. Use sunscreen of at least 30 SPF and wear a hat when venturing into the backcountry.

Ticks: Tiny spiderlike creatures devastated human populations in parts of Montana at the turn of the previous century by transmitting Rocky Mountain spotted fever. Though the fever is rare, it's still possible to acquire it. Also rare, but of slightly greater concern, is Lyme disease, which was identified in the East but has since moved west. Cover as much skin as possible when walking through brushy areas. After a day in the woods, spend some extra time in the shower checking yourself carefully, especially your hair. If you find one, use tweezers to "unscrew" them. Make sure you get the head and don't leave the mouthparts. Neosporin or the natural tea tree oil applied to the bite should reduce swelling. Keep a close eye on any bites. The ramifications can last a lifetime, and perhaps even be deadly.

Columbine plants are part of a dazzling display of wildflower colors in June. NPS

West Nile Virus: Several cases of West Nile virus are reported each summer, and the mosquito-borne disease appears to be on the rise in the Northern Rockies. Most mosquitoes don't carry the virus, but if you plan to hike in areas where they are common, especially around standing or slow-moving water, you have some options. Use insect repellants with DEET or, if you prefer to avoid chemicals, try citronella or other natural mosquito deterrents.

Luckily for this photographer, this bison isn't agitated—yet.

Wildlife: We have saved perhaps the most important for last—important for your safety, but also for the health and well-being of wildlife. All too often, humans have displayed a cavalier attitude toward animals that appear docile. And all too often, they have paid a price. Inevitably, wildlife pay a price, too, usually with their lives. Though most visitors would guess grizzly bears to be the most dangerous creature, most injuries to visitors involve bison. People get too close to these incredibly athletic animals, and before they know what hit them—literally—an agitated bison has vented its fury. Moose are cantankerous and will pursue a human for no apparent reason; conflicts are rare in part because moose numbers have declined. An increase in grizzly bear populations combined with rising tourism means more conflicts are inevitable. *Park regulations require visitors to stay at least 100 yards from bears and wolves, and it's 25 yards for other wildlife. But we recommend 100 yards for bison, elk, and deer as well. Grand Teton National Park in 2011 controversially altered its regulations to include vehicular traffic being required to be at least 100 yards from grizzlies.*

Protecting Greater Yellowstone for future generations is an ongoing struggle against overdevelopment and other threats. Following are a few conservation-oriented organizations with a variety of missions.

Buffalo Field Campaign (406-646-0070, www.buffalofieldcampaign.org) has hunkered down in West Yellowstone, one hub of the controversy involving the many bison that wander from the park. They're often seen protesting or handing out leaflets, especially during hazing of bison by the Montana Department of Livestock in the spring. In some ways, this passionate group is a throwback to the tree sit-in days of antilogging in the Pacific Northwest.

Grand Teton National Park Foundation (307-732-0629, www.gtnpf.org) in Moose is a nonprofit outfit that raises money from private entities to help with a variety of projects in the park. It is partially supported by the profits from Grand Teton Bottled Water.

Grand Teton Natural History Association (307-739-3403, www.grandtetonpark .org) is based in Moose and is the park's equivalent of the Yellowstone Association. Its emphasis is education and it is supported through classes and book sales.

Greater Yellowstone Coalition (406-586-1593, www.greateryellowstone.org) keeps an eye on all things Yellowstone and the park's periphery from its headquarters in Bozeman plus offices in Idaho Falls, Idaho, and Cody and Jackson, Wyoming.

National Parks Conservation Association (406-222-2268 or 406-585-1471 or 307-733-4680, www.npca.org) has a Yellowstone Field Office in Bozeman and a Grand Teton Field Office in Jackson.

Yellowstone Association (406-848-2400, www.yellowstoneassociation.org) emphasizes education and understanding of the park's goals. It offers classes through the Yellowstone Association Institute and sells books at a variety of places, including the Buffalo Ranch in the Lamar Valley and a new campus on a bluff overlooking the Yellowstone River in Gardiner, Montana.

Yellowstone Park Foundation (406-586-6303, www.ypf.org), located in Bozeman, helps finance infrastructure improvements within the park by tapping businesses and private individuals. This is where your money goes if you use a Yellowstone National Park Visa.

ANNUAL FESTIVALS

Alta, Wyoming

Grand Targhee Bluegrass Festival (1-800-827-4433, mid-Aug.): Three days of bluegrass music, arts and crafts, food booths, and children's entertainment

Cody, Wyoming

Buffalo Bill Art Show and Sale (1-888-598-8119 or 307-587-5002, www.buffalo billartshow.com, late Sept.): Fine art with Western themes is shown at the Buffalo Bill Historical Center; proceeds benefit the center.

Old West Show and Auction (307-587-9014, www.codyoldwest.com, late June): Collectors from around the country gather to buy old cowboy gear in the Robbie Powwow Garden at the Buffalo Bill Historical Center.

Plains Indian Museum Powwow (307-587-4771, www.bbhc.org/events, mid-June): Singing, dancing, arts and crafts, and Indian food from all over the region are featured at the Robbie Powwow Garden at the Buffalo Bill Historical Center.

Rendezvous Royale (1-888-598-8119 or 307-587-5002, www.rendezvousroyale.org, late Sept.): This celebration of the arts combines the Buffalo Bill Art Show and Sale, Buffalo Bill Historical Center's Patrons Ball fund-raiser, and the Western Design Conference—which features Western fashions in the Riley Arena.

Yellowstone Jazz Festival (307-587-4771, www.yellowstonejazz.com, mid-July): Jazz aficionados have converged from around the nation for 20 years at this event funded by the Wyoming Arts Council. Venues are the Cody City Park, Buffalo Bill Historical Center, and Powell High School.

Gardiner, Montana

Yellowstone Music Festival and Art Show (406-848-7971, www.yellowstonemusic fest.com, Labor Day): Live bluegrass, rock, and folk music are all performed in the shadows of the famed Roosevelt Arch at Arch Park.

Jackson, Wyoming

Elkfest (307-733-3316, www.elkfest.org, late May): Elk-antler auction and mountain-man rendezvous are the highlights of the annual Elkfest at the Teton County Fairgrounds. Antlers are collected by Boy Scouts from the nearby National Elk Refuge and are sold to help with the feeding of the elk.

Grand Teton Music Festival (307-733-1128, www.gtmf.org, mid-July to late Aug.): Nightly classical-music concerts featuring internationally renowned symphony musicians are held in newly renovated Walk Festival Hall in Teton Village. Included is a free concert each July 4.

Jackson Hole Film Festival (1-800-733-8144 or 307-733-8144, www.jhff.org, early June): Each year, about 80 independent films are screened for competition in seven categories, followed by round-table discussions and other events at the Center for the Arts downtown.

Jackson Hole Scottish Festival (www.wyohighlanders.net, mid-Aug.): People of Scottish ancestry celebrate their roots with a variety of events over two days at the Teton County Fairgrounds. Featured are vendors, drumming, dancing, music, sports, and clan-related events. The Wyoming Highlanders are a nonprofit group that celebrates the Scottish and Celtic mountain men who came to northwest Wyoming more than two hundred years ago.

Jackson Hole Fall Arts Festival (307-733-3316, www.jacksonholechamber.com, early Sept.): A wide array of music, cowboy poetry and cuisine, along with gallery walks, workshops, and artist receptions are featured at this festival. The highlight is the "Taste of the Tetons" food expo.

Jackson Hole Wildlife Film Festival (307-733-7016, www.jhfestival.org, early Oct.): Some seven hundred filmmakers from more than 30 countries gather at Jackson Lake Lodge with scientists, naturalists, and other wildlife enthusiasts to view and discuss wildlife films. Event culminates with an awards ceremony.

Art Fair Jackson Hole (307-733-8792, www.artassociation.org, late July): A competitive arts and crafts fair that takes place at Miller Park.

Hikers traverse the Observation Peak Trail in Yellowstone National Park.

Old West Days (307-733-3316, www.jacksonholechamber.com/old_west_days/, Memorial Day Weekend): Lots of old West activities—including mountain-man rendezvous, chuckwagon dinners, horses, shootouts, etc.—take place at the Teton County Fairgrounds.

Spring Earth Festival (307-739-2246, www.muriecenter.org/programs.html, mid-Apr.): The conservation-oriented Murie Foundation offers its Teton Sustainability Project and other adventures during this festival. The event culminates with an ecofair at the Murie Center in Moose.

Teton County Fair (307-733-5289, www.tetoncountyfair.com, late July): A week-long event at the Teton County Fairgrounds that includes the usual fair fare—rodeo, 4-H competitions, beauty queens, a demolition derby, wildlife, food, music, and exhibits—all with a Western flair.

Driggs, Idaho

Teton Valley Summer Festival (208-354-2500, www.tetonvalleychamber.com, early July): This annual event at the Driggs airport is famed for the launch of hot-air balloons, but also features a crafts fair, parade, fireworks, and other activities.

West Yellowstone, Montana

Knothead Jamboree (406-646-1093, www.hkcaller.com/knotheadjamboree, Labor Day weekend): Up to one thousand square dancers have been gathering annually for a half-century at the Union Pacific Dining Lodge for this dancing event. The event is so-named because once upon a time anybody who journeyed more than 100 miles to go square dancing was considered a "knothead."

World Snowmobile Expo (406-646-7701, www.snowmobileexpo.com, mid-Mar.): Six days of racing in the self-proclaimed snowmobile capital of the world—conducted at Expo Central, the Snocross track, and the airport—make this one of the area's more unique festivals.

Yellowstone Ski Festival (406-646-7097, www.yellowstoneskifestival.com, late Nov.): More than three thousand Nordic skiers gather at the Rendezvous Ski Trails to celebrate the beginning of the season with races, shows, sales, etc.

Index